Advance Praise for *Contested Curriculum*

"A much-needed, accessibly written, and deeply insightful account of one of the key issues in America's current culture wars."

—John D'Emilio, author of *Memories of a Gay Catholic Boyhood*

"A much-needed primer on the decades-long struggle for LGBTQ history education, a first-rate lesson plan on how to improve our classrooms, and an A+ answer to the question of whether more inclusive history education can support democracy."

—Marc Stein, author of *Queer Public History: Essays on Scholarly Activism*

"In this accessible and powerful book, Romesburg reminds us that the long, ongoing fight for LGBTQ+ equality and justice has often happened in schools, in classrooms, and by teachers. The lesson Romesburg offers is that battles over LGBTQ+ representation in the history curriculum are ultimately disputes over whether queer and trans people matter. And history education, he argues, is an ideal place to insist that LGBTQ+ perspectives and experiences are woven into the very idea of the nation."

—Jen Gilbert, author of *Sexuality in School: The Limits of Education*

"*Contested Curriculum* is a detailed chronology of the passage and implementation of the first legislation to establish LGBTQ-inclusive K–12 history education in the United States. Romesburg deftly places this California story in the national political context and fills in a heretofore missing piece of LGBTQ education history. A thorough update on the contemporary battle between inclusive and anti-LGBTQ curriculum laws leaves readers with an understanding of the importance of sound educational policy that expands students' thinking, improves school climate, and simply tells the truth about gender and sexual diversity."

—Karen L. Graves, author of *Mad River,
Marjorie Rowland, and the Quest for
LGBTQ Teachers' Rights* (Rutgers
University Press, 2022)

"*Contested Curriculum* makes a powerful case for LGBTQ inclusion in K–12 social studies and tells a compelling story about how dedicated collective action led to that breakthrough in California. It reminds us that LGBTQ history is a necessary part of all young people's access to high-quality history instruction. Romesburg provides an insider's perspective, scholarly analysis, and a roadmap for change that will inspire readers to continue working for LGBTQ curricular inclusion, whether at the grassroots or statewide level."

—David M. Donahue, professor in the
School of Education at the University
of San Francisco

Contested Curriculum

Q+ Public

Series editors: E. G. Crichton, Jeffrey Escoffier (2018–2022)

Editorial Board

E. G. Crichton (chair), University of California Santa Cruz; co-founder of *OUT/LOOK* journal

Jeffrey Escoffier (co-chair 2018–2022), co-founder of *OUT/LOOK* journal

Shantel Gabrieal Buggs, Florida State University, Tallahassee

Julian Carter, California College of the Arts, San Francisco

Wilfredo Flores, University of North Carolina at Charlotte; Queering Medicine

Stephanie Hsu, Pace University, New York; Center for LGBTQ Studies (CLAGS); Q-Wave

Ajuan Mance, Mills College, Oakland, CA

Maya Manvi, San Francisco Museum of Modern Art

Don Romesburg, Sonoma State University, Rohnert Park, CA; GLBT Historical Society

Andrew Spieldenner, California State University, San Marcos; MPact: Global Action for Gay Health & Rights; United States People Living with HIV Caucus

The Q+ Public books are a limited series of curated volumes, based on the seminal journal *OUT/LOOK: National Lesbian and Gay Quarterly*. *OUT/LOOK* was a political and cultural quarterly published out of San Francisco from 1988 to 1992. It was the first new publication to bring together lesbians and gay men after a decade or more of political and cultural separatism. It was consciously multigender and racially inclusive, addressed politics and culture, wrested with controversial topics, and emphasized visual material along with scholarly and creative writing. *OUT/LOOK* built a bridge between academic inquiry and the broader community. Q+ Public promises to revive *OUT/LOOK*'s political and cultural agenda in a new format, and revitalize a queer public sphere to bring together academics, intellectuals, and artists to explore questions that urgently concern all LGBTQ+ communities.

For a complete list of titles in the series, please see the last page of the book.

Contested Curriculum

LGBTQ History Goes to School

DON ROMESBURG

Rutgers University Press
New Brunswick, Camden, and Newark, New Jersey
London and Oxford

Rutgers University Press is a department of Rutgers, The State University of New Jersey, one of the leading public research universities in the nation. By publishing worldwide, it furthers the University's mission of dedication to excellence in teaching, scholarship, research, and clinical care.

Library of Congress Cataloging-in-Publication Data

Names: Romesburg, Don, author.
Title: Contested curriculum : LGBTQ history goes to school /
Don Romesburg. Description: New Brunswick, New Jersey : Rutgers
University Press, 2025. | Series: Q+ public | Includes index.
Identifiers: LCCN 2024040388 | ISBN 9781978824102 (cloth) |
ISBN 9781978824096 (paperback) | ISBN 9781978824119 (epub) |
ISBN 9781978824133 (pdf)
Subjects: LCSH: Sexual minorities—Education—United States. |
Homosexuality and education—United States. | Sexual minorities—
United States—History—Study and teaching. | Education—Curricula—
Social aspects—United States.
Classification: LCC LC2574 .R66 2025 | DDC 306.76071/073—dc23/
eng/20241211116
LC record available at https://lccn.loc.gov/2024040388

A British Cataloging-in-Publication record for this book is available
from the British Library.

Copyright © 2025 by Don Romesburg
All rights reserved
No part of this book may be reproduced or utilized in any form or by any
means, electronic or mechanical, or by any information storage and retrieval
system, without written permission from the publisher. Please contact Rutgers
University Press, 106 Somerset Street, New Brunswick, NJ 08901. The only
exception to this prohibition is "fair use" as defined by U.S. copyright law.

References to internet websites (URLs) were accurate at the time of writing.
Neither the author nor Rutgers University Press is responsible for URLs that
may have expired or changed since the manuscript was prepared.

♾ The paper used in this publication meets the requirements of the American
National Standard for Information Sciences—Permanence of Paper for
Printed Library Materials, ANSI Z39.48-1992.

rutgersuniversitypress.org

For my mom and all the rest of the public school teachers
For my daughters and all the rest of the public school kids
For all the LGBTQ+ history education visionaries across
the decades and to come

Contents

Notes on the Art	xi
Series Foreword	xvii
E. G. CRICHTON	
Introduction: Can LGBTQ History Education Save Democracy?	1
1. The Prehistory of LGBTQ History Education	27
2. The State's the Place? Sidelined Reforms Become Opt-In History	55
3. Making California FAIR	95
WITH CAROLYN LAUB	
4. Resource FAIR: Materials and Trainings Empower Educators	139
WITH RICK OCULTO	
Conclusion: As California Goes . . . ?	177
Acknowledgments	197
Notes	201
Index	247

Notes on the Art

The artwork on the cover and chapter openers (as well as at the end of the conclusion) are all part of the Queer Ancestors Project. Since 2011, the project, led by printmaking artist, queer history scholar, and novelist Katie Gilmartin, has used history to build community by providing queer and trans people, age eighteen to twenty-six, free interdisciplinary workshops in printmaking, writing, and queer history. Public and online exhibitions provide a creative window on the past through which the larger community can glimpse a shared future. For more information on the Queer Ancestors Project and more extensive artist statements and bios, visit queerancestorsproject.org.

Cover   Kimiko Goeller, *descent*, 2020. Artist statement: I wanted to capture the isolation I feel knowing that the ancestors I am seeking out exist but have gone through history nameless and faceless, while also conveying the support I feel knowing that my existence is built upon those legacies. I represent that using the spider lilies and chrysanthemums, which are the flowers of death in Japanese culture. These flowers act as a reminder that I have inherited both the resilience and the flaws of my ancestors. Even with all of these thoughts that come up related to ancestry, there is so much hope for the future.

I.1 Cedar Kerwin, *Queer Heroes* (James Baldwin, Audre Lorde, Sylvia Rivera, Leslie Feinberg, and Marsha P. Johnson), 2018. Artist statement: I hope to honor all of these individuals' works, ideologies, and teachings with this print. It is also meant as a reminder to our queer and trans siblings today that we have beautiful powerful ancestors to lend us their strength through their words, actions, and wisdom.   xxii

1.1 Two-spirit artist Canelo Cabrera Lopez, *Always Have, Always Will*, 2021. Artist statement: This piece was inspired by the statement "Give us our flowers while we're still here." I want Black and Brown queer and trans people to be celebrated. We are queer and trans ancestors in the making and those that came after us deserve to know that we have always existed and we will continue to do so, as history has shown us.   26

1.2 Laurie Casa Grande, "Unfortunately, History Has Set the Record a Little Too Straight," poster, 1988. Created to commemorate the first National Coming Out Day. 49

2.1 Alan Gutirrez, *Bayard Rustin*, 2012. Artist statement: Bayard Rustin is seldom recognized for his leadership role in organizing the historic March on Washington. His activism and identity as an African American gay man is absent from many history lessons of the civil rights movement. This piece is dedicated to his leadership, his radical sex politics, and his inclusion into school curriculum via California's FAIR Education Act. 54

2.2 Photo of Jessea Greenman counterprotesting against anti-gay demonstrators opposing Project 10 at a San Francisco school board meeting, May 29, 1990. 70

2.3 Robert Birle, "LGB Historical Figures and Events," poster, 1992. Created for Project 21 and featuring fifty-seven diverse lesbian, gay, and bisexual historical figures and seven events. 77

3.1 Ess, *Public Universal Friend (I am that I am)*, 2021. Artist statement: The Public Universal Friend was an American preacher who rejected all genders and even a personal identity. In late 1776, the Friend had an intense religious experience and proclaimed that the Friend's previous identity, Jemima Wilkinson, was dead. The Friend now had a new spirit to preach the word of God. This story was jaw-dropping to me. I felt seen and understood, as an agender nonbinary person. The Friend was a queer ancestor that intensely rejected gender and gained self-determination and respect. When questioned about the Friend's gender, the Friend is quoted as simply stating, "I am that I am." 94

3.2 Photo of Don Romesburg in front of the California Department of Education in Sacramento holding *Making the Framework FAIR*, December 18, 2014. 123

4.1 Maria Olivia Davalos Stanton, *Sally Ride's Adventures on Planet Lesbos*, 2021. Artist statement: This print is inspired by Sally Ride, queer pulp fiction, retro sci-fi comics, and queer futurisms. It imagines a future where Ride is able to go off on space adventures without needing to leave behind a part of her identity. It is constructing a future in which we venture into the stars because we have embraced what is beautiful and nurturing and wish to find more and give more to our cosmos. A queer science fiction story affirms a queer now, affirms a queer me becoming an ancestor to future queer and trans peoples. 138

4.2 Charley Parkhurst, Los Gatos Footbridge Mural Project, 2017. 148

4.3 Photo of FAIR Education Act Implementation Coalition members after testifying before the Instructional

Quality Commission at the California Department of Education in Sacramento, August 17, 2017.   155

C.1   Striff Striffolino, *Part of Me*, 2020. Artist statement: To Leslie Feinberg, author of *Stone Butch Blues* (1993), which includes the sentence "If it wasn't for you, I'd never have known I had a right to be me." Your words are the ones that have allowed me to express myself best. They've brought me to a closer understanding of who I am and what my identity is and have given me comfort in knowing that may be in constant transition. Thank you for holding me through it all and for being a part of me forever. Love, Striff.   176

C.2   Mar Valle-Remond, *The Great Work Begins*, 2022. Artist statement: This print is a tribute to the living and the grieving, the dead and the dying, the ancestors who are remembered and forgotten, and everyone in between. For me, certainty during pandemic times lies in the knowledge that my queer ancestors have faced similar situations in the past. Grief, death, life, and health are all nonbinary. When thinking about the future, Prior Walter's final line in *Angels in America* comes to mind: "The great work begins"—there is an opportunity for radical change, it's up to us to take it.   196

Series Foreword

Q+ Public is a series of small thematic books in which leading scholars, artists, community leaders and activists, independent writers and thinkers engage in critical reflection on contemporary LGBTQ political, social, and cultural issues.

Q+ Public is about elevating the challenges of thinking about gender, sex, and sexuality across complex and diverse identities to offer a forum for public dialogue. It asserts the need and existence of a queer public space.

Q+ Public is an outgrowth, after a long hibernation, of *OUT/LOOK Lesbian and Gay Quarterly*, a pioneering political and cultural journal that sparked intense national debate over the five years it was published, 1988 to 1992. As an early though incomplete model of intersectional inclusion, *OUT/LOOK* was the first publication since the early 1970s to bring together lesbians and gay men after years of separate movements. The visual and written content of *OUT/LOOK* addressed complex gender roles (with a blind spot about transgender issues), was racially diverse, embraced political and cultural topics that were controversial or had not yet been articulated, and emphasized visual art along with scholarly and creative writing. In a period when LGBTQ studies and queer theory were coalescing but not yet established,

OUT/LOOK built a bridge between academic inquiry and broader community.

The Q+ Public book series was initially conceived by E. G. Crichton and Jeffrey Escoffier, two of the six founders of *OUT/LOOK*. They brought together a diverse and highly qualified editorial collective. The plan is to issue two books a year in which engaged research, art and critical reflection address difficult and challenging topics.

The idea of a complicated and radical queer public has long been part of the vision and writing of Jeffrey Escoffier. Sadly, Jeffrey died unexpectedly in May 2022 at age 79, leaving behind Q+ Public, as well as several other publishing projects. Prolific, full of ideas and vision to the end, he is widely missed. The Q+ Public collective continues this work in his honor.

Each book in the Q+ Public series finds a way to dive into the deep nuances and discomforts of a topic. Each book features multiple points of view, strong art, and a strong editorial concept. In this era of new political dangers, Q+ Public takes on the challenges we face and offers new hope for public dialogue.

Contested Curriculum: LGBTQ History Goes to School explores the history of LGBTQ-inclusive K–12 history education in the United States. What began in fits and starts across the late twentieth century led to the passage of California's FAIR Education Act in 2011 and subsequent implementation across the country. In *Contested Curriculum*, historian Don Romesburg, the lead scholar working with LGBTQ+ advocacy organizations on the FAIR Education Act and related textbooks and teaching, tells the compelling story of the struggle to make history education more accurate and relevant. His insights are all the more urgent in this era of anti-LGBTQ+ book bans, "Don't Say Gay" legislation, and other attempts to diminish the powerful role that inclusive and honest history education should play in our diverse democracy.

E. G. Crichton

Contested Curriculum

FIG. I.1. Cedar Kerwin, *Queer Heroes* (James Baldwin, Audre Lorde, Sylvia Rivera, Leslie Feinberg, and Marsha P. Johnson), 2018.

Introduction

Can LGBTQ History Education Save Democracy?

In 1995, seventeen-year-old Allison Holzer of Richmond, Indiana, beat out thirty-four students from across the United States to win the Gay, Lesbian, and Straight Teachers Network's first annual Lesbian, Gay, and Bisexual History Month Essay Contest. She wrote, "[My friends] have their rich family and cultural histories, as do I, but most of them also have the history of their heterosexuality. . . . A big part of me and many other young people in this world is not taught to us." She added, "Knowing our history would not automatically make us happy, healthy human beings . . . but it gives us a source of strength: something to fall back on when we falter. . . . Gay, lesbian, and bisexual history is important to me because it is a part of who I am and who I wish to become."[1]

Written just a year and a half after she had come out to herself, Allison's essay highlighted the total absence of lesbian, gay, and bisexual subjects in her history curriculum. For most of her K–12 years, it had not occurred to her that past people had taken similar journeys. (Her omission of transgender was an artifact of that era, when the "T" was still being reincorporated into the "LGB."[2]) She saw both the potential and limits of history education as a vehicle for necessary identity work. Beyond just instilling a sense of "pride" through the introduction of historical "role models," inclusive K–12 history education could have helped her pave pathways into the future. History gave her "a connection with others who have the same roots. . . . people who I might otherwise have nothing in common with." By studying the queer past, she understood how she belonged to a diverse, forward-looking community rooted in mutual support, struggle, and celebration.

Over time, the Gay, Lesbian, and Straight Teachers Network became the Gay, Lesbian and Straight Education Network, and, later, just GLSEN. In 2017, GLSEN National Student Council member James Van Kuilenburg, a transgender high school student from West Virginia and Maryland, wrote a similar essay for the organization's blog. "We, as students and educators, must make a concerted effort to highlight the stories of transgender people, which have often been erased from our history textbooks, especially the stories of folks with multiple marginalized identities, like trans folks of color," he wrote. He recounted how in seventh grade, he had won first place in his school's Social Science Fair with a biography of trans Civil War veteran Albert Cashier, despite a teacher who had told him that "he had never heard of something like that." James added that while "the history of trans people is very important to me as a history nerd," it was also "important to every young person." Like Allison, he endorsed LGBTQ-inclusive K–12 history education as "proof of existence and the affirmation of identity." Yet, he added, the "benefits of teaching trans-inclusive history reach further than trans students themselves."

Echoing two decades of Safe Schools rhetoric and research between Allison's essay and his, James asserted it "can alter the school climate for the better."[3]

LGBTQ-inclusive K–12 history education does a lot of work simultaneously. For LGBTQ+ students, inclusive history education can enrich their identity, community, safety, and success. For all students, it facilitates a school climate of belonging across differences. For our society's emerging citizens, such an education promotes civic engagement, tools for navigating a pluralistic democracy, and critical citizenship skills.

Contested Curriculum explores the history of LGBTQ-inclusive K–12 history education in the United States. What began in fits and starts across the late twentieth century led to formalization of an inclusive curriculum through legislation, first with the passage of California's Fair, Accurate, Inclusive, and Respectful (FAIR) Education Act in 2011. Subsequent implementation of the law presented its own challenges and opportunities. As the lead scholar working with Californian LGBTQ+ advocacy organizations on the FAIR Education Act's passage and implementation, I have learned a lot about the gaping canyon between such a bill becoming law and curriculum showing up in classrooms and textbooks. I have talked to dozens of educators who have, either enthusiastically or reluctantly, educated themselves and their students about a field of history in which few received prior training. As a historian, I have wondered why the 2010s were the era when this deceptively simple idea—that all students, across elementary, middle, and high school, should receive LGBTQ-inclusive history education—finally broke into the mainstream. As a queer person who grew up through the AIDS crisis and its related culture wars, I had been waiting since 2011 for the backlash. And here we are.

Introduction   3

Since 2021, we have endured an unprecedented legislative assault against LGBTQ+ people and a moral panic over what the right imagines to be "critical race theory" being taught in K–12 public schools. Attacks on the rights and health of trans youth and attempts to censor discussions of racial inequity and justice understandably overshadow a wave of bills across the nation that propose the banning of (or requiring parental permission for) teaching about sexual orientation and gender identity in all subjects, including history. In sixteen states these have become law as of October 2024. Meanwhile, in 2024, Washington became the seventh state, following California, New Jersey, Illinois, Colorado, Oregon, and Nevada, to require the inclusion of LGBT content in K–12 history education. The existence of this history in classrooms clearly matters, even to those who mobilize against it. But why?

Why History Education Matters

The Founders understood that free common schools were necessary to build an educated citizenry in a democratic republic. Some viewed the study of history as moral and religious training. Thomas Jefferson, however, saw history education as a bulwark against demagoguery or tyranny. In a 1779 proposal to establish Virginia's public schools, he wrote that the study of the past enabled young people "as judges of the actions and designs of men" to "know ambition under every disguise . . . and . . . defeat its views."[4]

As many education scholars have observed, from then to now, there has been a tension between history education as an expression of nationalist patriotism and as a mechanism through which to transform diverse young people into engaged democratic citizens. These two approaches are not

4   Contested Curriculum

mutually exclusive. Neither necessarily precludes incorporation of LGBTQ history.

In 1981, the California Department of Education (CDE) issued its first History-Social Science Framework—previously the California Framework for the Social Sciences—signaling history's renewed prominence. Its introduction states, "The central purpose of history/social science education is to prepare students to become human, rational, understanding, and participating citizens in a diverse society and an increasingly interdependent world—students who will preserve and continue to advance progress toward a just society."[5]

A 1984 conference at the University of California, Berkeley, kicked off the Clio Project, a collaboration between the university's School of Education and the CDE that sought to bring more rigor, depth, and quality to the state's K–12 history education. Among the 650 college professors and K–12 educators in attendance was State Superintendent of Public Instruction Bill Honig's special guest, National Endowment for the Humanities chair (and Reagan appointee) William Bennett. Six years prior, Bennett had made his opinion clear on bringing LGBT content into K–12 curriculum, in an essay entitled "The Homosexual Teacher." He argued that discrete gay educators, if otherwise talented and never speaking of anything gay related, were acceptable. However, if a community "does not favor proselytization for homosexuality as a bona fide part of the curriculum, it can act to prevent it from being taught." He equated this with "the teacher proselytizer for 'swinging,' or 'asexuality,' or the teacher who recommends the life of alcohol- or drug-induced stupor." At the conference, Bennett advocated history education for a "common culture," stating that "the public school is not principally an international food fair for the mind." There was a thread between Bennett's desire to censor gay presence in the

Introduction   5

curriculum and his tasking of history education with a patriotic "common culture" without too many presented options for difference. His phrasing echoed the words of education reformer Diane Ravitch, who would go on to draft the 1987 California History-Social Science Framework. She spoke at the conference in favor of a "common story" based in Western Civilization. This would become central not just to the Framework, but to her 1985 book, *The Schools We Deserve*. So, too, did it gesture to the Reagan Administration's widely read 1983 *A Nation at Risk* report.[6]

After Bennett's Clio talk, several K–12 teachers pushed back. One questioned the lack of discussion of racism or poverty and criticized the "limited view of American history presented" in an early draft of California's history curriculum standards. Another suggested that multiple interpretations and lenses rather than a single "common story" would improve students' preparation for civic engagement. Historian Peter Stearns urged California K–12 history education to embrace social history. "All groups in society"—and he explicitly named "homosexuals" among those groups—"deserve historical study in their own right and as contributors to the broader processes of social change."[7] Stearns's call reflected how scholarly and popular history across the 1970s and 1980s was transformed by social history, along with histories that centered women, people of color, class, Indigenous peoples, and, indeed, gay men and lesbians. His vision, like that of the teachers responding to Bennett and Ravitch, understood diversity and central to the project of meaningful and relevant U.S. history education.

From the 1980s to the present, history education has remained core to a curriculum charged with preparing students for civic engagement in a pluralistic democratic

6 Contested Curriculum

society. As the tension at the 1984 Clio conference suggests, it has been a contested site regarding the kinds of identity and community it should help foster. When women, people of color, and LGBTQ people show up in the K–12 U.S. history narrative, they transform it. That transformation can take many possible forms. A *pluralistic* model of "e pluribus unum" tends toward an assimilative march toward progress. This assumes a historical process by which marginalized peoples move toward equality and, over time, take their place in the "common story." More *identity-based* models of multiculturalism assume the distinct histories of different communities can be braided into a collective tapestry, a shared American story. *Intersectional* models explore how changing and mutually constitutive social power dynamics produce evolving processes of marginalization, belonging, and incorporation. They emphasize the interconnectedness of all people, institutions, and cultural arrangements across shifting conditions and positions of privilege and oppression. This, too, produces a "common story," although far afield from those imagined by Bennett and Ravitch in the 1980s. In reality, none of these three paths to a shared narrative requires hegemony or exclusivity. Each serves powerful purposes in terms of why we need K–12 history education in the first place. LGBTQ history can—and should—fit into any of these models.

History Wars Are Culture Wars

In the United States, "history wars," what some have called the culture wars over history education, have been periodically fought for the last century. In each of these conflicts, "heritage" and "historical" models of a usable past have competed. Those who advocate a heritage model tend to view history education as tasked with instilling patriotism through inspirational stories, unifying national identity, transmitting principles stemming from the Founding Fathers and the Constitution, and conserving the American past as a series of knowable facts that possess a fixed merit. The historical model nurtures critical thinking skills, empowering developing citizens to understand how history can help them engage with the present. As such, the historical model invites an investment in the country's ongoing improvement. It encourages multiple perspectives and identities. It highlights a tension between national principles and their implementation. It appreciates how details of the past are subject to continual reinterpretation through historical inquiry and scholarship.[8]

In this sense, the heritage model is conservative, while the historical model is progressive. Neither is apolitical. As education scholar Larry Cuban notes, in legislation, policy, and media punditry, the battle between the heritage and history models plays out time and again as a curricular embodiment of the "strain between stability and change at the very core of tax-supported public schools in a democracy." In the classroom, Cuban argues, the struggle is a "false choice." All teachers try to pair stable content with applied skills. While many content-heavy teachers lean conservative in the material delivered, others are liberal or progressive. Similarly, skills-heavy educators might skew liberal or progressive, but the idea that this would lead students away from applying conservative lessons to dilemmas of the present is far from inevitable. In a recent major report by the American Historical Association, surveyed secondary school history teachers across many states, red, blue, and purple, had near unanimity in their goals of building students' critical thinking, democratic citizenship, and ability to make connections between past and present. Above 80 percent also emphasized cause and

8   Contested Curriculum

effect, multiple perspectives, and primary source analysis. Only a quarter saw as important framing history as "a story of violence, oppression, and/or injustice" or as "fulfillment of the promises of the nation's founding." In other words, in the classroom, a commonality of priorities far outweighs the battle over history war ideologies.[9]

As this book demonstrates, since at least the 1980s, LGBTQ history has been one of the key battlegrounds between the heritage and historical models. Both proponents and opponents of LGBTQ-inclusive history education claim that it is inherently progressive rather than conservative in its aim and outcome. I assert, rather, that LGBTQ-inclusive K–12 history education belongs in *both* models, and in all classrooms. This is especially important to acknowledge because, throughout the different history wars that have sprung up over the past century, the charge of "un-Americanism" or "anti-Americanism" has floated as a signifier of various concepts figured as harmful or inappropriate to K–12 history education. This charge has almost inevitably been made by heritage advocates against more historical models. When LGBTQ history has come up, detractors have assumed it to be somehow threatening to "real" American history.

From the 1940s through the 1960s in California, Cold War anxieties related to the Soviet Union and civil rights for people of color produced a particularly intense wave of un-Americanism accusations. In 1962, following a call by civil rights leaders to address treatment of Black people in K–12 textbooks, the California Legislature passed Senate Concurrent Resolution No. 29, requesting that the CDE take steps to ensure textbooks "give due regard to sound intergroup relations." The California State Curriculum Committee subsequently issued related guidelines.[10]

Introduction   9

It was in this context that historian John Hope Franklin wrote his eighth-grade textbook *Land of the Free* (1966) to meet these state laws and policies. For this, it was attacked as un-American. One familiar accusation was that its mild criticism of capitalism "foments class hatred." Added was the charge that it placed an "overemphasis on Negro participation in American history," including favorable mentions of W.E.B. DuBois and Martin Luther King Jr. Another was that its lens on the American past produced a "guilt complex" in students who would otherwise have a "good feeling" about the nation. As one Californian lamented, "Why play up our mistakes, downgrade our heroes, and please our enemies?"[11]

Resistance to *Land of the Free* was an episode in the periodic history wars of the twentieth century, which have now re-emerged in the early twenty-first. It was also a building block for California's central place in what would soon come to be known as the New Right. The coalition of conservative Christians, cultural nationalists, John Birchers, white supremacists, free-market corporatists, Cold Warriors, and anti-tax libertarians would see its ultimate ascendance in the 1980 presidential election of Ronald Reagan. In the winter of 1966–1967, Reagan came into California's governorship just as *Land of the Free* was adopted. He chose to stay out of the textbook fray.[12]

The California Board of Education nonetheless adopted the paradigm-shifting textbook because it was singularly responsive to the state's inclusionary legislation and policy. In other words, it would not have been written the way it was, nor approved, had legislative groundwork not been laid. Here we can see a key historical lesson for our present: Grassroots activism sowed the seeds for inclusive curricular transformation. Without legislative mandates, *Land of the Free* would not have withstood structural intransigence and right-wing opposition. Even Dr. Maxwell Rafferty, California's arch-conservative state superintendent of public instruction, endorsed its adoption.[13]

In 1967, while Rafferty was endorsing *Land of the Free*, he was eagerly combatting the influence of homosexuality and gender diversity in public education. As he recalled a decade later about his chairing of the state's education credentials commission, "We took for granted the self-evident proposition that a homosexual in a school job was as preposterously out of question as a heroin mainliner working in the local drug store." He added that it was "the ultimate in jackass queries" to ask, "Should the school curriculum be 'modified' to reflect current changes in life-styles?" He suggested one might as well ask, "Should the school curriculum be modified to reflect practices . . . that are considered vicious by every great religion on earth and that are outlawed by every civilized country in the world?"[14] While Rafferty's tenure as state superintendent had passed, his rant came in the wake of Anita Bryant's successful anti-gay "Save Our Children" campaign in Dade County, Florida. California's battle over the anti-gay educator Proposition 6 (the "Briggs Initiative") was just heating up. Chapter 1 elaborates on why LGBTQ-inclusive history education was essentially impossible in this era.

In the 1980s and 1990s, the history wars shifted from an emphasis primarily on textbooks to standards and frameworks. The *A Nation at Risk* report sparked federal, state, and local reforms to a K–12 education supposedly lacking rigor and patriotism. "Un-Americanism" was signified by some of the usual suspects, such as the multiple perspectives that Bennett had decried as an "international food fair for the mind." Often, government and media debate centered on a tension between "multiculturalism" (or "inclusion") and "unity" (or a "common culture"). Bill Honig and the CDE declared that a "consensus" process yielded the state's 1987 History-Social Science Framework, state standards, and textbook adoptions. The process was actually quite contentious. The outcomes were an amalgam of a "common story" and far more inclusion of people of color, women, and class-based analysis than any state had previously achieved.[15]

Largely untold in histories of this time is the intentional exclusion of LGBTQ history by Framework authors, the CDE, and textbook publishers.[16] As detailed in chapter 2, this state-sanctioned "cancel culture" happened despite an organized movement to counter it. California's overt exclusion of LGBTQ content in its standards, frameworks, and approved educational materials sent shockwaves across the country. They impacted Massachusetts governor William Weld's excising of inclusive curriculum from the state's 1993 *Making Schools Safe for Gay and Lesbian Youth* report. They also resulted in the near-total absence of LGBTQ history in proposed 1994 National History Standards.

LGBTQ-inclusive history education, sitting at the nexus of the history wars and the religious right's culture war against multiculturalism, feminism, LGBTQ civic and cultural belonging, and comprehensive sex education, was largely shut out. It was in this context that Lesbian and Gay History Month (now officially LGBT History Month) was born as a voluntary, opt-in K–12 alternative to systemic exclusion.

As recently as 2010, Diane Ravitch called history wars a "distant memory."[17] Heritage models, along with some degree of multicultural representation and methods of historical thinking, continued to be popularized and adapted in the 2000s. In the 2010s, however, Texas and California stoked the fire. In Texas, the state's right-wing Republican-controlled Board of Education cherry-picked the past to

12   Contested Curriculum

affirm contemporary Republican political philosophies and a white, evangelical Christian "national genesis" claim to U.S. exceptionalism.[18] As detailed in Chapters 3 and 4, in California, the passage of the FAIR Education Act had a profound impact on formalizing LGBTQ-inclusive history education, first in that state and then around the country. By the end of the decade, the state had once again positioned its history education policy as a national leader. Key to this was its unprecedented LGBTQ inclusion across elementary, middle, and high school U.S. history curriculums. It also embraced the historical model without abandoning the heritage essence of the 1987 Framework.

By the beginning of the 2020s, the Trump wing of the Republican Party was collaborating with the Heritage Foundation, the American Legislative Exchange Council, and conservative media outlets to stoke a full-fledged history war. Seizing on materials related to the *New York Times*' 1619 Project and the catchphrase "critical race theory," Trump Republicans, right-wing think tanks, and lobbying groups such as Parents Defending Education stirred up a moral panic over the prospect of K–12 history education inclusive of gender, class, and, especially, race through the lens of intersectional analysis of power and change over time. Republican politicians continued to build culture war momentum across the early 2020s. At local, state, and national levels, they proposed or passed laws and created policies to ban the 1619 Project from schools (or withheld funding from districts and states that used it).[19]

The scope of attack has been far broader. Tennessee, for example, passed Senate Bill (SB) 0623, banning K–12 teaching that could lead a student to "feel discomfort, guilt, anguish or another form of psychological distress solely because of the individual's race or sex." It also prohibits curriculum that leads to "division between, or resentment of, a race, sex, religion, creed, nonviolent political affiliation, social class or class of people." The state also passed SB 1229, which requires a thirty-day parental notification prior to any curriculum, including in history and social studies classes, that mentions sexual orientation or gender identity.[20] This is "heritage" on steroids. Long after the fever of this history war subsides, it will have downstream effects in state and local elections, policy, and classrooms.

Why LGBTQ History Education Matters

While LGBTQ content is still woefully underrepresented in K–12 education, history has continued to be the place it likely appears. Sometimes, it only shows up in student-initiated work, as with James Van Kuilenburg's trans Civil War soldier project mentioned earlier. Still, because history education is closely linked with citizenship development, teachers who might otherwise be reluctant to teach about gender and sexuality can recognize its place in the classroom. Empowering students to become engaged in a diverse democracy necessitates a curriculum inclusive of the historical processes by which the modern LGBTQ+ rights movement emerged and LGBTQ+ peoples moved away from persistent criminalization and pathologization. History education, unlike sex education, fits more clearly into the "pedagogic frame" of what sociologist Janice Irvine calls the "culture-based model," as opposed to the "public health model." Because of this, LGBTQ history can be taught in terms of rights, restrictions, and cultural expressions in relation to other forms of difference and belonging. Rather than being "about sex" or compelling educators to take contemporary political positions in regard to LGBTQ issues, history education provides both the difference in subject matter and time that might make inclusion feel safer than in other subject areas.[21]

How, specifically, does inclusive history education matter to LGBTQ+ youth? First, curricular *exclusion* teaches them, intentionally or otherwise, that they also do not matter. As former Chicago Public Schools student Stephanie Gentry-Fernandez recalled in 2008, "My teachers repeatedly showed me that queer issues . . . were not of any importance to them. Queer history . . . was never covered in class, and many of us were silenced when we tried to bring [it] up."[22] With California's passage of the FAIR Education Act, some savvy students have been able to successfully advocate for their teachers to incorporate LGBTQ content. Such inclusion should not rest on the shoulders of already structurally vulnerable students.

Second, inclusive education can make schools safer. Back in the early 1980s, educator and curriculum studies scholar James T. Sears appealed to teachers to incorporate lesbian and gay history, in part as a means of making schools more affirming for "those [gay] students who have been the butt of locker-room jokes."[23] Sears was an early advocate of what by the 1990s would become known as the Safe Schools movement. Undoubtedly, students needed (and need) safer schools and greater personal resilience. LGBTQ-inclusive history education makes a meaningful intervention.[24]

Third, it can make LGBTQ+ students more successful. By the 2010s, student focus groups affirmed what social science research was already concluding: LGBTQ-inclusive curriculum helped students see themselves "in historical contexts and as historical actors and, therefore, relevant in the future as well." Such students were "more likely to be engaged as active learners and develop a greater understanding of the material." Research indicates that inclusive curriculum can improve attendance, grade point average, and educational attainment. More intersectional LGBTQ-inclusive curriculum can have even deeper impacts for queer and trans students of color.[25]

Beyond safe schools and student success, LGBTQ-inclusive history education also provides a set of resources particular to queer and trans students. As Allison Holzer recognized in her prize-winning essay that kicked of this introduction, most students count on home cultures and families to augment school history curriculums. Such familial and cultural histories are a source of grounding and resilience for young people from a diversity of backgrounds. Most LGBTQ+ youth, however, do not grow up in homes and cultures that center LGBTQ+ histories as affirmations of their own identities, search for communities, and sense of futurity. For queer and trans youth, schools should play a role in transmitting LGBTQ history across generations, because families and cultures of origin often do not. Moreover, by building LGBTQ-inclusive history education for all, students need not self-identify or opt-in in order to learn this history. It becomes accessible to everyone.

LGBTQ-inclusive history education also provides queer and trans youth with tools for thriving. At the most basic level, showcasing historical contributions by LGBTQ figures provides role models. This rationale is mentioned time and again in inclusive curriculum scholarship and activism since the 1980s. It is striking how much this reasoning aligned back then with the appeals of heritage model advocates such as Diane Ravitch, who called for compelling history education filled with inspiring "biographies [and] hero tales."[26]

LGBTQ-inclusive K–12 history education also demonstrates how contemporary lesbian, gay, bisexual, transgender,

16   Contested Curriculum

queer, and other communities came to be. Exploring movements and cultures shifts LGBTQ+ students' understandings from the desiring self to communities of belonging and resistance. Such history education can empower queer and trans students to question how heteronormativity and cisnormativity congealed and changed, and who benefitted. Through intersectional lenses, such history education equips youth with greater efficacy to promote social justice and examine power relations. Drawing on the historical model, LGBTQ-inclusive history education facilitates capacities for queer and trans youth to become more engaged citizens.[27]

If LGBTQ-inclusive education only mattered to queer and trans youth, one might program it primarily through, say, Gay-Straight Alliance clubs. Yet this history is important to all students. It shapes school climate, improves historical thinking skills, and connects broader histories to diverse genders, sexualities, families, and movements. An LGBTQ-inclusive history education underscores forces of oppression, forms of resistance, and cultural expressions beyond heteronormative expectations. This allows non-LGBTQ students windows into experiences different from their own. All students can also trace the origins and development of misconceptions and stereotypes. Consideration of how LGBTQ struggles relate to other movements for civil and human rights invites all students into open dialogue about our lives and issues in the present. This improves intergroup relations and reduces stigma.

Since the 1980s, some lesbian and gay history advocates recognized the intersectionality with gender, race, and class. In 1983, a remarkable issue of the *Interracial Books for Children Bulletin* centered Black queer voices, including Audre Lorde, Leonard Andrews Jr., and Barbara Smith. In Smith's essay, she echoed her work in the Combahee River Collective by encouraging "intertwining 'isms'" to build teaching about lesbians and gays into curriculum addressing racism and sexism. This approach would also counter perceptions of homosexuality as a "white disease" or just about "white men with large discretionary incomes." Leonore Gordon, the issue's guest editor, added that interconnected K–12 curriculum was central to the struggle to "eliminate oppression and achieve human liberation."[28]

Intersectional LGBTQ-inclusive history education demonstrates for all students how queerness and transness have been policed and managed in relation to race, class, ability, indigeneity, and colonialism. It models historical thinking that explores multiple perspectives, connections between LGBTQ-specific and other major events, the use of diverse primary and secondary sources, and the application of history to the questioning of dominant paradigms. It encourages consideration of past alternative expressions of sexuality, gender, and family. These allow all students to think beyond contemporary social and familial norms. Such practices make history education exciting and engaging for all students. They nurture critical thinking and democratic education skills to the benefit of all.

LGBTQ history matters to students of all ages. It can and should be taught in developmentally and age-appropriate ways in grade school, middle school, and high school. Early grade social science and history education is centered on both burgeoning collective belonging and appreciation for diversity. Incorporating LGBTQ-inclusive history into this model can be seamless, as shown by the 2016 California History-Social Science Framework. While this is addressed at length in chapter 3, a couple of illustrative examples here are helpful.

In second grade, when kids learn about heroes and role models, California's Framework includes LGBTQ ones.

18 Contested Curriculum

When second graders explore how their families connect to their communities and the wider world, they also appreciate family diversity past and present. That means they also learn that some kids have one parent, some have two dads, and some have multigenerational households.

In fourth grade, California state history has shifted away from sugar cube models of Spanish missions. The Framework now suggests project-based learning should emphasize how waves of colonization brought transformations to Indigenous societies, without glossing over devastating consequences or Native resilience. Such lessons can acknowledge Indigenous gender diversity, including two-spirit roles, and how that changed with European-American settler colonialism. In addition, fourth-grade lessons on California civil rights history now include the state's particular place in the modern LGBTQ rights movement.

By early primary grades, students are already discerning the social differences of gender role and can appreciate that families come in diverse configurations and affectional arrangements. Key moments in gender identity development happen in both early primary and middle school years. Self-identification of sexual orientation intensifies in later primary and middle school. Unless they are given the resources to do otherwise, even the youngest elementary students assume and police heteronormativity and gender normativity in themselves and others. History and social science lessons in those grades that are inclusive of gender diversity and the roles and contributions of diverse LGBTQ+ people give all students conceptual, practical, and historical vocabularies and tools to apply to the past and present, for themselves and each other. Postponing this curriculum until high school helps no one, misrepresents history, and contributes to a risky, harmful school culture.[29]

So ... *Can* LGBTQ History Education Save Democracy?

Okay, so no. It can't, not all by itself. Still, I hope I've established the importance of inclusive history education generally and LGBTQ history education specifically to the training of a capable citizenry in a diverse society. LGBTQ-inclusive history education can fit into a variety of modalities, ranging from the conservative to the transformative. Some very real obstacles must be overcome.

First, while history as a subject is highly politicized, it is structurally undervalued. The standards and testing movement, with its emphasis on English language arts (ELA), math, and science, has deprioritized history education and dampened innovative inclusive curriculum. This has been especially true at the elementary level, where over the last two decades class time spent on social studies has been reduced. Even as statewide history and social studies standards have included some racial and gender diversity, standardization has stymied more expansive multicultural and/or intersectional curriculums. On the bright side, the Common Core movement and related College, Career, and Civic Life (C3) Framework for Social Studies State Standards have encouraged more historical thinking, critical thought, source analysis, and consideration of multiple perspectives. These are good for a diverse history education that moves beyond a dull march through required dates and facts. In 2014, California eliminated its state history exams aligned to state standards. On the one hand, this has freed up educators considerably in terms of teaching diverse (including LGBTQ) histories. On the other, the elimination of history testing (while retaining testing in ELA and math) signals the subject's lower prioritization.[30]

20   Contested Curriculum

Second, LGBTQ history education in particular faces many hurdles. In most parts of the country, LGBTQ history is either passively excluded or overtly restricted. Only a handful of states mandate its inclusion. Educators in other states are vulnerable to district, school, and community-based challenges. Far more widely available LGBTQ-specific or -inclusive educational materials exist now than even a decade ago. These range from primary source collections and lesson plans to textbooks and teaching guides. Still, most teachers feel ill-prepared to teach the content. Most preservice programs and professional development give some attention to LGBTQ+ students as a vulnerable population. But very few prepare teachers in LGBTQ history education. Many teachers also simply believe that LGBTQ content does not belong in curriculum at their grade levels. Finally, in every state there is a vocal minority of the population that is actively opposed to its inclusion, which generally makes otherwise reluctant educators avoid it.[31]

If all of that can be overcome—and I adamantly believe that it should—the potential is profound. In 2020, Frame-Works Institute published a strategic brief in partnership with the Organization of American Historians to clarify the essential roles of history education. The "ongoing process of description, analysis and interpretation of the past involving critical examination of multiple perspectives" can confront "authoritarian and neo-fascist recastings," it asserts. It acknowledges that K–12 history education plays a key role, adding that "inclusive, shared history" could "bring people together" to move past the renewed culture wars.[32] LGBTQ-inclusive curriculum is surely vital to this project.

From my experience collaborating with teachers and historians, LGBTQ history education can exist through multiple modalities, whether conservative (patriotic/nationalistic), liberal (pluralist/democratic), multicultural (identitarian/democratic), or transformative (intersectional/democratic). Through any of these modalities you can teach, for example, about the Lavender Scare's mid-twentieth-century systemic governmental persecution and the nation's capacity to subsequently accommodate basic protections for sexual and gender minorities.

While this history can inspire students to consider its relationship to contemporary political and social concerns, it need not prescribe a particular position. You can teach about the existence of gender diversity in the American past regardless of your beliefs related to contemporary trans youth's access to gender-affirming healthcare. You can teach about the Harlem Renaissance's queer dynamics whether or not you think Lil Nas X or Janelle Monáe are good or bad influences on today's cultural landscape. Even modest inclusion, such as incorporating the rise of the LGBTQ freedom struggle into existing civil rights–era curriculums, improves our schools and society. All of these elements of American history were important in their time. They shape where we are—all of us—today.

What would a transformative LGBTQ-inclusive K–12 history education look like? In 2014, David Donahue analyzed elementary-level materials on gay politician Harvey Milk according to James Banks's four levels of multicultural inclusion. Donahue argued that most Milk curriculum remained at the lowest level, "Heros and Holidays." He urged materials that were transformational (level three). Such an approach helps students "understand *why* injustice and inequality exist and *how* political and social change for LGBTQ justice can be made." It also takes Milk from being a "heroic individual to part of a bigger story of

22   Contested Curriculum

ongoing collective action among coalitions of diverse people."[33] Donahue's insight informed LGBT inclusion in California's 2016 History-Social Science Framework.

LGBTQ-transformative history education invites multiple perspectives and moves beyond individuals to movements. It emphasizes intersecting systems of oppression and coalitional approaches to confronting them. Social studies education scholar Stephen Camacia describes a transformative K–12 history curriculum as one that supports critical democratic examinations of dominant structuring narratives and links these to contemporary social justice efforts. This is not just an additive approach that brings LGBTQ+ identities into existing curriculums. It's a way in which to explore the whole history curriculum through lenses of gender and sexual diversity as well as queer- and trans-inclusive intersectionality.[34] Interrogating how normative structures and systems evolved, how policing and enforcement mechanisms worked, and how people and movements navigated, resisted, and transformed them is a fundamentally historical project. It challenges students to imagine what has been—and could be otherwise.

LGBTQ-transformative history education could also satisfy the concerns of Gary Nash and Charlotte Crabtree, who oversaw the proposed National History Standards in the 1990s. They called for an inclusive history yet one that avoided "an excessive emphasis . . . on differences, distinctions, and separate experiences."[35] An LGBTQ-transformative history education has the potential to move K–12 curriculum beyond cultural pluralism and identity politics. It can take us toward a comprehensive exploration of how we all have been shaped, albeit in uneven ways, by an American past filled with changing social power arrangements related to gender, sexuality, race, and other forms of difference.

Beyond content and pedagogy, an LGBTQ-transformative history education has to move beyond individual classrooms and teachers to a coordinated process that is both bottom-up and top-down. Students and educators must have the freedom to explore and innovate in age-appropriate ways. That requires school, district, and state policies that facilitate LGBTQ curricular inclusion. Such policies drive a host of processes, from textbook revision and adoption to professional development priorities and funding, all of which are discussed in chapter 4.

Without these policies, educators who want to do this work are vulnerable to a host of attacks. Educators who are reluctant or actively resistant to doing the work will have few incentives—and no training—to change. Still, as Debra Fowler, executive director of the LGBTQ history education nonprofit History UnErased says, "Policy mandates are terrific but unless systems are in place to make them happen, they don't get us very far."[36] A truly LGBTQ-transformative history education is one where policy implementation is funded to build aligned curriculum and educational materials. Leadership must foster an enduring commitment from state and local school officials, administrators, and teachers' organizations, as well as outreach to parents, students, and other stakeholders. The struggle for this history has been many decades in the making. We still have a long road ahead.

In 1968, James Baldwin testified before the House Select Subcommittee on Labor to speak about history education. "My history," he told congressional leaders, "contains the truth about America. It is going to be hard to teach it. . . . I am the flesh of your flesh and bone of your bone. . . . My history and culture has got to be taught. It is yours." He warned that such a history lesson would be transformative: "This would involve a change in your institutions. It is not

24   Contested Curriculum

just a matter of passing a bill. It is not a matter of letting me into it, it has to change. This is true for all American institutions—including schools and the textbook industry."[37]

We can achieve an LGBTQ-transformative K–12 history education with powerful content, concepts, curriculum, materials, policies, and people. Our democracy needs it. Now is the time.

FIG. 1.1. Two-spirit artist Canelo Cabrera Lopez, *Always Have, Always Will*, 2021.

1

The Prehistory of LGBTQ History Education

In 2011, the California State Legislature passed Senate Bill 48: the Fair, Accurate, Inclusive, and Respectful (FAIR) Education Act. Preceding that moment were over four decades of work to bring LGBTQ history education into public schools. The structures and practices enabling its possibility extend back even further. A series of cofactors prevented meaningful implementation of LGBTQ-inclusive K–12 history education from the 1970s through the 1980s. Still, tentative successes demonstrated that teaching age-appropriate, diverse history generally and LGBTQ history specifically was both possible and important. The challenges revealed the many obstacles confronting those advocating its inclusion.

To make sense of how LGBTQ-inclusive history education made its way into K–12 policy, we have to start a century ago. In the 1920s, a nationwide push to modernize textbooks led the California Department of Education to create the Curriculum Commission in 1927. It was tasked with evaluating textbooks for state adoption across subjects, including history and social studies.[1] This body would later be known at the Curriculum Development and Supplemental Materials Commission and, more recently, the Instructional Quality Commission. It became the key structure for not just determining what history textbooks the state would adopt, but also developing the History-Social Science Framework and related state standards. The prehistory of LGBTQ history education also has roots in the 1930s and 1940s, when advocates tried to bring more Black history into textbooks. Starting in 1932, the National Association for the Advancement of Colored People (NAACP) Committee on Public School Textbooks lobbied textbook publishers with its *Anti-Negro Propaganda in School Textbooks* report. By the 1950s, history textbooks made tokenizing changes. Racist frames and narratives persisted. California's fifth graders still learned that enslaved children played happily with the children of slave owners and had "snug cabins to live in, plenty to eat, and work that was not too hard." Southern textbooks well into the 1960s called the white supremacist rollback of Reconstruction "Redemption" and cast the Ku Klux Klan as heroic. Progress in this era was hampered by anti-communist attacks on inclusionary textbooks. These conflated fears about what attackers saw as "collectivist" propaganda with content that might further racial integration.[2]

In the postwar era, hundreds of small "watchdog" groups had sprung up across the United States to ferret out "subversive" elements in education. In California, Pasadena and later Orange County became key to right-wing organizing regarding textbook selection. In the mid-1950s, fueled by McCarthyism, they secured loyalty oaths from all social studies textbook authors. By the 1960s, through the language of anti-communism, minimizing racial inclusion became one of the main fronts in textbook fights. This was rarely linked

28   Contested Curriculum

directly with concerns regarding sexuality, although claims that racial inclusion in history textbooks would further "race mixing" among America's youth had embedded within it an implicit anxiety about a breakdown in the nation's racialized sexual order. No proposed history textbooks meaningfully addressed women's history, beyond mention of suffrage and a handful of "worthies." There was no discussion of gender as a social force or what would later become known as LGBTQ history.

Many of the same people who mobilized to fight inclusive history textbooks battled against sex education. Across the 1960s, even the relatively liberal Mary Calderone and her organization SIECUS (Sex Information and Education Council of the United States) emphasized that a comprehensive curriculum should have monogamous heterosexuality and sex within marriage as its goals. She also suggested that such education could help prevent nonmarital heterosexual sex and homosexuality. Nonetheless, critics attacked SEICUS and comprehensive sex education for stirring up the very activities they purported to prevent. Californian activism in this era became a crucial bridge between disparate 1950s and 1960s anticommunist forces regarding textbooks and curriculum and the late 1970s anti-gay "Save Our Children" campaign in Florida and California's related Briggs Initiative. With Orange County as the center of resistance to John Hope Franklin's eighth-grade textbook *Land of the Free* (1966) and comprehensive sex education, the New Right built a powerful base of grievance that would later elect Ronald Reagan to the U.S. presidency.[3]

Despite emergent New Right forces, during the 1960s and 1970s pressure mounted for history textbooks and related policy to become more inclusive. The civil rights movement's ongoing curricular efforts combined with major scholarly reassessments of the histories of slavery and its aftermath, as well as the histories of Native Americans, Latino/as, and Asian Americans. Activists asserted that accurate textbooks would both help ill-informed Americans reconsider the basis of their racism and bolster Black students' resilience against feelings of inferiority and exclusion. In September 1965, the California State Legislature revised Education Code Section 9310.5 to mandate that K–8 U.S. and California history textbooks "correctly portray the role and contribution of the American Negro and members of other ethnic groups in the total development of the United States and of the State of California." In 1974, thanks to the organizing of feminists in the California Federation of Teachers, this was updated to include women's contributions and prohibit curriculum that reflected "adversely on persons" on the basis of "sex." In 2011, a more contemporary version of this became the scaffolding that the FAIR Education Act used to mandate the inclusion of the "role and contributions of . . . lesbian, gay, bisexual, and transgender Americans" and "persons with disabilities" to the "economic, political, and social development of California and the United States of America."[4]

At the national level, Vice President Hubert Humphrey decried the "Negro history gap" and Congress passed the Elementary and Secondary School Education Act of 1965. In this law, $400 million was earmarked for schools and libraries to purchase "multi-racial" and "multi-ethnic" books. Even so, many districts opted for noninclusive textbooks. In the early to mid-1970s, the federal government committed to diversifying K–12 history curriculum. Congress passed the 1972 Ethnic Heritage Studies Act (EHSA) as Title IX amendments to the Elementary and Secondary Education Act of 1965. It funded projects that emphasized the "contributions of . . . ethnic groups to the American heritage" in history education. In addition to Black, Native American, and Latino/a efforts, it supported ethnic European subgroups (such as Italian Americans and Polish Americans).[5]

Also in the 1970s, feminist critiques of K–12 schools revealed how sexism structured curriculum. For history education particularly, feminists demonstrated how curriculum and textbooks rendered women invisible or unimportant to major historical events and change over time. They pushed for the inclusion of women's lives, accomplishments, and impacts, examined where and why omission occurred, and called for new lenses of gender. Feminists also raised many other concerns about gender stereotypes in institutional norms and practices, classroom arrangements, and policies. In 1973, representatives of the California Federation of Teachers founded the Women in Education Committee and testified before the State Board of Education's Curriculum Commission to present evidence of sexism in textbooks. This led the next year to laws updating the Education Code to mandate inclusion of the roles and contributions of women in U.S. history education and textbooks.[6]

The landmark federal Women's Education Equity Act (WEEA) of 1974 sought to fight sex-role stereotyping and the underrepresentation of women in K–12 education. It funded studies revealing the absence of women's history in K–12 textbooks and suggested places for inclusion. WEEA grants underwrote *In Search of Our Past* (1980), a widely disseminated project out of Berkeley Unified School District for junior high schools. Its lesson plans, contextual material, and resources substantially covered precontact Native women, Black and white southern antebellum women, and diverse women's labor in nineteenth- and early twentieth-century industrialization. *In Search of Our Past* features multiple examples of women pushing against racialized white, middle-class feminine ideals. There are also mentions of historical structures of Native and Black family diversity beyond nuclear family models. It demonstrates intersections between movements such as abolitionism and feminism. Students are urged to consider how race, class, and sex structure linked oppressions, and how women resisted and reformed institutions and systems.[7] For all its strengths, *In Search of Our Past* neither had material on same-sex relationships/identities nor gender diversity beyond the conventional male/female binary. Moreover, because it was a supplemental resource rather than a survey textbook such as *Land of the Free*, it was not core curriculum. During the Reagan administration, funding for EHSA and WEEA was drastically cut or rolled into other U.S. Department of Education block grants. Related projects gradually faded from history classrooms.

As a result of textbook reforms, curricular changes, and governmental practices, K–12 history textbooks across the 1970s and 1980s generally became more inclusive of nonwhite, women, immigrant, and/or working-class "worthies." Highlighted individuals emphasized a patriotic narrative of continual improvement toward opportunity, freedom, and national exceptionalism. Plopping "inspirational" figures in without critical context avoided questions about what the experiences of people of color, immigrants, or women might tell students about ongoing U.S. exclusions and struggles for transformation. Race, gender, and class as analytic lenses through which to explore the entire American past remained sidelined.[8] LGBTQ representation and analysis was wholly absent. Nonetheless, feminist and racial justice achievements built organizing, legislative, and curriculum precedents for the eventual passage of the FAIR Education Act.

32   Contested Curriculum

Preliminary Lesbian and Gay Lessons

The invisibility of K–12 LGBTQ history through the 1970s resulted from several factors. First, LGBTQ scholarly history was in its infancy. Second, LGBTQ+ educators and students faced profound marginalization and discrimination. Third, many viewed even modest efforts to bring LGBTQ content into K–12 classrooms as harmful to young people's development. Still, initial building blocks in scholarship, law, and advocacy sowed the possibility of inclusion.

What was then called "lesbian and gay history" was at its academic beginnings. While some homophile activists did historical research in the 1950s and 1960s, foundational scholarly works were not published until the mid-1970s. In that sense, Carroll Smith-Rosenberg's article "The Female World of Love and Ritual" (1975) and Jonathan Ned Katz's *Gay American History* (1976) represent the origins of the subfield. The Gay Academic Union, formed in 1973, featured scholars doing historical research, including Katz, Joan Nestle, Barbara Gittings, Martin Duberman, and John D'Emilio. The Committee on Lesbian and Gay History (which became the Committee on LGBT History and is now the LGBTQ+ History Association, an affiliate of the American Historical Association), did not form until 1979.[9]

From the late 1940s through the 1970s, stigma, discrimination, and policing of homosexuality and gender variance in teachers and students foreclosed inclusion of LGBTQ history education. In the postwar era, returning veteran men replaced women in school administration. Married women came to outnumber the single women who had long dominated the teaching profession. This set up a heteronormative gender binary within school cultures at the same time that "spinsterhood" was increasingly associated with pathologized lesbianism. Expert discourse viewed homosexuality among youth as an environmental and psychosocial contagion requiring scrutiny.[10]

In the early 1950s, the California State Legislature made it the only state to require police to coordinate with school officials and the state agency tasked with approving teaching licenses whenever educators were arrested on gay-related charges. In states such as Idaho and Florida, sex panics during the 1950s and 1960s ensnared educators in anti-gay witch hunts. These were justified through postwar medical, social scientific, popular—and empirically wrong—beliefs linking sexual "perversion" with psychopathy and pedophilia. Educators, regardless of sexual orientation or gender identity, had to embody the "model citizen," espouse the virtues of heteronormativity, and disavow anything in the classroom that might implicate them. Rumors could and did destroy careers.[11]

There were no prospects of inclusive curriculum, unless one counts the anti-gay scaremongering health education film *Boys Beware* (1961), which was shown in classrooms across Southern California. In Anaheim, it was shown as part of what was a fairly liberal Family Life and Sex Education program until conservatives mobilized against that program in the late 1960s. Prior to the rollback, the ninth-grade curriculum taught that homosexuality "had been known throughout human history" but certainly did not teach about that history. The instructional guide for teachers, in a position that was relatively sympathetic for the time, urged tolerance for what it viewed as a "problem" or deviation.[12]

Rather than educating about the existence of LGBT lives and themes in history, experts generally urged teachers to surveil students for signs of homosexual tendencies. In health class, teachers might mention homosexuality to caution

34   Contested Curriculum

students against it but otherwise were to stay away from the subject. "The role of the classroom teacher is one of noting the problem," asserted psychiatrist George Kriegman, "and bringing it to the attention of the appropriate school counselor or health educator." By virtue of not being involved in "daily tutorial activity," he explained, counselors and health educators could discuss suspicions with students. They could then seek preventative measures that would redirect most youth back onto the straight and narrow. He advised counselors assign more "extreme" cases to intensive psychological or psychiatric intervention.[13]

Even though lesbian and gay educators gained more personal rights and professional protections between the mid-1960s and the mid-1970s, this did not translate into curricular inclusion. In many cases, victories were predicated on the assumption that teachers would not bring LGBT content into their classrooms. In 1969, the California Supreme Court ruled in the landmark 4–3 *Morrison v. State Board of Education* decision that a teacher could not lose his credentials based solely on his "homosexual character" or on prior noncriminal same-sex activities (i.e., private, consensual, and neither illegal sodomy nor resulting in arrest). As the majority stated, "There was no evidence that petitioner had failed to impress upon the minds of his pupils the principles of morality as required."[14] In other words, the court ruled for Morrison in part because the teacher did not discuss homosexuality with his students and his sexual orientation did not affect his curriculum or pedagogy.

A flurry of other cases from the late 1960s through the mid-1970s solidified *Morrison* as a precedent, but few educators victorious in court were able to return to classroom teaching. Joe Acanfora, the plaintiff in the Fourth Circuit's *Acanfora v. Board of Education of Montgomery County* (1974) decision, was a Maryland teacher reassigned out of the classroom due to his gay public activism. While the court ruled that his speech was protected because it occurred outside of the classroom, he lost anyway on a technicality. He never returned to teaching. Several trans K–12 educators, including New Jersey elementary band teacher Paula Grossman, Pennsylvania art teacher Jenelle Ashlie, and California high school gym teacher Steve Dain, either lost their cases outright or received compensation but not the right to return to the classroom, based on fears that their presence could psychologically harm or confuse students. No successful cases directly affirmed the right of educators to teach LGBTQ-inclusive curriculum. Case law continued to build a fragile status protection based on sexual orientation but not gender identity, and public speech, but only beyond school walls.[15]

Beyond court cases, organizing not only gave lesbian, gay, and bisexual educators social support and a political voice, it furthered the dialogue about bringing content into classrooms. In 1969 and 1970, long before such actions happened in other states, the California Federation of Teachers passed several resolutions. One urged "life and sex education" that "explains the various American life-styles" and denounced systemic oppression against gay people. After a heated floor debate, the organization's convention also passed a resolution supporting gay-affirming school counseling. In 1972, New Jersey high school English teacher and Gay Activist Alliance member John Gish organized the Gay Teachers Caucus of the National Education Association (NEA). In 1974, the NEA added "sexual preference" to its nondiscrimination statement, a year after the American Psychiatric Association (APA) depathologized homosexuality. From then on, the NEA offered teachers funding to fight employment discrimination. A year after the 1974 formation of the New York

36   Contested Curriculum

Gay Teachers Association (GTA), educators secured a commitment from the city's Board of Education that it would not discriminate in employment on the grounds of someone being gay. By the late 1970s, the GTA's newsletter regularly voiced gay teachers' responsibility to lesbian and gay students and the related importance of being out in the classroom.[16]

In spring 1975, educators Hank Wilson, Tom Ammiano, and Ron Lanza formed the Bay Area Gay Teachers Caucus (soon after renamed the Gay Teachers and School Workers Coalition). According to Ammiano, they organized out of anger. Lanza had quit his Walnut Creek job when administrators told him he could not invite a gay speaker into his class. In June, outraged by the San Francisco Board of Education's 7–0 vote against adding sexual orientation to its employment nondiscrimination policy, the Bay Area Gay Teachers Caucus mobilized over three hundred people, including students and straight teachers, to descend on the chambers, singing "When the Gays Go Marching In." The board, citing the *Morrison* case, APA depathologization, and inclusive NEA policy, unanimously reversed their vote. The crowd erupted into sustained applause. A middle school girl at the rally, asked how she felt about having a gay teacher, replied, "I like it a lot because they have more reasonable answers, and they wouldn't just say 'Men do this and men do that,' they'd probably say, 'Both' [men and women can do anything]." In his memoir, Ammiano recalls, "That was the first time that we won anything big. We were crying." During the rest of the 1970s and into the 1980s, similar organizations formed around the state and across the country.[17]

Throughout the 1970s and into the 1980s, much inclusion was necessarily, as educator Stephen Lane notes, "meant to escape the notice of school leadership." Lane writes that some brave teachers informally included something in "a lesson plan . . . or reading chosen with particular care." In 1976, for example, elementary school teacher Eric Rofes was reading with his students when the word "gay" elicited giggles. In the ensuing discussion, he acknowledged that while it meant "happy" in this context, it could also mean "homosexual," and that was not something to laugh about. The following year, two students in his class independently chose anti-gay crusader Anita Bryant as their "Important Person" to write about, one favorable and the other critical. Rofes facilitated a spirited discussion as a result. These moments are illustrative of informal ways teachers invited LGBTQ content at personal risk but often without raising the eyebrows of staff, administrators, or parents. (There were, of course, many instances where casual history "lessons" were decidedly discriminatory. In October 1978, activists protested a Honolulu high school history teacher who, while teaching the fall of Rome, was asked his thoughts on homosexuals. By his own account, he told his students, "If I were king . . . I would line them up and shoot them." He faced no disciplinary action.)[18]

There were more visible advocacy advances. In 1971, the local Board of Education fired an eighth-grade Iowa City sex education teacher for having members of the Gay Liberation Front speak, but the community rallied around him and he was reinstated. In Massachusetts and California, lesbian and gay speakers bureaus organized and brought advocates, experts, and "everyday" gay men and lesbians into high school classrooms. Members of the Homophile Union of Boston and the local Daughters of Bilitis chapter in 1972 founded the Boston Gay Speakers Bureau (now SpeakOUT Boston). Soon after, they began giving talks at local high schools to provide positive gay and lesbian role models. Around the same time, in Santa Barbara, gay men and lesbians organized

38   Contested Curriculum

a similar speakers bureau. This occurred initially through "family life" and health education. In places such as San Francisco and Palo Alto, mandated units included content on sex roles and sexual orientation. At one Oregon high school, students had a day devoted to choosing from speakers on a variety of sexuality and relationship subjects. The gay and lesbian panel was so popular they had to turn students away, so speakers repeated the session six times throughout the day to meet demand. "There has been no criticism of this program by the community and a minimum of questioning," observers remarked. Through guest speakers and teachers' informal mentioning of past lesbian and gay individuals and events, social studies and history content also began to occasionally appear. Even so, the focus was on the elimination of derogatory stereotypes rather than presenting homosexuality as equivalent to heterosexuality.[19]

Despite this sunny account, bringing guest speakers came with risk for teachers. Shortly after the Gay Teachers Speakers Bureau formed in San Francisco, an educator at Everett Middle School was fired and lost his credential after the daughter of an anti-gay activist claimed a speaker brought out a sex toy during a talk. The allegation was groundless and the teacher won on appeal. Still, he was reassigned to the library rather than being allowed to return to the classroom.[20]

Beyond Briggs: Advances and Setbacks in the 1980s

In 1977, anti-gay crusader Anita Bryant's successful Save Our Children campaign had led to the repeal of sexual orientation protections in the nondiscrimination ordinance of Dade County, Florida. Riding this momentum, California state senator John Briggs proposed a law to fire or deny employment to school employees whose "public homosexual activity and/or public homosexual conduct" was "directed at, or likely to come to the attention of, school children or other school employees." Briggs, an Orange County Republican whose ambitions were fused with the New Right, put this before voters in 1978 as a ballot initiative after a failed effort to move it through the legislature. Proponents attempted to portray lesbian, gay, and bisexual educators as bad role models. They suggested that such teachers' open presence in schools could encourage kids to be gay and (relying on long-standing false stereotypes) lead to child molestation. The passage of Proposition 6 (informally known as the Briggs Initiative) would have derailed the nascent inclusive curriculum. At first, a majority of Californians seemed likely to approve the measure. Ultimately, however, Proposition 6 lost in a landslide, due to the grassroots organizing efforts of lesbian, gay, and bisexual activists, educators, labor allies, and a diverse array of other movements.

In some towns, the Briggs battle clarified why an inclusive curriculum was one way to foster a democracy that embraced diversity. In Healdsburg, the local school board president joined Briggs at a September 1978 press conference to target Fitch Mountain Elementary School second-grade teacher Larry Berner. Briggs raved that "put[ting] a second-grade child with a homosexual" was like letting "necrophiliacs . . . be morticians." The attack backfired when hundreds of fellow teachers, parents, faith leaders, and community members rallied to Berner's defense. Mothers testified that they wanted teachers like him so their children would not "grow up to be bigots." A dad added that his son was "very happy in [Berner's] class" and that he trusted Berner more than "many heterosexual teachers." Berner, previously soft-spoken and discreet, went on to be an activist with SCRAP 6 (Sonoma County Residents Against Prop 6), even debating Briggs.[21]

Many educators, regardless of sexual orientation, became more vocal about the dignity and worth of lesbian, gay, and bisexual teachers and began to consider the value of relevant classroom content. In 1977, Lester Kirkendall, an emeritus professor of family life at Oregon State in Corvallis, and Len Trisch, a health education specialist for the Oregon Department of Education, argued that, at least in secondary school, social studies classes should "examine the pros and cons of issues that agitate communities, states, or the nation—for example, the civil rights of homosexuals." They suggested that in history classes students could learn about ancient "Greek attitudes about women and homosexual relations." They saw this as part of a "supportive and integrative" approach to homosexuality across the curriculum. Students, as developing citizens, should learn about homosexuality, they explained, adding that "discriminatory practices will need to be explored and discarded, as will the various myths and stereotypes that have made the lives of homosexuals difficult."[22] As the growing lesbian, gay, and bisexual movement and rise of the New Right brought related issues more persistently into the public square, it became self-evident to some that K–12 students should acquire tools to consider and contextualize them.

Even in its defeat, the Briggs campaign had negative reverberations for inclusive curriculum. In California, the Briggs Initiative cast a long shadow. Reverend Lou Sheldon, an Orange County evangelical leader, was deeply involved in Proposition 6. He went on to found the California Coalition for Traditional Values. By 1984, this had morphed into Traditional Values Coalition (TVC), an anti-gay organization with national ambitions. Across the 1980s and 1990s, TVC obsessively fought against LGBT students, teachers, and curriculum. This organizing helped accelerate the Christian Right's national movement.

In 1978, Oklahoma passed the Briggs-style House Bill 1629. The bill was introduced by Democratic state representative John Monks and Republican state senator Mary Helm. Monks referred to homosexuals as "degenerate" and "mentally deranged." He reassured citizens that the bill would apply to "both queers and lesbians" as well as others who "promoted homosexuality." After the bill sailed through the Oklahoma House with an 88–2 vote, Senator Helm flew Anita Bryant out for a three-thousand-strong "Oklahomans for Anita" rally at the State Fair Arena. In April, the state senate unanimously passed the bill, and the governor signed it into law.

In court, the law was less successful. Although the state won in U.S. district court, Judge Luther Eubanks warned that trying to fire a teacher who simply "assigns for class study articles and books written by advocates of gay rights" would almost certainly be ruled unconstitutional. In 1984, the Tenth Circuit Court of Appeals overturned this ruling in a 2–1 decision on First Amendment grounds, even as it upheld the right to deny employment to homosexuals for overt, public sexual conduct. The opinion tempered the law's curricular implications. In part because "the statute does not require that the teacher's public utterance occur in the classroom," the court declared the law overly broad. In 1985, the U.S. Supreme Court affirmed the decision without a written opinion by the narrowest of margins, a 4–4 ruling (with one justice out for medical care).[23]

Meanwhile in Maine, Madison High School social studies teacher David Solmitz sought to hold a schoolwide "Tolerance Day" in the fall of 1984 that would include gay and lesbian speakers. It was to be in response to the recent murder of a gay man by high school students yelling anti-gay epithets. When community uproar led to the cancellation of Tolerance Day, the local school board cited student safety and preventing educational disruption as its rationales. In 1985, the Supreme Court of Maine found against the teacher, a proposed lesbian speaker, and a high school history student, who all alleged that the cancellation violated their constitutional rights. Still, the court stressed what the case did not involve: The school board, it wrote, "did not tell Solmitz how he was to teach his history course. It did not restrict Solmitz in any way in freely expressing his views on any subject within or without the school. Similarly, the Board did not prohibit any other discussions of tolerance or of prejudice against homosexuals, whether in Solmitz's classes or otherwise within Madison High School."[24] While hardly a full-throated defense of the right of teachers to bring LGBT-inclusive curriculum into their history classrooms, the opinion suggests the court's hesitancy to make curricular content an issue from which to parse First Amendment rights. From all of these cases, the extent to which LGBT-inclusive curriculum could be protected speech remained ambiguous.

In terms of post-Briggs federal legislation, the November 1980 election that swept Reagan into the presidency also gave Republicans a Senate majority for the first time since 1953. In 1981, capitalizing on the convergence in the New Right between evangelical, conservative Catholic, and Mormon agendas to promote abstinence-only health education, Senators Orrin Hatch (R-UT) and Jeremiah Denton (R-AL) introduced the Adolescent Family Life Act (AFLA). The act was immensely consequential for LGBT-inclusive curriculum beyond sex education. While AFLA did not explicitly mention homosexuality, its intent, like that of the whole abstinence-only sex education movement, singularly promoted a wait-until-marriage approach. This not only sought to prohibit all nonmarital sex but also rejected considering same-sex couples as legitimate.

This de facto exclusion of homosexuality from health curriculums became more formalized across the country as the AIDS epidemic gave cultural conservatives new fodder. In 1987, notoriously anti-gay senator Jesse Helms (R-NC) introduced an amendment to an appropriations bill that banned federal funds "to provide AIDS education, information, or prevention materials and activities that promote or encourage, directly or indirectly, homosexual sexual activities." This utilized Briggs-style language. The logic of AFLA and the Helms Amendment was then extended by state legislatures to anti-gay curriculum laws. From 1987 to 1988, nine states, including California, passed laws that either imposed "abstinence only until marriage" requirements for health education or established bans on the "promotion of homosexuality" or teaching that homosexuality was an acceptable "lifestyle." From 1989 through 1996, another seven states passed anti-gay curriculum laws.[25] While these "No Promo Homo" laws targeted sex education, they had a chilling effect across subjects.

Even though the Briggs Initiative cast a long shadow well into the 1990s, the campaign also produced new LGBTQ-inclusive curricular possibilities. After the defeat of Proposition 6, the Gay Teachers and School Workers Coalition supported development of gay-friendly K–12 curriculum. The San Francisco-based Save Our Human Rights Foundation, which had begun during the campaign, transformed into the Human Rights Foundation (HRF). With a focus on making public schools supportive environments for lesbian and gay students, HRF recognized the importance of curriculum. Attracting the interest of the Columbia Foundation, HRF secured grants to expand its speakers bureau and produce a

K–12 lesbian and gay curriculum guide.[26] In 1984, this became *Demystifying Homosexuality: A Teaching Guide about Lesbians and Gay Men*. This 175-page book primarily focused on health education curriculum, but managing editor (and HRF executive director) José Gómez also featured a chapter on "Gay or Bisexual Historical Figures." Mostly it took a heritage-based "heroes/role models" approach. Its anachronistic "we are everywhere" approach labeled prominent historical figures as forebears to contemporary lesbians, gays, and bisexuals. In this, it emulated a similar move made in *Young, Gay and Proud!*, a book directed to youth (rather than educators) that saw its first U.S. publication in 1980.[27]

Nonetheless, *Demystifying Homosexuality*'s history chapter begins by considering Jonathan Ned Katz's *Gay American History*, which, it explains, uses a gay historical lens to formulate a "new basis for a radical critique of society." Quoting Katz, Gómez asserts that, at its best, lesbian- and gay-inclusive history education should produce more expansive, interlinked kinds of historical thinking about labor, power, sex roles, sexism, family and marriage, and "the role of the religious, legislative, judicial, medical, and psychological professions in the social creation of pain." Ultimately, such education might, as Katz argues, raise "the question of whether this society can accommodate the demands of America's dispossessed for power and control over the machinery by which they make their lives."[28]

A chapter on "Lesbian and Gay Male Literature" explains nineteenth-century traditions of same-sex romantic friendships, how late nineteenth- and early twentieth-century sexology categorized and pathologized sexual and gender diversity, and how archival and personal censorship leaves much of the queer past hidden. As such, *Demystifying*

Homosexuality demonstrated to educators how age-appropriate inclusive history was possible through both heritage / heroes / role models and historical inquiry approaches (see the introduction). It is unclear how much teachers used this book, but it was distributed nationally and even internationally.

Across the 1980s, gay youth protectionist discourse also justified K–12 curricular inclusion. In the mid-1980s, legal scholars Donna Dennis and Ruth Harlow made the argument that mandated "inclusive curriculum" should be one legal remedy for school-based discrimination. They wrote, "Courts should require schools" to "use texts that discuss the long-standing persecution of gay persons, and that include the contributions of gay persons to history."[29] While this novel legal strategy remained untested, educators and advocates made multiple efforts to get inclusive history into classrooms.

In 1984, following a violent incident, School District of Philadelphia superintendent Dr. Constance Clayton (the first woman and African American to hold the post) invited the Philadelphia Lesbian and Gay Task Force (PLGTF) to make suggestions on how to make schools safer for gay students. Among other calls, PLGTF executive director Rita Addessa suggested a Board of Education policy prohibiting sexual orientation discrimination in curriculum and instructional materials. Moreover, Addessa urged "mandates" for "the fair and representative treatment of gay and lesbian people, along with women, racial and ethnic minorities, as part of the ongoing process of curricular revision," citing history as a key subject area. In 1986, Addessa requested that funding for ongoing curricular revision be built into the district's long-range budget. In 1988, PLGTF folded these recommendations in a general ask for anti-discrimination measures from the Commonwealth of Pennsylvania. No action was taken. Finally, in 1994, the School District of Philadelphia passed some of her suggestions, bundled into Policy 102, "Multiracial-Multicultural-Gender Education." In the late 1990s, Addessa was still demanding the district embrace "its spirit or its mandate . . . around gay and lesbian issues."[30]

Educators were more successful in creating distinct organizations to serve LGBT students. The Institute for the Protection of Lesbian and Gay Youth (later Hetrick-Martin Institute), founded in 1979 in New York, launched Harvey Milk High School in 1985, primarily to serve at-risk sexual-minority youth who struggled in the city's public schools. The year prior in Los Angeles, Fairfax High School science teacher Dr. Virginia Uribe founded Project 10, which had a similar mission. In Massachusetts in 1987, Cambridge Rindge and Latin School English teacher Arthur Lipkin and auto shop teacher Al Ferreria pushed for faculty training on anti-gay bias. The following year, after the suicide of a recent graduate, Ferreria started Project 10 East as an early kind of Gay-Straight Alliance group.[31] None of these institutional efforts centered on history education per se. But all acknowledged curriculum as one part of the larger puzzle of protecting sexual-minority students.

Institutional interventions were met with pushback. In California, the Traditional Values Coalition launched an ultimately unsuccessful multiyear media and legislative campaign against Project 10. Other attempts at institutional change stalled before even getting off the ground. One straight Boston high school social studies teacher recalled in the mid-1980s requesting that the school's students and staff "be taught about homosexuality, educated against common stereotypes, and be encouraged to create a supportive environment for homosexual students." In response, a fellow faculty member called him the "fag in social studies" and the proposal went nowhere. In addition, it was far easier for administrators to dismiss student needs and educators' professional development than face what they anticipated would be substantial resistance. For this reason, unlike many major school reforms of the late twentieth- and early twenty-first centuries, the Gay-Straight Alliance and subsequent Safe Schools movements would largely be bottom-up (from students and teachers) rather than top-down (from administrators and policymakers).[32]

Some teachers continued to quietly make informal interventions throughout the 1980s. Lane suggests that gay teachers and straight allies tried to help students through three strategies: becoming the known "safe" person at school for students, finding nonjudgmental and nonconfrontational ways to bring gay and lesbian awareness into the classroom, and avoiding controversy. Sometimes, these efforts propelled teachers into activism. Most notably, New England private school teacher Kevin Jennings went from showing his eleventh-grade U.S. history class *The Times of Harvey Milk* in the spring of 1987 to, the next year, coming out to his class before showing the documentary. In 1990, he founded the Gay and Lesbian Independent School Teachers Network (GLISTN). GLISTN would soon after become GLSTN (the Gay and Lesbian School Teachers Network), with Jennings as its first full-time executive director, and, by 1997, GLSEN (the Gay, Lesbian, and Straight Educators Network). Across the 1990s, Jennings would be instrumental in the first sustained push for LGBTQ-inclusive K–12 history education.[33]

In addition to informal and institutional strategies, educators and others sought to craft history curriculum

48 Contested Curriculum

FIG. 1.2. Laurie Casa Grande, "Unfortunately, History Has Set the Record a Little Too Straight" poster (Minneapolis: Gay and Lesbian Community Action Council, 1988). Courtesy of the GLBT Historical Society.

supplements like *Demystifying Homosexuality*. In 1988, to commemorate the first National Coming Out Day, the Gay and Lesbian Community Action Council of Minneapolis printed a widely distributed poster of ten famous historical figures, with the headline, "Unfortunately, History Has Set the Record a Little Too Straight." Using the role model/ heritage approach, the poster's images of people such as James Baldwin, Willa Cather, Eleanor Roosevelt, Bessie Smith, and Walt Whitman implies that they were in some fashion queer (some more openly and avowedly than others). The caption reads, "Assume that all important contributions are made by heterosexuals, and you're not only thinking straight, but narrow. Sexual orientation has nothing to do with the ability to make a mark, let alone make history."[34]

The poster's ambiguity about labeling its subjects makes it a somewhat ironic expression of National Coming Out Day. A viewer might reasonably wonder, "Well, were they or weren't they?" Implicitly, the tactic suggests the challenge of claiming people from the past as "like us" in a contemporary identitarian sense of sexual orientation. The poster's coyness also signals, without explaining, the unreliability of the archive and historical record to "prove" people were gay, lesbian, or bisexual. Still, even with its winking refusal to spell out how and why these figures constitute LGBTQ-inclusive history—and bearing in mind that labeling them through contemporary identity categories would have produced its own set of problems—it found its way into classrooms without raising too many eyebrows. As a selective conversation starter, and as a nod to students who might identify an educator who posted it as "safe," it made a lasting contribution.

More substantial was *Struggle for Equality: Lesbian and Gay Community*. The New York City Mayor's Office for the Lesbian and Gay Community developed this optional supplement for seventh- and eighth-grade social studies in fall 1989. It was created in conjunction with the New York City Board of Education's "Statement of Policy on Multicultural Education and Promotion of Positive Intergroup Relations," which was inclusive of sexual orientation.

Struggle for Equality presents a series of learning activities that frame the attainment of lesbian and gay civil rights and social acceptance. Three sections cover lesbian and gay social history directly. One explores the "hidden identities" of gay men and lesbians before Stonewall. Another has students track the growth of a lesbian and gay political movement from the homophile era through gay liberation and the development of national organizing. The third, in a remarkably nuanced set of sources, explores the particular challenges of "breaking the silence" for queer people of color, centering on blues singer Gladys Bentley's move from Harlem Renaissance top hat, tuxedo, and open relationships with women through her 1950s performative heterosexual domesticity in *Ebony* magazine. It also features late 1970s speeches by Audre Lorde and the socially conscious music of Tracy Chapman, who then (as now) refused to discuss publicly her sexuality while otherwise presenting as a Black queer woman.[35]

Struggle for Equality was a major advancement for inclusive K–12 history education. It went far beyond showcasing "role models." Instead, it linked past to present though historical inquiry about civic recognition and rights, social movement development, and the ways in which individual lives and identities are shaped by their historical contexts. It demonstrated how this content can easily and appropriately be taught not just in high school, but also in middle grades. On behalf of the Mayor's Office for the Lesbian and Gay Community, over the next two years psychologist Philip Spivey and nurse Ellen Zaltzberg gave workshops linking history with health in order to confront "heterosexism and homophobia." Among advocates for inclusive curriculum, it was widely cited. In the first year and a half, twenty-six of the thirty-two community districts within the New York public school system expressed a willingness to consider lesbian- and gay-affirmative materials. In 1991, building on this momentum, New York Public Library's first official celebration of Pride featured "Pride and Prejudice," a weeklong series of films and lectures designed to develop and distribute an "audio and visual Gay high school history curriculum." Curated by writer and activist Alan Hertzberg, the week had the endorsement of the Mayor's Office for the Lesbian and Gay Community and featured lectures by historians Joan Nestle and Martin Duberman, among others.[36]

Unfortunately, *Struggle for Equality*'s success was undermined by larger political forces. In late 1991 and 1992, a national controversy regarding the city's multicultural Children of the Rainbow Curriculum erupted due to three brief mentions of gay- and lesbian-parented families. Under pressure, the Board of Education backpedaled. In 1995, it wrote LGBTQ content out of its multicultural education policy. While *Struggle for Equality* was republished in 1994 as a supplemental resource, the withdrawal of administrative support blunted its impact.[37]

From the 1960s through the 1980s, government policy, educational reform, and labor advocacy brought about substantial changes to history education in terms of women and people of color. While these inclusionary processes left much to be desired, they nonetheless gave LGBTQ curriculum advocates a conceptual space to argue for something similar. Across the 1970s and 1980s, openly LGBTQ educators gained some labor protections and free speech rights, but their direct impact on LGBTQ-inclusive curriculum was mixed. For history education, this was complicated by the fact that LGBTQ history as a field of scholarship was still formative. Even so, advocacy for teachers and sexual-minority youth led to modest, sporadic, and generally short-lived curricular interventions. Bottom-up and localized historical curriculums and materials were undoubtedly groundbreaking, whether they took a heritage/role model or

52 Contested Curriculum

historical/movement approach. To gain a lasting foothold, however, LGBTQ-inclusive history education required both state action and community-based efforts at local and national scales. As chapter 2 shows, transforming these strategies into successful outcomes was considerably harder than advocates hoped.

FIG. 2.1. Alan Gutirrez, *Bayard Rustin*, 2012.

2

The State's the Place?

Sidelined Reforms Become Opt-In History

During the late 1980s and early 1990s, while a handful of cities initiated supplemental K–12 lesbian and gay history curricula, California and Massachusetts activists took their efforts statewide. Changing state policy held the promise of facilitating widespread implementation, baking in inclusion. Still, even as Safe Schools models of LGBTQ+ student advocacy found traction, state-level inclusive history education became collateral damage in wider culture war battles. Over the 1990s, this led to a shift away from the state and toward opt-in models for LGBT history education, such as the creation of Lesbian and Gay History Month. Real state-level change would have to wait until the 2010s.

California's First Framework Fight

Nearly three decades before California's LGBT-inclusive 2016 History-Social Science Framework, advocates made a concerted effort to get lesbian and gay history into an earlier version. Widely seen as a signal achievement in state education policy, California's 1987 History-Social Science Framework was a crown jewel of Bill Honig's decade-long tenure as state superintendent of public instruction. In November 1982, Honig, a former lawyer and teacher, beat three-term incumbent Wilson C. Riles, the first African American elected to statewide office in California, for the nonpartisan post. In 1982, Riles was the establishment candidate and enjoyed the backing of teachers unions. Honig, a centrist liberal with a reform message of systemic transformation, "educational excellence," and scholarship-grounded curriculum, attracted support from a constellation of conservatives, business leaders, and parents. Honig had served previously on the state's Board of Education. There, he came to believe that curricular reform could be the basis for improved teacher development, textbooks, and assessment. He touted recentering history in social studies and called for a common curriculum that would enhance civic engagement and shared values.[1]

In 1983, passage of California Senate Bill 813, the Hart-Hughes Educational Improvement Act, largely based on Honig's agenda, brought sweeping changes. The law set into motion subject-area Model Curriculum Standards, crafted through advisory committees mixing K–12 educators with university scholars. These were to be aligned with new frameworks that would direct academic content, textbook guidelines, and testing criteria.[2]

Honig's vision resonated with the Reagan administration's *A Nation at Risk* report, which came out the same year. This report suggested that failing schools were an issue of national security and global economic competition. In addition to calling for renewed academic rigor, it urged history curriculum that would promote, as mentioned in the introduction, a "common culture" for the pluralistic United

States. By 1985, when William Bennett became Reagan's secretary of education, he had, as chair of the National Endowment for the Humanities (NEH), already been a key speaker at Honig's 1984 Clio Conference at the University of California, Berkeley.

Also presenting at the Clio Conference was Diane Ravitch, a historian and educational reformer who became a central architect of California's History-Social Science Framework. At the conference, Ravitch presented a call for history teaching to "awaken . . . youngsters to the universality of the human experience as well as the magnificence and the brutality of which humans are capable." She believed that "properly taught, history encourages the development of intelligence, civility, and a sense of perspective. It endows students with a broad knowledge of other times, other cultures, other places; it presents cultural resources on which students may draw for the rest of their lives."[3] Ravitch's concept of history education went beyond instilling patriotism, morals, or civic decision-making. Honig's vision more closely aligned with Ravitch's than that of neoconservatives such as Bennett. Still, all three believed history education should strengthen common American culture. Shared values, they imagined, could bridge differences of a multicultural population struggling to overcome past inequalities.

In March 1986, Honig assembled historians and social studies teachers on the History-Social Science Curriculum Framework Committee. Ravitch and University of California, Los Angeles (UCLA), education professor Charlotte Crabtree were the new Framework's principal drafters. On July 9, 1987, the California Board of Education unanimously approved its new History-Social Science Framework. It was heralded for balancing multiculturalism with the need for a "common story" and instilling democratic civic values, citizenship rights, and responsibilities. It was to be the basis for a multiyear process of educator development, textbook alignment, and student assessment. These would culminate in a rigorous and inclusive social studies education centered in history as the "great integrative discipline."[4]

Some disagreed with the State Board of Education's (and Honig's) characterization of the Framework as a "consensus document." During the June 10 public comment at the Board of Education meeting, thirty-nine people spoke, many from communities of color and ethnic groups who expressed their concerns with limited representation. As education professor Duane Campbell later observed, it assumed that the frame for ethnic European immigrant assimilation could explain the dynamics of Mexican Americans, Indigenous people, and Asian Americans. As such, it gave those histories short shrift, preferring what Ravitch called "a story well told." Ravitch also left out anything LGBTQ, a personal irony given that, when this process was underway, she and her husband divorced (in 1986) and she began (in 1988) a long-term relationship with Mary Butz, a New York City educator she would legally marry in 2012.[5]

By framing minorities through a melting pot model, the 1987 Framework upheld an American progress narrative toward a more perfect union. As a both/and document, it purported, as Honig put it, to "present students with the goods and the bads of history" while "interweaving the stories of the many different groups who constitute the American people" into a "remarkable synthesis." It portrayed an inclusive, if homogenizing, mainstream liberalism. Culturally conservative education reformers such as Bennett and Lynne Cheney, his NEH successor, celebrated it, precisely because it allowed for difference but heralded assimilation, centered history as a civic project of "e pluribus unum," and leaned hard into that "unum."[6]

Meanwhile, in 1985, Robert Birle, a student teacher at San Francisco's George Washington High School, organized fellow teachers into what became the Bay Area Network of Gay and Lesbian Educators (BANGLE). The social group quickly grew to an advocacy organization with over forty members. By 1986, BANGLE recognized that the California Department of Education (CDE) was key to developing lesbian- and gay-inclusive education.[7] Birle requested a meeting with Honig.

By coincidence, in April 1986, the state attorney general's Commission on Racial, Ethnic, Religious, and Minority Violence issued its *Final Report*. The report had wide-ranging recommendations regarding race, religion, age, disability, and refugee status protections. In its education strategy, however, the report highlighted lesbians and gay men. It found, based on testimony from the San Francisco-based organization Community United Against Violence, that "much of the violence motivated by bigotry against gays and lesbians is perpetrated by school aged youth and that many young gays and lesbians are victimized in schools." Because of this, it urged the CDE to work with "gay and lesbian community representatives to prepare materials on myths and stereotypes" and "develop a handbook to provide information on gay and lesbian lifestyles" that could be distributed to educators.[8] BANGLE used these recommendations to advocate for greater inclusion in Honig's process.

In July, pressure from BANGLE led Honig to sit down with the *Bay Area Reporter*, a San Francisco gay community newspaper. In the article, Honig agreed to the general idea of "tolerance." He said that "kids shouldn't develop negative

The State's the Place?   59

feelings" toward lesbians and gays, adding that the CDE should "make sure that all people are treated with respect." Still, he argued, "I don't agree with the position that all lifestyles are . . . as good as the other." In an awkwardly phrased analogy, he explained, "I can not know anything about Nigerian culture but I can [still] know not to beat up Nigerians." Honig called more direct teaching about lesbians and gays "proselytizing" and added that "a literature of gay stories [with] gay protagonists . . . would be divisive." He conceded that "there should be information about the gay rights movement in high school [history] textbooks."[9] Difference, Honig believed, should be met with "respect," a term he used multiple times in the interview. Gay and lesbian subjects were to be included as long as they could transcend differences that might exclude them from heteronormative "tolerance." Honig's assimilative logic allowed examples of marginalization insofar as they demonstrated America's exceptional capacity to overcome them.

In any case, openly identified LGBTQ people and/or events did not show up in the 1987 History-Social Science Framework. They almost did not appear in any related materials either. Following a 1985 law that mandated the state's students learn about human rights and genocide, the CDE crafted its *Model Curriculum Guide for Human Rights and Genocide*. In early 1987, when the initial draft was released for public comment, it made no mention of historic persecution of homosexuals. BANGLE and Parents and Friends of Lesbians and Gays (PFLAG) protested, mounting a successful letter-writing campaign.

When the final guide was published later that year, gay people appeared twice, both in a bullet-pointed list of "examples of *extreme human rights violations*" (emphasis in original). First, among specific U.S. events such as slavery, the 1882

60 Contested Curriculum

Chinese Exclusion Act, and World War II Japanese American internment, was a general statement that educators should also teach about "discrimination against blacks, Asians, Hispanics, American Indians, women, the handicapped, and homosexuals." Second, "homosexuals" were included in a list of those victimized by "totalitarian policies" in Nazi Germany and Stalinist Russia. Related teaching materials, however, did not mention them, leaving teachers without implementation guidance.[10]

In 1988, Honig agreed to regular meetings with BANGLE to address the needs of gay, lesbian, and bisexual students. After the first one in August, he initiated the process to establish an Advisory Committee for the Gay and Lesbian Community, in line with other minorities' advisory committees. In January 1989, as plans were being made for a public ceremony to launch the committee, the CDE backed away. Deputy Superintendent of Public Instruction David Gordon told Birle that Honig was too busy with other priorities. He assured BANGLE there was an "open door." In reality, Honig refused to meet with representatives again until 1992.[11]

Birle joined forces with Jessea Greenman, who volunteered with the San Francisco Bay Area chapter of the Gay and Lesbian Alliance Against Defamation (GLAAD/ SFBA), and Hank Wilson, the educator who had helped cofound the Bay Area Gay Teachers Caucus fifteen years prior. Together, they became Project 21, named after its mission to make "public school curricula and textbooks across the USA inclusive of lesbian, bisexual and gay concerns by the twenty-first century." In a recent interview, Greenman noted that by the name "you can see that [we] knew it would take a long time." While Project 21 was California-focused, organizers understood that, given the federal nature of education, eventually groundwork would need to be laid in all fifty states.[12]

Project 21 was housed at and funded by GLAAD/SFBA, then primarily a media watchdog organization. As Greenman reasoned, textbooks were a powerful form of media that required GLAAD's activism to insure fair, accurate, and inclusive representation of lesbian, gay, and bisexual people. (Their conception of the project did not yet include transgender people, although that thinking evolved across the mid-1990s.) In 1990, the CDE engaged in a new round of K–8 History-Social Science textbook adoptions, aligned with the 1987 Framework and the *Model Curriculum Guide for Human Rights and Genocide*. When it came to changing school curriculums, Project 21 saw textbook reform as efficient because the community "could not afford the time and the resources to fight . . . in every school district in the state, let alone the country."[13]

To change textbooks, Project 21 had to engage state agencies tasked with their approval. Even with the advantage of several years of lobbying, the process was daunting. In the days before online review, publishers distributed proposed textbooks to the CDE's appointed Instructional Materials Evaluation Panels, which were made up primarily of K–12 educators and scholars. The public could review proposed textbooks at Instructional Material Display Centers across the state. People could make comments either in writing or during public meetings. The CDE and its evaluative bodies took most seriously those that addressed either of two concerns: legal compliance with Education Code and CDE policy, including mandates on "cultural and racial diversity"; and content evaluation, including factual accuracy and educational value. Evaluation Panels scored textbooks on these factors. Publishers responded to concerns and made minor related revisions. The Subject Matter Committee created a report of textbooks recommended (or not) for adoption. The Curriculum Commission considered this, heard additional public comment, and requested more publisher edits. After one more round of public hearings, the State Board of Education made its final list of approved textbooks.[14]

Project 21 entered the process during the Curriculum Commission's public comment. Even before heading to Sacramento, Greenman conceded at the time that their efforts were likely more "consciousness raising" rather than transformative, and later reflected, "I looked at this as planting the seeds." Birle also saw their campaign as the start of a "long-term battle" that was "part of a larger national movement aimed at improving the school conditions for gay youth."[15] Still, advocates made full-throated critiques and demands.

On July 19, 1990, a handful of lesbians and gay men were among the clamorous ninety-plus people testifying before the Curriculum Commission. San Francisco teacher Kevin Davis pointed to textbooks' failure to identify prominent historical figures as gay and urged a more "honest" history. California State University, Sacramento, communications professor Lee Nichols asserted that until the commission approved inclusive texts, students would "acquire their knowledge" about lesbian and gay people "from the streets." He accused commissioners of being "intimidated by demagogues, racists, and homophobes." Greenman, in a gesture to respectability politics, was dressed in the one business suit she owned. She called for Alexander Hamilton, Willa Cather, Oscar Wilde, Alan Turing, and others be named as gay so they might become role models for LGB youth. Hank Wilson waved a rainbow flag and held up informational posters, characterizing the friendship between the Marquis de

The State's the Place?   63

Lafayette and George Washington as romantic. According to one report, some Muslim advocates, there to push for better representation in sixth-grade world history textbooks, shook their head at Wilson's claim and said, "Shame! Shame!" Reverend Lou Sheldon of the Traditional Values Coalition viewed Project 21's testimony as "the homosexual community's way of overhauling straight America." When Greenman attempted to formally introduce herself to Sheldon, he refused to shake her hand.[16]

One surprise of the hearing was a coiffed blonde woman that Greenman recalled "looked like Anita Bryant," who stepped up to the speaker's podium "with her pearls and make-up," and, to everyone's surprise, said she had a gay son and that schools needed inclusive textbooks. This woman, whom Greenman only remembers as Carla, was a PFLAG mom from Santa Cruz who became a supporter of the Project 21 cause, along with the "absolutely fabulous" Julia and Sam Thoron, who had recently joined PFLAG's San Francisco chapter after their nineteen-year-old daughter had come out to them as a lesbian that summer while home from college. PFLAG, Greenman said, was the only organization besides BANGLE and GLAAD/SFBA that really "got" Project 21. At the time, many LGBT organizations saw the curriculum issue as too controversial.[17] In the end, the commission only advanced two publishers' educational materials to the next round: Houghton-Mifflin's K–8 series and Holt, Rinehart, and Winston's eighth-grade U.S. history textbook. Neither had gay content.

The California Board of Education's September 13 meeting was the final level of approval. Project 21 held a rally outside the CDE before testifying inside. At the rally, Birle called on fellow gay, lesbian, and bisexual people to "raise our voices in protest against a system which has denied our existence, robbed us of our heroes and heroines, pandered to religious intolerance . . . and nurtured the conditions which led to our persecution." He called on the Board of Education to meet its "obligation to prepare the citizens of this state to function in the real world." In his meeting testimony, Birle added, "Students should not be forced to read between the lines to know that some of this country's greatest citizens were gay, lesbian, or bisexual." He exhorted the Board to "get on with the job of educating our youth without bias or distortion."[18]

Greenman recalled the meeting as "heated and tense." She believed it was the first time that lesbian and gay people had appeared before the State Board of Education directly calling for curricular inclusion. In her testimony, she accused Board members of endorsing "lie by omission" and called them complicit in violence against lesbian, gay, and bisexual people. She pushed not just for "famous figures and front-page events" but the movements of "a courageous people."[19] Like the Curriculum Commission, the Board of Education made no LGB changes.

The History-Social Science Framework required curriculums to "accurately portray the cultural and racial diversity of our society." Project 21 saw, within "cultural diversity," a place for LGB-inclusive history education. The state's decision-making bodies followed the CDE's very different interpretation. "The framework does not establish homosexuals as a minority or cultural group," it asserted. It added, "To identify and treat them as such is not within the scope of the framework or this adoption." Moreover, Curriculum Committee members felt that K–8 was too young for such content. If it were to be included, they argued, it should appear in high school educational materials, which were conveniently outside of the scope of the state's textbook approval process.[20]

Californian LGBTQ-inclusive history education advocates faced gatekeepers who viewed all who pushed for more multicultural textbook representation as part of the same threat to "common culture" history education. As Dan Chernow, vice chairman of the Curriculum Committee, said, decision-makers tended to see the diverse people testifying as "interest groups" who "want to see history taught strictly from their perspective."[21] This was not true for lesbian, gay, and bisexual advocates, who were fighting against total erasure, not misrepresentation. That distinction was lost on those who pulled the levers.

At the same time, as rhetoric scholar Thomas Dunn notes in his analysis of this campaign, BANGLE and Project 21 "articulated a public memory of *liberation*." They insisted that "if a single story of American history was to be proclaimed, then gays and lesbians [and bisexuals] had to be included." They aligned themselves with activists of color seeking to widen the narrow lens through which they collectively asserted that much of the History-Social Science Framework and aligned textbooks narrated the American past. Birle and Greenman also wanted racially diverse LGB men and women included in a history education that would "place heteronormative reactions against sexual minorities under inspection and, at times, condemnation."[22]

Accessible education advocate Laurie Olsen usefully framed the debate into which lesbian, gay, and bisexual advocates plunged as one between "inclusionists" and "pluralists." In the 1990 textbook battle, inclusionists included representatives of the National Association for the Advancement of Colored People (NAACP), the National Chicano Human Rights Commission, and professors in San Francisco State University's Women's Studies Department and School of Ethnic Studies. They wanted history education that

66   Contested Curriculum

described the roots of contemporary inequalities and the development of distinct cultural identities. They also believed students' self-esteem would "thrive" when they appreciated each other's "full heritage and history." Teaching difference would instill the importance of "working together as equals," which inclusionists saw as essential to a successful society. Pluralists included Honig, Ravitch, historian Arthur Schlesinger Jr., and others who embraced multiculturalism so long as it was in the service of a common cultural narrative. People of color, and particularly African Americans and Native Americans, were assimilable into this history through their contributions to the larger U.S. culture. Ravitch worried that demands for textbooks that centered Afrocentric and Indigenous perspectives or too much content based on difference would "neglect the bonds of mutuality that exist among people of different groups" in favor of "primary identity in the cultures and homelands of their ancestry."[23]

Lost on Ravitch and many others was the particularity of LGB communities and histories, which fell outside of this framing of diaspora. They lacked "primary" identarian homelands—from where do lesbians "come"?—from which to transcend difference (as pluralists desired) or through which they might locate identity beyond national unity (against which pluralists cautioned). Project 21 and related lesbian, gay, and bisexual activists spoke in solidarity with inclusionists, often centering people of color. In hindsight, however, their demand was quite modest compared to other calls for change. Rather than seeking a history education based on multiple lenses of difference, as was the call of some, Greenman, Birle, and their collaborators simply wanted a basic acknowledgment that LGB people had existed, that their struggle for rights and recognition was historically meaningful. Because the pluralist-versus-inclusionist battle

The State's the Place?   67

was so heated, this nuance was ignored. Over and over, state decision-makers and the mainstream media represented lesbian and gay claims not as an exemplar of the pluralist understanding of assimilable difference, which in some forms it could certainly be. Rather, the claims were framed as the radical extreme to which identity politics would take history education if it acceded to multicultural demands. *Even* queer people might be included, they seemed to fear.

In 1991, efforts regarding textbooks shifted away from the CDE and toward local adoption processes. Districts determined whether to opt into K–8 grades for the state-approved Houghton Mifflin educational materials or to forego state funding. They also determined which grade 9–12 textbooks to adopt. More choices existed here, since the state did not vet high school textbooks. The Berkeley, Hayward, Oakland, and East Palo Alto School Districts made national headlines for rejecting Houghton-Mifflin textbooks because of criticisms over their representations of people of color and Indigenous people. Greenman asked Project 21 supporters to endorse this campaign whenever they condemned lesbian, gay, and bisexual omission. San Francisco Unified School District adopted the Houghton-Mifflin series anyway, but pledged, in response to Black, Native American, Asian/Pacific Islander, Jewish, and lesbian, gay, and bisexual pushback, to develop supplemental materials.[24]

Meanwhile, when the San Francisco Unified School District selected Gary Nash's *American Odyssey: The United States in the Twentieth Century*, activists noted that gay people received but one brief mention. Where it listed AIDS among "health concerns of the 1980s," it explained, "most of its earliest victims were homosexual men and intravenous drug users, people to whom the general population paid little attention." Greenman and others demanded incorporation of

68   Contested Curriculum

lesbian, gay, and bisexual people as historical actors and agents of change, not just victims of circumstance and intolerance. She pointed to the Prentice-Hall high school textbook *A History of the United States since 1865* as a favorable alternative, because it had a page dedicated to "Gay and Lesbian Rights" and "The AIDS Crisis." She urged people to call on their local school boards to adopt it.[25]

In May 1990, San Francisco youth advocates had proposed a Project 10-style program for lesbian, gay, and bisexual inclusion for the city's public schools, based on the Los Angeles program described in chapter 1. Superintendent Ramon Cortines opposed it, saying, "We have to be very, very careful about enticing young people as it relates to their sexual orientation." Greenman and allies mounted a successful campaign for approval, battling against anti-gay fundamentalist Christians and others who sought to sink it.

In October of that year, San Francisco Board of Education commissioner Leland Yee introduced a resolution for which Project 21 lobbied. Noting that Houghton-Mifflin textbooks contained "various distortions and omissions," the resolution called upon the superintendent of schools to "develop and secure" supplemental materials. These would "provide a more accurate portrayal of ethnic, religious, and gay and lesbian groups and their contributions to the life of this State and nation." This resolution became district policy.[26] In November 1990, the effort was given more heft when San Franciscans elected former teacher (and Gay Teachers and School Workers Coalition organizer) Tom Ammiano as the first openly LGBTQ+ person to serve on the school board.

By August 1991, the Board of Education had approved over two hundred supplemental materials, incorporating five gay and lesbian reading lists, including "Gays in America,"

FIG. 2.2. Jessea Greenman counterprotesting against antigay demonstrators opposing Project 10 at a San Francisco School Board meeting, May 29, 1990. Photo by Rick Gerharter. Note the use of the educational poster discussed in chapter 1 (Figure 1.2).

"Homophobia: Discrimination Based on Sexual Orientation," "The Rise of the Gay and Lesbian Movement," "Multicultural Education Curriculum: Lesbian and Gay Community," and "Before Stonewall." Still, as educator Lily Gee Hickman lamented, "The material won't even be used by students, and who knows if teachers [will] integrate [them] into regular studies?"[27]

The district also established Support Services for Gay and Lesbian Youth (later Support Services for Sexual Minority Youth), now with Cortines's enthusiastic support. Staffer Kevin Gogin and Lowell High School history teacher Barbara Blinick piloted related lesson plans for high school social studies teachers. These included "Homophobia and Heterosexism," "In the Life: Lesbians, Gay Men, and Bisexuals in the Harlem Renaissance," a lesson on homosexuals targeted during the Holocaust, and a three-day unit on lesbian and gay organizing in the context of 1960s and 1970s social movements from Black Power to feminism. For health classes and elementary grades, they also had materials about family diversity that included same-sex parented ones. In 1995, the lessons became a published series distributed to educators by the district's School Health Programs Department.[28] For its efforts, San Francisco Unified School District was held up as a model of how local districts could launch history education initiatives.

At the state level, while history progress fizzled, health framework revision succeeded. Project 21's experience with the opaque machinations of CDE bureaucracy helped. Birle and others began lobbying Honig in early 1991, demanding meetings. They rejected Honig's efforts to funnel their concerns through a scheduled Curriculum Committee open forum, calling the tactic "completely unsatisfactory . . . given the previous framework adoption process." A public letter-writing campaign to pressure Honig succeeded. A meeting was held in April 1992.[29]

At the meeting, Honig affirmed that the Health Education Framework being drafted by the Curriculum Commission should address "slurs, self-esteem," and "risk behaviors." While he urged the advocates to avoid "proselytizing," he added, "I have no problem saying to the Board of Education that we are generally supportive." Jessea Greenman viewed the meeting as successful, despite some of Honig's other comments, such as "We aren't going to say that all lifestyles are equal no matter what."[30]

Backed by public health and social science research on suicidality, HIV/AIDS risk, bullying, and harassment, the Curriculum Committee in May unanimously approved its first LGB-inclusive Health Education Framework. It endorsed a "factual, substantiated discussion on homosexuality." It also taught respect for "teenagers questioning their sexual orientation" and that people can "feel affection for both women and men." The first Health Education Framework to acknowledge sexual orientation also strongly encouraged abstinence as "the healthiest course of action for young people." It affirmed the existence of diverse families even as it asserted that the "best" model was a father and a mother in a stable environment. As such, it was endorsed both by Greenman as a "great step forward" and Reverend Sheldon, who said he was "quite pleased" with the Framework's "abstinence emphasis and the pro-family position." The state's Board of Education unanimously approved it.[31]

Why did Project 21 succeed with the Health Education Framework when it struggled with the History-Social Science Framework and textbook adoption? Despite the polarizing culture war discourse, health education was, in this context, an affirmation of child protectionism, while

72 Contested Curriculum

inclusive history education got framed as overzealous multiculturalism. This was mirrored in Massachusetts during the launching of the Safe Schools movement.

Massachusetts Safe Schools Make (and Sideline) History

Massachusetts led the early Safe Schools movement and helped determine what shape it would—and would not—take. Educators there had already built early Gay-Straight Alliance (GSA) clubs and were developing and teaching inclusive curriculum. In 1993, they successfully appealed for state buy-in. This achievement cannot be overstated. It accelerated a shift nationally from a 1980s discourse of viewing sexual-minority youth as "at-risk" to the 1990s Safe Schools model. Rather than managing problem students, schools came to be understood as problem environments. Groundwork by educators was bolstered by a 1989 publication by U.S. Department of Health and Human Services, *Report of the Secretary's Task Force on Youth Suicide*, which quantified the disproportionately high rates of suicide attempts by lesbian and gay students.[32] Safe Schools promoted institutional supports such as nondiscrimination policies, GSAs, and culturally competent staff providing "Safe Zones." Curriculum was generally not in the mix.

Massachusetts set this precedent. During the 1992 hearings to establish the Governor's Commission on Gay and Lesbian Youth, the Gay, Lesbian, and Straight Teachers Network (GLSTN) lobbied for "age-appropriate inclusion of gay and lesbian issues in school curricula." Kevin Jennings and Arthur Lipkin provided detailed recommendations, especially in history. Unfortunately, in the wake of the controversy in New York over the Children of the Rainbow

Curriculum's inclusion of brief mentions of lesbian and gay-headed families (see chapter 1), the majority of the commission saw inclusive curriculum as politically untenable. Governor William Weld, a moderate Republican who was otherwise very supportive of Safe Schools efforts, ordered it dropped from the report. On May 20, 1993, the *Boston Herald*'s front-page headline read, "There'll Be No Gay School Lessons."[33]

As Jennings wrote in his memoir, "The curriculum loss was a bitter pill, but the sweeping endorsement [of the other recommendations] was far more than I hoped for." The absence of curricular reforms or mandates came to characterize the Safe Schools movement overall. In 2016, Jennings reiterated that the removal of curriculum in Massachusetts' otherwise groundbreaking initiative had "nagged" him for "more than two decades." He added, "I have always regretted that we settled for less than what we knew was required." This would have lasting consequences. In 1995, the state's Social Studies Framework Committee recommended that students should analyze "individual and cultural components of identity," including sexual orientation. Because the Governor's Commission on Gay and Lesbian Youth had not addressed curriculum, the Massachusetts Board of Education eliminated the final version.[34]

Jennings and Lipkin would continue to make lesbian and gay history more accessible for districts, schools, libraries, teachers, and students across the 1990s. They were leaders in a strategy to develop materials that would allow for motivated educators to opt into this content despite the lack of a curricular mandate. Jennings, a former history teacher, would, in addition to helming GLSTN, edit the 1994 book *Becoming Visible: A Reader in Gay and Lesbian History for High School and College Students*. He combined excerpts of scholarly

74   Contested Curriculum

histories with his own introductory text and select primary sources on premodern Greece and Rome and China, colonial encounters with Native America, Revolutionary War soldiers, nineteenth-century "passing women," sexology, the Holocaust, postwar U.S. persecution of gays, the homophile movement, gay liberation, manifestos and platforms, major Supreme Court cases, contemporary "gays around the globe," and gay and lesbian youth testimony.

In the introduction, Jennings suggests that inclusion provides students (LGBTQ and otherwise) with tools to acknowledge the reality of gay people and, in turn, reduce suicide, violence, and discrimination. Jennings discusses the debate of seeing the queer past as "we are everywhere" essentialism versus social constructionist historical and cultural specificity. He also describes tensions between telling the history through well-known figures or through social history and movements, and he provides teacher notes, signposting material best suited for college. Each section features discussion questions and activities.

Several aspects of *Becoming Visible* are jarring today. The total lack of a trans analysis, fleeting glances at bisexual frames of interpretation, and overwhelming whiteness of the material stand out. At least on the first two counts, Jennings was in line with much of the lesbian and gay history scholarship of the 1980s and early 1990s. On the third, he acknowledged that the book is "weighted to the experience of white gay men." He looked forward to scholarship that would overcome his book's "shortcomings." All in all, *Becoming Visible* succeeds in its intention to supply tools and empower educators and students to make the leap into inclusive curriculum. Across the early and mid-1990s, Jennings juggled building GLSTN with providing *Becoming Visible*-related outreach to educators. In them, he shared ideas on how to incorporate

The State's the Place?   75

content into survey U.S. history classes and provided supplemental resources.[35]

Similarly in the early 1990s, former Cambridge Rindge and Latin School English teacher Arthur Lipkin, through the Harvard Graduate School of Education, began developing lesbian- and gay-centered curricular materials in history, English, and science. His Gay/Lesbian High School Curriculum Project featured *The Stonewall Riots and the History of Gay and Lesbians in the United States*, a forty-page report that began with Stonewall as a "turning point." It equipped educators to take students from the colonial era through the AIDS crisis. Lipkin ran a two-week model curriculum in a Cambridge high school U.S. history class. Gay and straight students gave overwhelmingly positive responses. As one student noted in a follow-up interview, "The more we talk about homosexuality in class, the more comfortable I am with the idea, with gay people, with my own sexuality, and with my own male identity." This straight-identified student suggested the lesson was "about as important as the desegregation of schools . . . and the abolition of slavery." Lipkin also gave many presentations to educators across the 1990s. In an early and important initiative, he coordinated across the mid-1990s with representatives from the International Foundation for Gender Education to incorporate transgender history. In 1997, the Massachusetts Department of Education contracted the two men to create sample opt-in lesson plans, bibliographies, and books.[36]

The same period saw a boom beyond Massachusetts in accessible high school history materials. In 1992, Project 21 created a full-color poster featuring fifty-seven diverse lesbian, gay, and bisexual figures and seven events. The poster, conceived of and hand-drawn by Robert Birle, included a coded key explaining historical significance, as

76   Contested Curriculum

FIG. 2.3. Robert Birle, "LGB Historical Figures and Events" poster (San Francisco: Project 21, 1992). Courtesy of the GLBT Historical Society.

well as a bibliography. Promoted by various social justice organizations around the country, hundreds of these posters continued to be sold out of GLAAD's San Francisco office through the late 1990s.[37] In terms of visibility, diversity, breadth, and content, this represented a significant evolution from the 1988 "Unfortunately, History Has Set the Record a Little Too Straight" poster discussed in chapter 1.

Also in 1992, young adult-directed Chelsea House Publishers contracted with historian Martin Duberman to direct an ambitious multivolume "Lives of Notable Gay Men and Lesbians" series for high school libraries and students. While some forty books were initially planned, by October 1995 just eleven had come out. The series was in the red due to the culture war, which also targeted children's books such as *Heather Has Two Mommies* and *Daddy's Roommate*. Many people were offended by the series' premise entirely. Others pushed back on centering a series around subjects' sexualities. Still, Duberman noted that it spoke to young audiences, including those "calling themselves queer." He added that many featured figures did not fit into "rigid gay/straight or male/female categories." That fluidity, he suggested, accurately represented gender and sexual identities in the past as well as the present. By 1996, the series had ceased publication. Those who did access the books had age-appropriate, readable biographies that neither only focused on heroes nor hid the sexualities of James Baldwin (the first in the series), Willa Cather, Rock Hudson, J. Edgar Hoover, and others.[38]

In 1998, another important educational resource became available to educators and, potentially, students. The award-winning documentary *Out of the Past*, designed for high school audiences, enjoyed a Sundance premiere and wide circulation on PBS and video/DVD. It threads the story of Utah student Kelli Peterson, who in 1995 led the fight to

78   Contested Curriculum

secure the right to form and maintain a high school GSA, with five historical profiles.[39] Celebrity voiceovers including Gwyneth Paltrow and Edward Norton recount seventeenth-century Puritan minister Michael Wigglesworth; the nineteenth-century "Boston marriage" of Sarah Orne Jewett and Annie Adams Fields; Henry Gerber's thwarted 1920s effort to launch a political organization for homosexual rights; Bayard Rustin's place in the Black freedom struggle; and Barbara Gittings's role in lesbian rights and the depathologization of homosexuality.[40] GLSTN (by then GLSEN) and Jennings were closely involved in *Out of the Past*. Eliza Byard, the film's writer, editor, and coproducer, went on to become GLSEN's deputy director and, from 2008 to 2021, executive director. In 1999, GLSEN produced a related teacher's guide for history, social studies, and English language arts.[41]

Lastly, in 2000, People About Changing Education (PACE) published *Transforming the Nation: A Teaching Guide to Lesbian, Gay, Bisexual, and Transgendered US Histories since the 1950s*. It was authored by activist-scholar N'Tanya Lee, who had been active in PACE's response to New York City's Children of the Rainbow Curriculum struggle, and American studies graduate student Alex Robertson Textor. During the Rainbow Curriculum fight, the religious right sought to divide families of color from LGBTQ people by claiming the latter were essentially white, privileged people seeking "special rights." In the preface, Lee writes, "We quickly recognized the need for educational materials about the history of LGBT persecution and resistance that also dealt with the history of race and racism." The authors intended the guide to be used by educators as well as older students. It emphasizes that "fighting gay persecution . . . alone will maintain racism, poverty and inequality,"

The State's the Place?   79

highlighting "the connections between forms of oppression, the role of mass movements . . . , the role that people on the margins play in challenging the mainstream." In each chapter, arranged by decade, broader LGBTQ history primers are accompanied by featured voices and images of queer and trans people of color, framing discussion questions, and primary and secondary sources for further study.[42] *Transforming the Nation* provided a much more intersectional and trans-inclusive approach than previous high school supplementals, setting a new standard. It did not, however, enjoy wide circulation.

Despite the lack of mandates in Massachusetts, California, or anywhere, Jennings, Lipkin, and others facilitated curricular changes, but only for those teachers eager to incorporate LGBTQ history. By the turn of the twenty-first century, numerous quality curricular supplements and workshops were available to educators and districts. The most coordinated opt-in push across the decade, however, was Lesbian and Gay History Month (now LGBT History Month).

LGBT History Month Stakes Its Claim

Building on Black History Month and National Women's History Month, advocates across the 1990s sought to incentivize the teaching of LGBTQ-inclusive history. While this effort was successful in raising the visibility of LGBTQ history, limited content actually appeared in K–12 schools. The campaign reveals the strengths and limits of an opt-in approach to inclusive history education.

In some ways, the history of LGBTQ History Month goes back to 1926, when historian Carter G. Woodson and the Association for the Study of Negro Life and History established a Negro History Week in February. By the late

1960s, many colleges recognized February as Black History Month and in 1976 Congress formalized it. By 1980, all states had adopted K–12 public school commemoration. In 1987, President Reagan declared National Women's History Month, which had begun as a weeklong local commemoration in Santa Rosa, California, in 1978. The next year, he declared Hispanic Heritage Month. In 1990, President George W. Bush approved National American Indian Heritage Month. In 1992 Congress endorsed Asian/Pacific Islander Heritage Month.[43] By the early 1990s, then, there was a well-established tradition through which marginalized histories found established times in the K–12 academic calendar when some (often token) effort would be made to tell stories of women and people of color.

In this context the California State Board of Education in January 1991 cited its History-Social Science Framework in establishing March as Women's History Month. GLAAD/SFBA called on community members to "write the board to urge them to designate June as Lesbian/Gay/Bisexual History Month" and to suggest that LGB people should be considered an ethnic/cultural group under the Framework. While not seriously considered, the effort signals how the idea for such a month was in the ether of this era. What ultimately took root as Lesbian and Gay History Month emerged in Missouri. Robert Birle had moved to Kansas City in 1992, struggling with the challenges of living with and also caring for a partner with AIDS. Jessea Greenman later marveled at how "energetic and smart" Birle was, and laughed recalling how, after his move, he apologized to her because he thought in his attempt to establish a midwestern chapter of Project 21 he could "only do six states."[44]

Meanwhile, Rodney Wilson, a nontenured history teacher at Mehlville High School in suburban St. Louis, had struggled with the anti-gay slurs he routinely heard. As Wilson later reflected, "I turned to history to make sense of it all. . . . LGBT history gave me self-confidence as a gay person and strengthened my resolve to live, as best I could, an honest, open and integrated life." Wilson used history months to diversify his curriculum. Wilson and Birle knew one another, as part of the small pool of regional educators active in the National Education Association (NEA)'s Lesbian and Gay Caucus. Wilson discussed with Birle the idea he had for a Lesbian and Gay History Month set in October, to coincide with National Coming Out Day (October 11) and commemorate the anniversaries of the community's first two Marches on Washington (in 1979 and 1987). Birle put him in contact with the GLAAD/SFBA activists. In early 1994, Kevin Jennings was traveling around the country to promote *Becoming Visible* and make GLSTN a national organization. Operating on a shoestring budget, he slept on Wilson's couch during his St. Louis stop—the two knew each other because Wilson wrote an essay for Jennings's anthology *One Teacher in Ten: Gay and Lesbian Educators Tell Their Stories.* Jennings became a key partner in launching Lesbian and Gay History Month.[45]

Around the same time, Wilson attended a workshop at an NEA conference titled "Affording Equal Opportunity to Lesbian and Gay Students through Teaching and Counseling." Coupled with his initial Lesbian and Gay History Month efforts, it moved him to become outspoken in his classroom. When teaching a Holocaust unit, he held up a poster of the patches Nazis used to label people in concentration camps. He explained that as a gay person, Nazis would have assigned him the pink triangle and killed him. To a stunned class, he linked Nazi persecution of homosexuals to contemporary U.S. violence, citing the 1978 assassination of Harvey Milk and the 1992 murder of gay sailor Allen Schindler Jr.[46]

Wilson's students were overwhelmingly supportive, as was, initially, his administration. After parental complaints, though, administration put a memo in his personnel file stating that it was "inappropriate conduct for a teacher to discuss facts of a personal nature . . . in the classroom." They also ordered him not to mention homosexuality unless it was part of existing curriculum, which by design it was not. With support from his local NEA chapter, he won tenure. Later that year he founded GLSTN-St. Louis, the organization's first chapter outside of Massachusetts. One of its first major actions was donating copies of *Becoming Visible* to area high schools and libraries. Many, including Mehlville High, refused to shelve them.[47]

Meanwhile, the idea for October 1994 as the first Lesbian and Gay History Month gained momentum. In a preliminary work plan, organizers believed the celebration would introduce role models to LGB youth. For all youth, it could "reduce the likelihood that fear and hatred of homosexuals will be propagated into the next generation." Wilson and Jennings coordinated with Kevin Boyer at Chicago's Gerber/Hart Gay and Lesbian Library and Archives to develop a National Coordinating Council. While Wilson and others anticipated that colleges and universities would be most likely to embrace the event, they also did outreach to community organizations, state and local governments, and teacher organizations and unions. Their High School Outreach Team consisted of Wilson, Jennings, Greenman, and Chicago area teacher Torey Wilson.[48]

Due to budgetary necessity, their "Secondary Schools Packet" was distributed by request (for five dollars) rather than mass-mailed free to districts or educators. This dulled its impact. Nonetheless, those who received it got a powerful introductory lesson in teaching lesbian and gay history. It urged educators to appreciate how sexual identities differ across cultures and eras. Teachers learned how to explain how historical figures' "homosexual orientation or behavior . . . affected [their] total biography." Teachers were guided to thread through their U.S. survey courses the evolution since the nineteenth century of "lesbian/gay identity and community" as well as the relationship between the development of a "lesbian/gay" movement and other social movements. The packet provided lessons on early America, the nineteenth century, the Roaring Twenties, McCarthyism, and the civil rights movement. It suggested ways high schools could celebrate, ranging from optional (extra credit for attending community lectures) to curricular (a group timeline project, student profiles of historical figures) to programmatic (assemblies).[49] Notably, there was no suggestion to reform curricular policies or textbooks.

The LGBTQ community applauded but also critiqued the rollout of the first Lesbian and Gay History Month. Historian Ginny Beemyn argued that bisexuals were omitted despite having "been a part of the queer liberation movement from the beginning." She also asserted that the naming of the month was behind the times, given that in 1993 a national demonstration had been titled the "March on Washington for Lesbian, Gay and Bi Equal Rights and Liberation." Greenman concurred. In response, the name changed in 1995 to "Lesbian, Gay, and Bisexual History Month." Greenman also requested that the secondary schools packet represent the ways historical subjects' racial backgrounds "influenced their g/l identity" and mark intersections between the LGBT movement and other social movements. Greenman continued to critique the official 1996 "Lesbian, Gay, and Bisexual

84   Contested Curriculum

History Month Primer" (then helmed by GLAAD) for being too white and largely omitting trans people and activism.[50]

In 1994, the NEA's Gay and Lesbian Educators Caucus got the association to pass a resolution endorsing the "accurate portrayal of the roles and contributions of gay, lesbian, and bisexual people throughout history." On July 6, 1995, the NEA General Assembly by a wide majority passed Resolution B-9, which called for educator trainings to "identify and eliminate sexual orientation stereotyping in the educational setting." Subsection (d) read: "Support for the celebration of a Lesbian and Gay History Month as a means of acknowledging the contributions of lesbians, gays, and bisexuals throughout history." The resolution mandated neither a curriculum nor local chapter declarations of October as Lesbian, Gay, and Bisexual History Month (which the NEA did not have the power to do). It provided no funding. Still, subsection (d) was controversial. The Virginia delegation, for example, opposed it out of fear that it would be polarizing. Virginia Education Association president Robley Jones argued this new visibility would be to the "disadvantage of the students we . . . wish to help." After B-9 passed, hundreds of NEA members threatened to quit their chapters.[51]

In the fall, what had been an intraorganizational debate became a national furor. In August, Christian conservatives began sounding the alarm about B-9, and especially subsection (d). By September the Concerned Women for America (CWA) began an attack on the NEA's support for "Lesbian and Gay History Month." Leader Beverly LaHaye dubbed it an "unprecedented stand promoting the homosexual agenda in our public schools." The CWA spoke out on Christian radio broadcasts and distributed fliers for local chapters to post in their communities, claiming that the NEA called for schools to engage in "celebrations of homosexuality."[52]

The State's the Place?   85

On October 13, the CWA escalated by taking out a half-page ad in the *Cleveland Plain Dealer*, *Des Moines Register*, *Sacramento Bee*, and many other newspapers across the country. In the ad, the CWA utilized what were predictable falsehoods and slippery-slope scare tactics in order to demonize the NEA; Lesbian, Gay, and Bisexual History Month; and, by extension, LGBTQ+ people. "They sincerely expect an entire nation of schoolchildren to accept the homosexual, lesbian, and bisexual lifestyle as normal," it warned, adding, "What is really frightening is the thought that our children will be celebrating the history of a group of people who historically prey on the innocence of minors."

Having established this right-wing dystopia of an "extremist" public employee union forcing pedophilic perverts upon school children, the ad urged readers to "just imagine" how history month speakers "are likely to present themselves," the "personal involvement your child will experience" studying and reporting on "a homosexual, lesbian, or bisexual," and the "pro-homosexual displays" students would have "to build in the classrooms." It ended with a warning: "Homosexual organizations have selected October as Lesbian and Gay History Month. It's already being celebrated in some schools. It may be celebrated at your school before the month is over."[53]

Excepting that advocates had indeed selected October as the month, nothing in the ad was based in reality. No school district in the country had even declared the month officially for its classrooms. Nonetheless, drawing on tropes established by Anita Bryant's 1977 "Save Our Children" campaign and contemporaneous anti-gay culture wars, the ad garnered mainstream media attention. It hardened the resolve of many districts and schools to reject any mandates toward LGBTQ-inclusive history education. In the mid-1990s, none were being proposed. It pressured teachers not to use related supplementals. And it suggested that the mere historical recognition was harmful to children. In Bend, Oregon, activists withdrew their request for the city council to proclaim Lesbian and Gay History Month after fundamentalist Christians opposed the measure, some threatening violence. In San Diego, a lesbian educator put up a Lesbian, Gay, and Bisexual History Month display at the district's central office, only to see the contents replaced a week later with a new, permanently dedicated "Teacher of the Year" display case. The national NEA offices received over twenty thousand letters and phone calls opposing Resolution B-9.[54]

LGBTQ activists, allies, and organizations organized a countercampaign. GLAAD issued a fact sheet countering the CWA's lies. It noted that such rhetoric was often linked to a rise in anti-LGBTQ violence. It pointed out that when people called the toll-free number in CWA's ad, their names were sold to other right-wing groups and they were "solicited continuously for donations." As a result, several newspapers, including the *Sacramento Bee*, apologized for having run the ad. Fears of NEA membership drops were overblown. Both nationally and in more conservative states' chapters, membership rose.[55]

At the NEA convention the next summer, however, Tennessee delegates successfully lobbied for the repeal of Resolution B-9 and any mention of Lesbian, Gay, and Bisexual History Month. The NEA also removed all references to Black History Month and National Women's History Month. In their place was Resolution B-7, a generic statement stating that "discrimination and stereotyping based on factors such as race, gender, physical disabilities, ethnicity, and sexual orientation must be eliminated" and endorsing "the equality of all." It added that schools should "integrate an accurate portrayal of the roles and contributions of all groups throughout history across the curriculum." Many LGBTQ education supporters saw it as teacher John Linder did, "caving in to demands of the religious right." Indeed, the erasure of history months did not appease the CWA. It issued a release lamenting that now the NEA sought to "celebrate the gay and lesbian lifestyle throughout the entire school year, rather than in one designated month."[56]

Meanwhile, the *National Standards for History*, published in 1996 by the National Center for History in the Schools at UCLA, included a brief mention of gay history. Authored by Charlotte Crabtree, who coauthored California's 1987 History-Social Science Framework, and fellow UCLA historian Gary Nash, the *National Standards* had been intended to serve as a blueprint for voluntary adoption by states. The final version, in the "Contemporary United States (1968 to the Present)" section, suggested that in grades 9–12 students should "examine the emergence of the Gay Liberation Movement and evaluate the invocation of democratic ideals concerning the civil rights of gay Americans." This, the report explained, advanced solid historical analysis and interpretation by considering multiple perspectives.[57]

Unfortunately, while the project had been developed and funded through the NEH and U.S. Department of Education, it, too, became embroiled in a history war. In 1994, Lynne Cheney, who had initiated the project in 1991 while serving as NEH chair, attacked its "political correctness" and lack of patriotism. Despite Crabtree and Nash's efforts to build consensus over thirty-two months of deliberation, Cheney and other right-wing activists represented the document as leftist, multiculturalist revisionism. Cheney's

88   Contested Curriculum

talking points were coordinated with Republican elected officials, the Christian Coalition, and the CWA. By the fall of 1995, the U.S. government's endorsement of the *National Standards* was dead. UCLA's publication, while well received within the profession, lacked large-scale professional development and state adoption.[58]

Over the next few years, the push for Lesbian, Gay, and Bisexual History Month's K–12 content lost steam. It had been buffeted by the NEA/CWA battle, the religious right's "special rights" framing of LGBTQ political and social recognition, and the history wars that sought to marginalize "multiculturalism" in favor of teaching a "common story." As such, history month organizing shifted toward public history and higher education. GLAAD took a leadership role in promoting LGBT History Month's voluntary commemoration and promotion, but by 2000 was doing very little with it. It continued without coordination until 2006, when the Equality Forum assumed responsibility, primarily through releasing short biographies of notable figures each year.[59]

Arthur Lipkin argues that the NEA/CWA history month controversy "illustrates the limited effectiveness of policymaking from above and afar," adding that "without local support they are window dressing, or worse, divisive and half-hearted."[60] This is correct, but only part of the story. While grassroots efforts are vital to the success of inclusive history education, without state policy, successes remain ephemeral. Getting bureaucratic and legislative endorsement or, more powerfully, mandates, to incorporate LGBTQ content is substantially harder than generating optional supplements. Lasting, structural change requires resources, training, and policies. In the late 1980s and 1990s, progress on one front meant withdrawing on another.

The State's the Place? 89

The Curricular Exception to California's Student Safety

Like Massachusetts' launch of the Safe Schools movement, California's struggle to pass legislation affirming LGBTQ students required an explicit insistence that such laws would not influence curriculum. Californian activists were thwarted once again during the 1994 History-Social Science Framework process, which ended with the Curriculum Commission and State Board of Education unanimously reaffirming the 1987 Framework with no substantive changes. When Greenman protested, she was referred to the old *Model Curriculum for Human Rights and Genocide* as the place for gay content.[61]

That same year, Assemblywoman Marguerite Archie-Hudson, a Democrat representing the Forty-Eighth District in Los Angeles, introduced Assembly Bill (AB) 22 to amend the state's Education Code to ensure that educational materials portray the "ethnic, cultural, and racial diversity" of society, including the contributions of men and women and changing old language about the "roles and contributions of American Indians, American Negroes, Mexican Americans, Asian Americans, and European Americans" to "Native-Americans, African-Americans, Mexican-Americans, Latinos, Asian-Americans, Pacific Islanders, European-Americans" and "members of other ethnic and cultural groups." Openly lesbian assembly member Sheila Kuehl thought Archie-Hudson "might be open to amending the bill in a way that would include gays and lesbians." Her staff reached out to Greenman asking for what terms to use, since, she assumed, "the role and contributions of lesbian, gay, bisexual, and transgendered people" would not "get through the legislature." Greenman suggested "portray the ethnic, cultural, racial, and affectional diversity of our society" or the roles and contributions of "sexual minorities."

90   Contested Curriculum

As it turned out, AB 22 died in committee.[62] It did, however, germinate an idea for Kuehl.

In the 1995–1996 legislative session, Kuehl introduced a bill to prohibit sexual-orientation discrimination in public schools, including textbooks and instruction. It failed to get out the assembly's education committee. The following year, she reintroduced it as AB 101, the "Dignity for All Students Act." Kuehl had to reassure fellow legislators that the bill would not "mandate curriculum or create special rights." Even with the support of Superintendent of Schools Diane Easton, it failed to pass. In 1999, Kuehl brought forward a similar bill, AB 222. Before it even came up for a vote, it was revised to eliminate any reference to inclusive curriculum. It, too, failed.[63]

In that same session, another LGBTQ student nondiscrimination bill passed. AB 587, "The California Student Safety and Violence Prevention Act of 2000," overtly rejected its application for any "curriculum, textbook, presentation, or other material in any program or activity conducted by an education institution."[64] California now codified curricular exception as a precondition of LGBTQ student protections.

In 1995, after Project 21 had fallen apart, Jessea Greenman tried to relaunch its efforts through her P.E.R.S.O.N. (Public Education Regarding Sexual Orientation Nationally) Project. It was largely an email list for people advocating for LGBTQ K–12 education. She also produced a remarkable guidebook for how to enact lasting state-level reform. *The P.E.R.S.O.N. Organizing Manual* packed its four-hundred-plus pages with state-by-state analyses of standards, frameworks, and textbook adoption processes as well as sample letters to education officials, strategies for engagement, and contact information for key bureaucrats. She freely distributed it on request.

The State's the Place?   91

In the introduction, Greenman explained that nationally coordinated state-level efforts would provide "mutual support, avoids reinventing the wheel, achieves economies of scale, matches the right-wing where it is organized . . . and interweaves the work of educational equity activism with the statewide work being done by existing LGBT and allied organizations." Reflecting, perhaps, her frustrating experiences with statewide history education reform in California, she noted, "This work is controversial still within our own community (too radical, recruiting, all that), so you may not win any popularity contests at first. But as FDR once said, 'We have nothing to fear but fear itself.'" Few activists around the country had the appetite to take on the fight, even with such a powerful tool at their disposal. One can imagine that with focus and funding, this manual and its strategy could have been a transformative roadmap to change. Instead, by the late 1990s, Kevin Jennings had stopped giving history workshops at conferences and was focusing his energies on GLSTN's successful Safe Schools model. Greenman and others had given up conducting curricular and policy advocacy workshops at the National Gay and Lesbian Task Force's annual Creating Change Conference, citing a lack of interest and lukewarm reception from the activists there.[65]

During the 1990s, supplementals, LGBT History Month, and scattered workshops provided resources for highly motivated teachers. The flowering GSA movement had more students than ever before collectively asking, "Where is our history?" The expanding academic fields of queer and trans history meant that scholarly content could be integrated into the major U.S. historical themes that were the foundation of rigorous K–12 curriculums, standards, and frameworks. By the late 1990s within the education field, scholar-practitioners were describing how this history could

92   Contested Curriculum

be taught in elementary, middle, and high school grades in age-appropriate ways that folded into existing curriculum.

As the California State Legislature was battling over what rights it would afford students—and how it would avoid curriculum to secure them—a brave few teachers were using supplemental materials to incorporate content into their history education. Stacie Brensilver Berman, who interviewed a number of these early adopters, describes how in Los Angeles and the San Francisco Bay Area, a handful of LGBTQ educators brought queer-inclusive elements into their history curriculums in the late 1990s and early 2000s. All those she interviewed were activists in other aspects of their lives. They believed in a social justice framework for history education. They were also aware that, without formal protections or inclusive curricular policies, their decisions left them vulnerable. The risk was one few felt called to take.[66] By the turn of the twenty-first century, K–12 history education was ripe with potential for LGBTQ inclusion, but also structurally designed for exclusion. The underlying challenge presented by a supplements-instead-of-policy strategy would stymie implementation for decades to come. The FAIR Education Act began to change all that.

FIG. 3.1. Ess, *Public Universal Friend (I am that I am)*, 2021.

3

Making California FAIR

WITH CAROLYN LAUB

Across the 2000s, advocates continued to unsuccessfully pursue state-level LGBTQ-inclusive history education. It was not until the 2011 Fair, Accurate, Inclusive, and Respectful (FAIR) Education Act that California finally won a threshold victory. In the subsequent decade, the California Department of Education (CDE), advocates, educators, and school districts began implementation at a scale unthinkable before. What changed?

This chapter is coauthored by two of the major players in the law's passage and its integration into California's 2016 History-Social Science Framework. Carolyn Laub began curricular advocacy work as executive director of what was then the Gay-Straight Alliance (GSA) Network, a youth advocacy organization she had founded in 1998 and led through 2014. After that, Our Family Coalition (OFC), another organization playing a key role in the FAIR Education Act's implementation, contracted Carolyn as a consultant. Carolyn brought Don into the process as the lead scholar working with LGBTQ advocacy organizations. This chapter contextualizes the sequence of events from our insider's perspective. We argue that LGBTQ history education advocates transformed an educational paradigm by making curriculum central to the Safe Schools approach. Simultaneously, they freed LGBTQ-inclusive history education from being considered as primarily about creating safer schools. In the process, advocates created a new model for curricular reform. It relies on state legislation and policy, bureaucratic investment by affiliated institutions, scholarly and advocacy commitments, and grassroots engagement. While this model is specific to California's way of doing education, it provided the foundation for momentum elsewhere.

In 2006, state senator Sheila Kuehl introduced the Bias-Free Curriculum Act (Senate Bill [SB] 1437), which would have mandated that instructional materials "portray the roles and contributions of people who are lesbian, gay, bisexual or transgender to the economic, political, and social development of the state and country." As chapter 2 details, across the late 1990s, Kuehl had, as an assemblymember, tried to bring about curricular reform prior to the California Student Safety and Violence Prevention Act of 2000. In the end, that law explicitly excluded any curricular impact. Still, it kicked off a series of laws affirming student equal opportunity and access to public schooling free of sexual orientation or gender identity harassment.

Making the argument in 2006, Senator Kuehl leaned into what communications professor Thomas Dunn dubs the "rhetorics of contribution." Bias-Free Curriculum Act advocates sought to "align their vision . . . with the monumental rhetoric of nationalism." Dunn analyzes legislative debates and media interviews to argue that this strategy had overlapping effects. First, the repetitive "contributions" language signaled that resulting curriculum would be about

96   Contested Curriculum

affirmative rather than negative historical representation. Second, it would downplay harms to LGBTQ+ people caused by the government and mainstream society. Third, "role models" would fit into an existing mold of "women worthies" and admirable people of color who advanced the American Dream. Fourth, this emphasis led inevitably to a public debate about why a person's sexuality should matter to their historic recognition. Outside of someone like Harvey Milk, whose contribution was overtly about gay electoral victory, why, many asked, was a figure's sexuality relevant to history education?[1]

Right-wing religious pundits zeroed in on the age-appropriateness of discussing the "sexual behavior" of "historical figures," as the Concerned Women of America's Cindy Moles put it. Kuehl and her supporters emphasized that teachers would mention figures' sexual orientations and gender identities rather than sex lives. Focus on the Family's Tom Minnery called the bill "sexual indoctrination" propaganda. He claimed it would have "forced all public school teachers to present a one-sided message about homosexuality, bisexuality and transgender issues to students as young as five."[2]

Mainstream media issued similar, if tempered, sentiments. The *Sacramento Bee*'s editorial board opposed the Bias-Free Curriculum Act because "history is history. It isn't necessarily gay or straight." It claimed that the bill sought "to view the public deeds of men and women based on their private sexual orientation," resulting in "imposing [a] gay rights agenda onto the telling of history." The editorial board of the *Los Angeles Times* decried the bill as mandating that textbooks "recount history in part through a gay and lesbian prism," something far more ambitious than the legislation sought.[3]

These criticisms were based on the assumption that the bill would result in mass historical outing, salacious sexual descriptions, and LGBTQ cheerleading. Such alarmist rhetoric stemmed, in part, from a general ignorance of how LGBTQ history was studied and taught. When called upon to consider what such an inclusive history education might entail, a heteronormative public was primed to fixate anxiously on queer sexual desires and acts.

The emphasis on heroes furthered a Safe Schools logic. Improving school climate for LGBTQ students was laudable. Still, centering Safe Schools in debates around curriculum left the bill open to criticism that it promoted what historian Jonathan Zimmerman dubbed "history as therapy." In 2006, as the bill was making its way through the legislature, Zimmerman published an op-ed in which he generally supported inclusive curriculum but opposed the Bias-Free Curriculum Act because, he claimed, it would "distort the past" by using it only to make LGBTQ youth feel good about themselves. He worried about such a feel-good education "exaggerating the exploits of historical gays." Meanwhile, he countered, "all of us—straights as well as gays" would "evade the complex and painful history that we share." He wanted students to ask questions such as "Why have gays suffered so much discrimination?" and "What does that say about our nation—about its conceptions of love, of family, and of 'freedom' itself?"[4] These questions belong in the curriculum. One wonders how Zimmerman imagined they would show up without laws mandating, or at least resourcing, inclusion.

The op-ed was an extension of Zimmerman's thesis in his 2002 book, *Whose America? Culture Wars in the Public Schools.* There, he acknowledged that bringing more racial and gender diversity into history education "must rank as one of the greatest triumphs of history activism." Inclusion, he argued, came at the cost of critical frames of the U.S. past. Rather than learning about the long legacy of anti-Blackness, for

98 Contested Curriculum

example, textbooks taught about African American heroes who extended our nation's exceptionalism and/or strove for assimilation into its "common story" of equality, freedom, prosperity, and justice.[5]

While Zimmerman's rationale for opposing SB 1437 sounds good on paper, it rang hollow in the classroom. As fourth-grade teacher Julian Grant noted in a *San Francisco Chronicle* letter to the editor, the social studies textbooks he used in his Daly City class featured "positive information on the roles of Native Americans and immigrants." But Grant also taught the ways Indigenous and immigrant peoples were subjected to violence and discrimination. Of the bill, he wrote, Zimmerman "shouldn't fear an overly 'positive spin'" on gay men and lesbians. Teachers would "make sure that their students learn" both the "positive and negative" of that history.[6] Zimmerman, Grant suggested, was attacking a straw man instead of acknowledging how the law could improve education.

In the California State Legislature, Kuehl's rhetorical strategy finally got the bill passed, but substantially pared back. Rather than mandate "roles and contributions," it would have prohibited instructional materials that reflected adversely on "persons because of their race or ethnicity, gender, disability, nationality, sexual orientation, or religion, as those terms are defined in Section 422.56 of the Penal Code." That code section, the state's hate crimes law, defined "gender" to include gender identity and expression, and spelled out that "sexual orientation" includes heterosexuality, homosexuality, or bisexuality. This had the advantage of mandating textbook nondiscrimination without spelling out "lesbian, gay, bisexual, and transgender" in education code, a bid for the support of legislators who worried their constituencies would dislike that. On September 6, 2006, Governor Arnold Schwarzenegger vetoed it. He claimed it was unnecessary because state education policy already prohibited discrimination. Supporters rejected this capitulation to the far right but were unable to overcome the veto.

In the subsequent year, Senator Kuehl, steadfast yet pragmatic, got the Student Civil Rights Act (SB 777) signed into law under the governor. It amended existing law prohibiting discrimination in instruction to include categories protected under state hate crimes law, including sexual orientation and gender. Additionally, it amended education code to align with hate crimes law.[7] Back in the Safe Schools model, it replaced inclusive education with a vague call for a curriculum free of bias.

In the next two years, two new conditions made the FAIR Education Act possible. First, in November 2008, Gus Van Sant's feature film *Milk* was released to box-office success and critical acclaim. Starring Sean Penn as Harvey Milk, the movie underscored the importance of the gay San Francisco politician as a powerful American historical figure. The resonance struck especially deeply given its wide release in the wake of California voters' endorsement the same month of Proposition 8, which amended the state's constitution to define marriage as between one man and one woman. Coming thirty years after Milk's instrumental role in the defeat of the Briggs Initiative, the film's poignancy was hard to miss.

Milk's impact on establishing May 22 as Harvey Milk Day is clear. In February 2008, Assemblymember Mark Leno led the California State LGBTQ Legislative Caucus to introduce Assembly Bill 2567, declaring Harvey Milk Day as a "day of special significance" for public schools. In September, prior to the film's release (and passage of Prop 8), Schwarzenegger vetoed the bill. By February 2009, when Leno, now a state senator, reintroduced the Harvey Milk Day bill as SB 572,

100   Contested Curriculum

Milk had won Oscars for Penn (Best Actor) and Dustin Lance Black (Original Screenplay). In the post-Prop 8 landscape, recognizing LGBT history through one of its heroes took on more political urgency. In April, Ramona Unified School District administrators had prevented a sixth-grader from doing her class presentation on Milk. After pushback, they allowed it, but not during class time. Attendees had to have signed parental permission. As the State Assembly Committee on Education noted, the bill "would provide clear authority for school districts to conduct suitable exercises, such as this student presentation." The law amended the state's Education Code to encourage all public schools to use the day to "familiarize pupils with the contributions [Milk] made to this state." Schwarzenegger, the consummate Hollywood politician, signed the bill into law on October 11, National Coming Out Day, smack in the middle of LGBT History Month.[8] This established California's first statewide legislative precedent for LGBTQ-inclusive history education.

The second critical event was actually a *non*event. In 2008, the CDE had initiated its scheduled revision process for the History-Social Science Framework, but it did not happen. Schwarzenegger shelved the process, one of many Great Recession budget reduction measures.[9] Revision to the Framework would not begin again until 2014. This ended up being fortuitous. There's little doubt that, given the pattern established since the 1987 Framework, LGBTQ-related history would have continued to be marginalized, with Milk possibly incorporated to hastily align with SB 572. Instead, the next History-Social Science Framework came into being five years after the FAIR Education Act. What could have been a story of missed opportunities became one of unforeseen possibilities. First, though, the law had to be passed.

The FAIR Education Act: Embracing Rhetorics of Success and Honesty

On December 13, 2010, California state senator Mark Leno stood before his fellow legislators to introduce SB 48, the Fair, Accurate, Inclusive, and Respectful (FAIR) Education Act. "We can't simultaneously tell youth it's okay to be yourself," he explained, "when we aren't even teaching students about historical LGBT figures or the LGBT equal rights movement."[10]

Timing mattered. In September, widespread attention to LGBTQ+ youth suicides had spurred the viral "It Gets Better" campaign. Everyone from students to celebrities urged young people to hang on for a better life after high school. In response, the California-based GSA Network launched its own "Make It Better" campaign. It demanded supportive and enriching conditions for LGBTQ+ students here and now. In November, voters elected Democrat Jerry Brown governor. While Democrats had yet to gain their supermajority in the state's legislature (that would come with the 2012 election), they expanded their majority. The sky had not fallen after the passage of Harvey Milk Day. Bringing the "roles and contributions of LGBT Americans" into education code now seemed to many a reasonable next step.

LGBTQ policy advocates perceived that the window of opportunity—commonly referred to in political theory as the "Overton window"—had opened. The Overton window, named after conservative political theorist Joseph Overton at the Mackinac Center for Public Policy, was originally used to describe how shifts in public opinion resulting from the work of a think tank could make possible new policies that would have previously been considered unreasonable or extreme. While Overton initially used the concept in an educational context (to describe "school choice"), it has gone mainstream. It has been applied to shifts in various directions politically, and expanded to the impacts of grassroots mobilization and other political speech and activities. Conservative pundits have warned against the Overton window, for example, shifting toward acceptance of transgender youth or LGBT books in libraries. This has fueled the current culture war against LGBTQ+ youth and curriculum.[11] In 2010 in California, though, a confluence of factors contributed to shifts in public opinion toward protection of LGBTQ+ young people and awareness of LGBTQ history. Codifying LGBTQ history education inclusion became reasonable.

Leno often applied a Safe Schools rhetoric, noting research had shown that inclusive curriculum improved school climate. To this, however, he added two new rhetorical elements. The first was student "success." Leno emphasized how LGBTQ+ youth, like all students, deserved tools to do well in school. A culturally relevant curriculum would also benefit all students. The second was "accuracy." He underscored how unfair and factually incorrect the teaching of LGBTQ-exclusionary history was.

Emphases on student success and curricular accuracy came from ten years of research-based strategy generated by GSA Network, GLSEN, and other members of the California Safe Schools Coalition (CSSC) following passage of the California Student Safety and Violence Prevention Act of 2000. Over the next decade, the CSSC issued thirteen research briefs geared toward educating parents, schools, districts, policymakers, and the media on evidence-based school needs for accountability and empathy. In 2006, the CSSC released two briefs. *LGBT Student Safety: Steps*

Schools Can Take found that a key intervention was to "introduce curriculum that includes LGBT people and information about sexual orientation and identity." *LGBT Issues in the Curriculum Promote School Safety* found that when LGBT issues are included in curriculum, climates improve overall.[12]

Lessons from the Bias-Free Curriculum Act also drove research on how LGBTQ-inclusive curriculum shaped student safety and belonging. Findings demonstrated that, for example, GSAs provided LGBTQ+ students a protective presence that also enhanced their academic achievement. At schools with high levels of victimization, however, the GSAs' effectiveness as a buffer lessened. Other evidence-based interventions were therefore necessary for student safety and success. Inclusive curriculum is just such a tool.[13]

Messaging was crucial. After the Bias-Free Curriculum Act veto, GSA Network's Carolyn Laub had a candid conversation with communications professional Robert Pérez, a close friend. He suggested that most people did not consider providing role models to LGBTQ+ youth or improving their self-esteem good enough reasons to justify LGBTQ-inclusive curriculum. Rather, they wanted history education to be "full, fair, and accurate." Inspired, Laub realized "FAIR" could capture all of these elements at once: Fair, Accurate, Inclusive, and Respectful. The FAIR Education Act was named.

Laub and others strategically built a new patternicity in public attitudes about LGBTQ-inclusive history education policy and curriculum. To address the concern that teaching history should be about "facts" and benefit all students rather than promote an anti-bullying message to serve a small minority, advocates discussed LGBTQ content as accurate, relevant, and in need of corrective legislation to counter systematic omission. They emphasized LGBTQ inclusion as a sensible improvement to education legislation that already mandated inclusion of women and people of color.

To counter the falsehood that any discussion of LGBTQ+ people would teach kids about sex acts, advocates showcased concrete, age-appropriate examples of historical figures and civil rights movements for elementary, middle, and high school levels. This strategy relied on building mutually beneficial relationships with leaders of racial justice movements and advocates for ethnic studies. Organizers garnered support from the Anti-Defamation League, Asian Americans for Civil Rights and Equality, the California Teachers Association, Los Angeles and San Francisco Unified School Districts, and the Mexican American Legal Defense Fund, among many others.

To counter the notion that such curriculum amounted to pro-gay propaganda that took away from "real" history education, advocates explained how LGBTQ content fit into existing lessons. This is when Carolyn brought Don on board. As a public California university–based scholar and educator in U.S. queer history, Don helped develop a list of significant individuals and events for legislators and reporters skeptical that scholarship-backed, age-appropriate, LGBT-inclusive K–12 history education existed. Rather than centering LGBTQ+ youth, advocates foregrounded the importance of accurate, inclusive, and relevant lessons for all teachers, administrators, and students.

This rhetorical shift can be found in legislative debates and media across the early months of 2011. When testifying to the Senate Education Committee, Laub emphasized it was the legislature's job to instruct the CDE to ensure that exclusionary curriculum be replaced with up-to-date and accurate history lessons, guidelines, and diverse role models for all students. During California Senate debates prior to the successful 23–14 vote along party lines, Leno linked anti-FAIR positions to opposition "a few decades ago" to inclusionary moves for Black and women's history. In an *Education Week* article about the bill's senate passage and move to the assembly, Los Angeles Unified School District legislative advocate Virginia Storm-Martin argued, "Inclusive curriculum supports all students. It helps families feel acknowledged, and it promotes cultural fluency."[14]

The Assembly Committee on Education's analysis also utilized this framing. It portrayed the FAIR Education Act as a logical next step in "existing law" by ensuring "equal representation of all people in the curriculum." It added that it would "have the effect of creating safer and more welcoming school environments." Assemblymember Tom Ammiano, who had played a key role in the LGBTQ teachers movement since the 1970s and come up through San Francisco politics after his election to the city's Board of Education, sponsored the bill in the assembly. He steered its July 5 passage by a 50–26 vote.[15]

GSA Network and the rest of the CSSC also centered the FAIR Education Act in their Queer Youth Advocacy Day. It brought LGBTQ+ young people from around the state to Sacramento. It trained them to talk to legislators, take a clear position, and speak to the bill's importance. While some asserted it would reduce bullying, others emphasized how it would have made them more academically engaged. Los Angeles Unified School District representatives and teachers from across the state testified about the importance of being able to include LGBTQ historical content in terms of accuracy and student engagement for all. Educators already doing that curricular work explained how effective and age-appropriate it was.[16]

The "safety and success" shift stymied the usual oppositional arguments. The Traditional Values Coalition (TVC) and Capital Resource Institute insisted that the bill was an anti-bullying initiative. Relying on anti–Safe Schools rhetoric, they questioned why history-social science education should be burdened with protecting youth. TVC hoped to shock Californians by framing the bill as a gay agenda that would "force" the "widespread acceptance of the homosexual, bisexual, and transgender lifestyles."[17] FAIR advocates countered that while the bill might produce downstream effects of improving school climate, it primarily corrected inaccurate, long-standing curricular exclusion. While Republican state senator Doug La Melfa asked, "Are we going to take Winston Churchill out" to make way for "this type of curriculum?" Leno and others touted the common-sense adjustments of LGBT inclusion to existing lessons on, for example, civil rights movements.

Some of the same liberal and centrist actors that had opposed Kuehl's past proposals lined up again to oppose the FAIR Education Act. In a widely picked up Associated Press story, education historian Jonathan Zimmerman rehashed his claim that while he was "100 percent for adding gay and lesbian history," he opposed SB 48 as being about "citizens groups who want to see themselves in the curriculum." He added that the law would mean teaching that "Langston Hughes and Walt Whitman [were] gay" rather than "really hard questions about how sexuality works in this country, who benefits and who is marginalized." Historian Gary Nash, coauthor of the sidelined National History Standards in the 1990s, said that he only thought gay history should be taught in eleventh grade. This was in line with where he had placed a brief mention in those standards as part of late twentieth-century social movements.[18]

Time has proven Zimmerman and Nash wrong. Because of the FAIR Education Act, scholars, teachers, and educational specialists have contributed to a carefully vetted LGBTQ-inclusive state framework, robust lesson plans, well-curated primary source sets with teaching guides, integrated survey textbooks, and engaging professional development. Rather than token exercises in hero worship, these align with major events and themes in early American, modern, and contemporary history, across elementary, middle, and high school.

On July 13, 2011, Governor Brown signed SB 48 into law, to take effect in January 2012. He emphasized the rhetorical shift, stating, "History should be honest. This bill . . . ensures that the important contributions of Americans from all backgrounds and walks of life are included in our history books. It represents an important step forward for our state." Senator Leno added, "Denying LGBT people their rightful place in history gives our young people an inaccurate and incomplete view of the world around them." He thanked Brown for "recognizing that the LGBT community, its accomplishments, and its ongoing efforts toward first-class citizenship are important components of California history."[19] The FAIR Education Act became the first law of its kind in the nation. It had been nearly fifteen years since some version of it had first been floated by Kuehl. It would be another eight years before any other states would follow.

Opposition continued after passage. Across 2011, the *Los Angeles Times* editorial board published three editorials opposing the act. The latter two, run during LGBT History Month after the law's passage, accompanied a news story about how little training educators and districts were receiving. Rather than calling for professional development funding, the *Times* clutched its pearls over unfounded fears that

108   Contested Curriculum

lower grades might be exposed to "too much detail." It suggested "this schooling" was only "appropriate" for "sex education" and, possibly, "civics classes." A week later, it doubled down: "We opposed that law—not because we think schools shouldn't teach about the contributions of people of all sexual orientations (they should!) but because we are concerned about the continuing politicization of California's classrooms." It concluded, "There will always be debates . . . over what history is important and whose interpretation ought to prevail. . . . But we'd feel more comfortable if that debate were conducted by scholars and educators rather than politicians."[20]

While reasonable on its face—who *doesn't* think scholars and educators rather than politicians should be planning K–12 history curriculum?—the *Times* set up a false dichotomy. As Senator Leno pointed out, it was as if the newspaper was "unaware that California's inclusive education laws started in the Legislature and can only be updated by the Legislature." The legislature then left it to the CDE, local districts, and educators to determine how to best meet general mandates in frameworks, textbooks, and lessons. To imagine that the law would force teachers to "stuff the curriculum with new politically correct requirements" and "fables" mischaracterized and overstated the function of the state's educational legislation.[21]

In an op-ed, C. Scott Miller, a longtime K–5 educator from Santa Ana, joined Los Angeles Gay and Lesbian [now LGBT] Center executive director Lorri Jean to assign the newspaper an "F." The FAIR Education Act "amends the state education code," they explained, but the "real action happens at the local level." In "history books [and] . . . social studies education, not sex education," students should learn not just about heroic figures but how "police imprisoned people simply because of their sexual orientation or gender identity." To exclude such lessons "suggests that something is so wrong with being LGBT that discussions about us . . . must be kept out of schools."[22] Like educator Julian Grant, Miller understood that laws were but one step in the long road toward implementation—and why each step mattered.

The *Los Angeles Times'* opposition was more than just sour grapes about a fait accompli. As soon as the law passed, Christian conservatives, inspired by Prop 8's success to (temporarily) beat back marriage equality, mounted "Stop SB 48." Taking a page from their 2008 campaign, they claimed, falsely, that the FAIR Education Act would expose young children to sexual content. They also argued, in ways that resonate with today's "Don't Say Gay" laws, that the law would disenfranchise parents by denying them the right to excise curricular content they did not want their children to learn. (This is a power parents do not generally possess regarding history curriculum.) Finally, they complained that the law would deny students and teachers the ability to denounce homosexuality as morally wrong. The FAIR Education Act did build anti-bias and nondiscrimination protections into curriculum and educational materials. Even prior to the law, though, educators would have been hard-pressed to defend overt discriminatory statements from the front of a Californian public school classroom.

The FAIR Education Act Coalition, led by Equality California, GSA Network, Courage Campaign, and National Center for Lesbian Rights, mounted a counteroffensive. First, a series of focus groups revealed that many participants had no understanding that LGBTQ+ people had a meaningful history or how it could be relevant to K–12 education. Researchers found that "people's patternicity regarding the concept of history . . . prevented them from supporting the bill." One straight dad, for example, even after two hours of discussion about age-appropriate LGBT history education that cited Harvey Milk and Bayard Rustin, still worried that it would amount to teaching sex acts. Others still stated that history education should be about "facts" rather than "a diversity lesson that promoted acceptance." Many thought LGBT history had nothing to do with children and would interfere with their education. Some parents concluded that inclusive history threatened their ability to direct their children's moral, intellectual, and civic upbringing.[23]

Focus group findings shaped the FAIR Education Act Coalition's strategy in media as well as on the ground. Its "Decline to Sign" initiative mostly involved a public education and online information campaign. In addition, when people reported a place where Stop SB 48 petitioners were gathering signatures, tactical "truth squads" mobilized to talk to potential signers about what the FAIR Education Act actually did.[24]

From the beginning, the repeal campaign struggled. Unlike Prop 8, the Catholic and Mormon Churches were not enthusiastic Stop SB 48 backers. Many parents who might be mobilized either homeschooled or had their children in religious schools. Capitol Resource Institute, which spearheaded the effort, had a string of other failures, including an attempt to overturn Harvey Milk Day. Petition gatherers had until October 2011 to secure half a million valid signatures to get a repeal referendum on the June 2012 ballot. They fell short, but made a second attempt to get it on the November ballot. By July, Stop SB 48 had again failed.[25] The FAIR Education Act was here to stay.

Organizers soon realized the real challenge was not repeal but implementation. The FAIR Education Act lacked carrot

Making California FAIR   111

and stick. No funding was attached for educator development. No consequence existed for districts that did not make changes. Some teachers were openly defiant. Grace Callway, a fifth- and sixth-grade teacher near Yuba City, told the *Los Angeles Times* she would refuse to include LGBT history because she viewed homosexuality as a "destructive lifestyle." Educators were still being punished for LGBT inclusion. In 2012, English teacher Julia Frost, a lesbian who advised Sultana High School's GSA in Hesperia Unified School District, did not have her contract renewed and was investigated for "teaching homosexuality."[26]

In January 2012, Tom Adams, CDE director of the Curriculum Frameworks and Instructional Resources, acknowledged he had "no plans to check districts are complying with the law until the new textbooks are available." While the FAIR Education Act prohibited instructional materials that "reflect adversely" on LGBT people, the ongoing effects of the Great Recession had pushed back the CDE's start of new textbook adoptions until at least 2015.[27] (These would ultimately be finalized in 2017. There is no evidence the CDE has subsequently surveyed districts for FAIR Education Act compliance.)

Initially, many educators and even some advocates were confused about how schools should proceed. GLBT Historical Society executive director Paul Boneberg mused to one reporter, "I'm not sure how we plug it into the curriculum at the grade school level, if at all." Some teachers in the early grades already taught about same-sex parents when teaching about diverse families. They sometimes drew on the Human Rights Campaign's Welcoming Schools program that had, since 2006, provided K–5 materials. Still, elementary teachers expressed uncertainty about how to move beyond that. The handful of high school teachers already teaching about LGBTQ justice movements as part of a mid-twentieth-century civil rights unit saw little difference with the new law. The College Board had recently added Stonewall to Advanced Placement U.S. History. A few textbooks already mentioned Stonewall and/or AIDS.[28]

GSA Network and OFC compiled links to relevant teaching materials. Most available were more centered on safe schools and teaching tolerance than on history, or were teaching guides connected to specific documentary films. These required educators to carve out substantial class time in order to utilize them and were not well aligned with other survey history course needs, state and Common Core standards, or the History-Social Science Framework. Still, in May 2012, OFC launched their important new website, then called faireducationact.com (later renamed Teaching LGBTQ History), as a central hub for resources.[29]

Bucking the trend of the many school districts doing nothing in the first couple of years after the FAIR Education Act's passage, Los Angeles Unified took a proactive approach. In addition to creating policy affirming age-appropriate LGBT-inclusive history education at primary and secondary levels and in newly adopted social studies materials, it developed a site for curricular resources across grade levels. Most substantially, Los Angeles Unified entered into a multiyear initiative with the ONE Foundation and the Los Angeles LGBT Center to develop diverse LGBT-centered lesson plans and teaching materials.[30] Educators did not initially adopt these widely, however.

By mid-2012, advocates confronted a new challenge: What if the law was just symbolic? Across 2012 and the early months of 2013, the renamed and reconfigured FAIR Education Act Implementation Coalition (hereafter the FAIR Coalition) strategized. The most active representatives were from OFC, the organization overseeing primary-grade implementation; GSA Network, the organization tasked with steering secondary school implementation; Equality California, which had been central to the law's passage and was key to understanding how law translated into educational policy; the Los Angeles LGBT Center; and the Committee on LGBT History, an affiliate of the American Historical Association representing scholars and university educators. Representatives from several disability advocacy organizations, including the California Foundation for Independent Living Centers, YO! Disabled and Proud, and the Partnership on Inclusive Apprenticeships, collaborated on strategies to implement disability history, which was also part of the FAIR Education Act's mandate.

Over a series of conference calls, several proposals were advanced. One idea was to assemble K–12 educators, LGBTQ and disability history scholars, and policy stakeholders for a symposium, possibly at University of California, Davis. Another was to hold multiple regional teacher workshops to make them aware of the law and suggest ways to bring LGBTQ and disability history education into curriculums. A third was to reach out to school boards and administrators to develop local implementation plans. A fourth was to generate a webinar series on any or all of the above.[31] Most of the possibilities surpassed the strained capacities of the organizations involved, none of whom previously had history-social studies curriculum as a programming or budgetary priority. Given limited resources and bandwidth, advocates struggled to harness the FAIR Education Act toward widespread and enduring change. Then, without realizing it, we returned to a strategy that had failed in the past. This time, we found success.

114   Contested Curriculum

Reframing the Framework

When the FAIR Coalition met, we were not actively aware of the efforts made in the late 1980s and early 1990s to bring lesbian, gay, and bisexual content into California's History-Social Science Framework and related textbook adoptions. This may seem all the more incredible given that both Carolyn and Don had occasional communications in the mid to late 1990s with Jessea Greenman, a leader of the earlier effort described in chapter 2. Still, when the working group landed on the idea of pushing for changes to the Framework, it seemed like an innovative strategy rather than a restart of a previously unsuccessful campaign. With new law backing it up, we hoped Framework reform was the right idea for the right time.

In late 2012 and early 2013, representatives from GSA Network and OFC held a series of meetings with Tom Adams and colleagues from the CDE. Initially, the FAIR Coalition envisioned that Framework inclusion would lead to incorporation into the state's History-Social Science Standards. That would, we imagined, translate into alignment with the next textbook editions adopted throughout the state. Institutional investment and infrastructure for training and resources would follow.

In the early stages we did not appreciate that changing the History-Social Science Standards, as opposed to the Framework, required the legislature's specific action and significant resource allocation. We came to understand that standards revision was highly unlikely to occur any time soon. (As of 2025, the standards have still not been aligned to the 2016 History-Social Science Framework. There is no indication the legislature sees this as a priority.)

From mid-2013 to mid-2014, when the state's History-Social Science Framework revision process officially began, LGBTQ history advocates hoped to influence its initial draft. From mid-2014 to 2016, the Framework would go through a series of revisions and levels of state review. At each stage, public comment provided chances for advocates to urge additions and edits. In 2016, the California State Board of Education would give its final approval.

We anticipated neither the steep learning curve involved in institutional change nor the intensive, long-term commitment required. What Carolyn and Don, specifically, *did* realize (in January 2013 at a friend's Obama second-term inauguration viewing party), was that we needed to recruit queer and trans historians to develop FAIR-aligned revisions to the Framework. We reasoned that highlighting scholarship-backed changes would lend our suggestions authority. We also hoped that including historians in the process would lead to their greater buy-in for supporting K–12 history education generally. At the time, Don was cochair of the Committee on LGBT History (now the LGBTQ+ History Association), which gave the state's framework revision process a national profile among the field's practitioners.

In May 2013, fortuitously, the California State Board of Education approved its new Standards for Evaluating Instructional Materials for Social Content (commonly referred to as the "Social Content Standards"), in part to align with the FAIR Education Act. This first CDE move to comply with the law was not history-specific; it guided districts and educators across the curriculum. Among other revisions (such as replacing "American Negroes" with "African Americans"), it included a section on "Sexual Orientation and Gender Identity." This forbade demeaning and/or stereotypical representations and encouraged inclusion of

116   Contested Curriculum

LGBT people in discussions of "achievements in art, science, and other fields." It also called for a "fair proportion" of the "roles and contributions of . . . diverse sexual orientations and gender identities" in instructional content.[32]

The language regarding sexual orientation and gender identity came about largely through the work of Carolyn, representing GSA Network, and OFC executive director Judy Appel. Done without fanfare or media notice, it built relationships between LGBTQ history advocates and key CDE officials such as Tom Adams. The social content standards bolstered justification for the revised History-Social Science Framework to apply the FAIR Education Act comprehensively.

By June, the plan was hatched: We could develop a report, entitled *Making the Framework FAIR: California's History-Social Science Framework Proposed LGBT Revisions Related to the FAIR Education Act*, under the auspices of the Committee on LGBT History. As lead project scholar, Don would coordinate the project with coeditors Leila Rupp (a prominent lesbian history professor at University of California, Santa Barbara) and David Donahue (a gay former secondary school teacher, education professor, and then-associate provost at Mills College). We would review the existing Framework and Standards by grade levels for places where inclusive revisions should be made (Early America, Reconstruction, Cold War, and so on). We would then reach out to historians working on those times/themes to provide line edits and scholarly justifications. Editors would review historians' input for grade-level appropriateness and fit into the Framework and Standards language and scope. By late 2013, a draft report would be presented to the CDE's Curriculum Framework and Evaluation Criteria Committee for consideration in writing their draft History-Social Science

Framework. We planned for the report's public distribution prior to the mid-2014 formal launch of the CDE's Framework revision process.[33]

Over the summer, the editors approached nearly thirty historians to address forty places in the existing Framework for consideration, spanning grades two, three, four, five, eight, ten, eleven, and twelve. These covered historical eras and topical themes across time (such as family diversity, LGBTQ heroes and role models, women's movement history, the history of immigration, and the history of religion). In the end, sixteen scholars contributed, including Peter Boag, Michael Bronski, Rebecca Davis, John D'Emilio, Stephanie Gilmore, Richard Godbeer, Kwame Holmes, Daniel Hurewitz, David Johnson, Priya Kandaswamy, Louise W. Knight, Mark Rifkin, Daniel Winunwe Rivers, Clare Sears, Marc Stein, and Timothy Stewart-Winter. In fall, the editors evaluated accuracy, grade-level relevance, and developmentally appropriate subject matter. We also sought general feedback from key scholars (such as trans historian Susan Stryker, Black queer historian Kevin Mumford, and feminist historian Estelle Freedman) as well as GSA Network and OFC stakeholders.

Finally, the editors crafted an introduction in which we laid out the pedagogical, curricular, and social justifications for a "transformational approach" to aligning the new Framework with the FAIR Education Act. We made three basic arguments. First, because "the field of scholarly LGBT history has, over the past forty years, established all the hallmarks of other areas of academic history," K–12 U.S. history "cannot be comprehended without understanding changing concepts of sexuality and gender, in conjunction with race, ethnicity, class, disability, age, and other categories of difference." Second, the Framework should reflect a "proper retelling of history . . . that incorporates . . . the profound influence and change over time of sexuality as a field of social power and meaning making." Third, a "transformational revision that includes LGBT history encourages the kinds of diverse forms of analysis, multiple forms of evidence, and exploration of causality, change, and continuity over time that makes the study of history a central aspect of student growth into engaged civic life."[34]

It was not until the very end of the introduction, after we had laid out solidly disciplinary and pedagogical rationales, that we mentioned that curricular inclusion could also lead to greater LGBT student safety and improved school climate overall.[35] This was an intentional pivot from a "Safe Schools" strategy. We deployed the "success and honesty" rhetoric utilized in passing the FAIR Education Act as a jumping off point, but centered our argument on Framework investment in civic purpose, relevance to contemporary historical scholarship, honesty about the past, and excellence in historical thinking and method.

Our report shifted what education scholar Jal Mehta calls the "problem definition." Mehta defines a problem definition in educational policy as "a particular way of understanding a complex reality." He asserts that the "way a problem is framed has significant implications for the types of policy solutions that will seem desirable," and will thus shape the terms of political argument. Compelling problem definitions reshape policymakers' cognitive maps in ways that transform the nature of the debate and the constellation of key actors. This, in turn, produces opportunities for substantial institutional change.[36]

As chapter 2 details, creating substantive change in change-resistant institutions, such as the CDE, and its enabling mechanisms, such as the History-Social Science

Framework, can be incredibly hard. Political scientist Paul Pierson's theory of "path dependence" is useful here. Pierson explains why institutions can be so resistant to intervention and why seemingly small changes, once adopted, can become "threshold effects" that lead over time to profound cumulative outcomes. Institutional path dependence is furthered by large start-up costs (such as Framework revision and rollout), complexity and opacity of bureaucratic processes (such as the Framework's layers of review, public comment processes, and decision-makers' reception), and the need for changes to be easily folded back into organizational design and flow. When changes occur in such a system, they are therefore mostly incremental. They unfold over long periods (such as the multiyear processes of Framework revision, approval, and alignment with professional development, textbooks, and, eventually, standards).[37]

Path dependency helps explain why LGBTQ history education advocates in the late 1980s and early 1990s found so little traction while advocates in the 2010s found so much. Those first efforts lacked legislative mandates. But both the CDE and mainstream media viewed LGBTQ-inclusive history as an extreme capitulation to multiculturalism. The appeal made by lesbian, gay, and bisexual advocates thus worked against the policymakers' problem definition, which asserted that diversity had to be disciplined into a shared American "common story." In that framing, lesbian, gay, and bisexual inclusion would (supposedly) interrupt the common story only to appease a special interest group, rather than advance the CDE's goals.

By the 2010s, conditions had changed. Beyond the state's general political shift toward a Democratic administration and legislative supermajority, LGBTQ issues in national news, from military nondiscrimination to marriage equality, made our place in mainstream America's past, present, and future far more obvious. Additionally, in 2014 California stopped standardized history testing. This made changing the Framework significantly more possible, as it would not require realignment of state assessments. The FAIR Education Act required the CDE to, at a minimum, include some LGBT content in their revised Framework and related bureaucratic processes. "The law gave a lot more backing," Tom Adams acknowledged, adding, "Even though the protection existed beforehand, the curriculum aspect [gave] teachers a lot more confidence."[38]

In December 2013, our initial meeting with Framework revision staff regarding the *Making the Framework FAIR* draft was unexpectedly tense. It became clear that they intended to contain FAIR alignment to a mention of Milk in fourth-grade California History and Stonewall, Milk, and marriage equality in eleventh-grade Modern U.S. History. They were particularly concerned that LGBTQ advocates would seek to label famous people, such as Abraham Lincoln, as "gay." For us, it was obvious that they had not fully digested our draft report. *Making the Framework FAIR* suggested incorporating diverse LGBTQ communities and civil rights movements into the existing U.S. history survey. For periods before the twentieth century, the draft highlighted how gender and sexuality lenses gave history more nuance and accuracy, and helped students understand how the past and present connected. At the meeting, we did our best to clarify these points and to demonstrate how they were supported by decades of scholarship, but left unsure how much had landed. When the CDE released the preliminary revised K–12 History-Social Science Framework in September 2014, the state's History-Social Science Subject Matter Committee's designated drafters added Milk, marriage, and a

Making California FAIR   121

reference to the mid-twentieth-century Lavender Scare (a government-driven systematic persecution and purging of those suspected of being homosexual). While it made liberal use of "LGBT" throughout its general guidelines, the Framework's narrative history told a decidedly spare, white, middle-class gay story, leaving intact the exclusion of lesbian, bisexual, and transgender people, as well as queer and trans people of color.[39]

Our work had just begun. At the same time that the CDE's Instructional Quality Commission (IQC) issued its initial revised framework, the Committee on LGBT History publicly released *Making the Framework FAIR*, in part to underscore the stark contrast between the two approaches to inclusion. Educating the CDE became, out of necessity, political, but, unlike a typical lobbying campaign, also intensively bureaucratic. We sought to change the institutional problem definition. Rather than "How does the new Framework include LGBT 'roles and contributions' in the least disruptive way to business as usual?" we pushed toward "How can LGBT inclusion in the new Framework advance its aspirations in historical thinking, literacy, inquiry, citizenship development, access, and equity across early, middle, and high school?"

It matters that the authors and editors of *Making the Framework FAIR* were professional historians and education scholars. We were well versed in the historical thinking methods coming out of the Stanford History Education Group, including its *Reading Like a Historian* curriculum. These were held in high esteem by the CDE staff and contracted writers of the revised Framework, who were based at the California History-Social Science Project. We demonstrated our attunement to other models that helped steer the updating of the Framework, such as the California

122   Contested Curriculum

FIG. 3.2. Don Romesburg in front of the California Department of Education in Sacramento holding *Making the Framework FAIR*, December 18, 2014, author selfie.

Common Core State Standards for English Language Arts and Literacy in History/Social Studies, Science, and Technical Subjects; the California English Language Development Standards; and the National Council for the Social Studies College, Career, and Civic Life (C3) Framework for Social Science State Standards.[40]

Finally, before publishing the final report, Rick Oculto from OFC and Hilary Burdge from GSA Network recruited teachers into "Make History, Teach History" listening sessions. They provided approximately twenty educators predominantly from the Los Angeles and San Francisco areas a stipend to participate. In two sessions, Oculto and Burdge went over content recommendations to ascertain classroom viability. Teachers were overwhelmingly positive, praising the revisions' alignment with Common Core priorities, integration into existing units, and easy ways to comply with the FAIR Education Act. The main concern they voiced was a need for accompanying textbooks, professional development, and other resources.[41]

Fundamentally, we approached our suggested revisions as a way to further the CDE's goals. We presented ourselves not as activists seeking to compel "our" version of the past but as experts and partners in history education excellence. Throughout the two-year Framework revision and public comment process, LGBTQ history advocates utilized a strategy of speaking to decision-makers through their own bureaucratic language.

At the most basic level, for public comment cycles, we translated *Making the Framework FAIR* line edits into easily digestible tables. With our line-by-line revisions, overwhelmed CDE committee members could see exactly where, one by one, we suggested changes. They could also immediately understand why they were important in terms

124   Contested Curriculum

of compliance with the law, historical importance, accuracy, and alignment to the stated values of the Framework. From draft to draft, we learned that specific line edits made the cut, whereas general exhortations for more inclusion of X or Y did not. We also continuously tracked which changes made it into each version of the draft Framework as it moved from the History-Social Science Subject Matter Committee to the IQC and, finally, to the State Board of Education. At each level, we targeted new, specific appeals for those recommendations that had not made it in (yet!), as well as more accurate language for elements that had.

This mattered because, just at the level of the IQC, the CDE received over 1,700 comments, many more than they were used to receiving. Two hundred—12 percent—were about the FAIR Education Act. For example, high school teacher Gerald O'Connor wrote that the IQC's proposed revisions were "incredibly limited" and insisted that a "more well-rounded approach" would necessarily include "representations of lesbians, bisexuals, transgender people, and LGBT people of color." Mona Twocats-Romero, "a great grandmother" with "many grandchildren throughout the school system," wrote that "our schools will be contributing to the reduction of prejudice and promoting tolerance in today's diverse world." In addition to LGBTQ+ advocates, the IQC heard from Sikh Americans, Polish Americans, Persian Americans, Hindu Americans, Korean Americans, South Asian Americans, Armenian Americans, disability advocates, and environmental advocates. Only thirteen comments were anti-LGBT. They were vague condemnations rather than specific suggestions.[42]

Additionally, we attended all of the CDE's public meetings in Sacramento. Across 2014, 2015, and 2016, Carolyn, Don, and other FAIR Education Act Implementation

Coalition members made many ninety-mile trips each way from the Bay Area and back, sometimes multiple days in a row. At our most productive, we used commuting time on calls with each other, strategizing about how each person would use their one-minute public comment to either emphasize particular changes or underscore adoptions' ethical, social, or pedagogical importance. Waiting to speak often entailed hours, as anyone familiar with this kind of system can attest. We also tried to get diverse Sacramento-area educators, youth, and parents to speak.

We mobilized scholars, educators, school board members, parents, students, and teachers unions. Organizations ranging from the American Civil Liberties Union and Transgender Law Center to the American Historical Association sent support letters. Collectively, hundreds of individuals and groups called upon the CDE to embrace substantial LGBT inclusion across elementary, middle, and high school history. Those giving comments also made clear that the FAIR Education Act required the CDE by law to represent, at a minimum, lesbians *and* gay men *and* bisexuals *and* transgender people in history. We insisted that our proposed line edits did this in historically rigorous ways following professional historians' best practices.

The process from the end of 2014 to the summer of 2016 was thus a hybrid of politics, activism, scholarship, and the steep learning curve of bureaucratic savvy. In the many times we testified before state committees and boards, Don was probably heard respectfully both because of *Making the Framework FAIR*'s solid scholarship and because of his standing as a California State University–based historian. Carolyn managed the tracking of line edits and public comment testimony, providing us with an essential organizational tool. OFC and Equality California (our state's main

126   Contested Curriculum

LGBTQ+ civil rights organization) arranged resources and behind-the-scenes coalition work with advocacy organizations, K–12 teachers, students, and parents. Media strategy drew in other coalition partners. The Overton window shifted as Framework revision advanced. Over time, elements not initially accepted by the new Framework's authors or History-Social Science Subject Committee were more acceptable to the IQC and State Board of Education. This was precisely because so much other LGBT-related content had been approved at prior levels, due to well-evidenced and community-supported efforts throughout the process, and, significantly, because no substantive opposing public opinion was advanced.

One illustrative example was the effort to include Indigenous gender and sexual diversity in the Framework where Native American history already existed, namely in fourth-grade California History, fifth-grade Early American History, and eighth-grade Nineteenth-Century History. We believed that it was important that the term "Two-Spirit" appear in the Framework. This signaled its importance as a scholarly and community-based historical and contemporary organizing descriptor across Indigenous nations for gender-diverse and same-sex/bi/pansexual–attracted Native Americans. As an umbrella term, "Two-Spirit" draws on long-standing, tribally specific roles beyond the gender binary and avoids settler-colonial terminology.

At that first tense December 2013 meeting with CDE representatives, they had expressed concern that Californian Indigenous communities might take offense at having LGBT content added in the Framework where their histories appeared. While we were skeptical about the generalizability of this claim, it shaped our approach in several ways. First, we partnered with Indigenous Californian two-spirit organizations, such as Bay Area American Indian Two-Spirits, who testified that Indigenous gender diversity should be a part of what students learn about Native American history. Greg Sarris, tribal chairman of the Federated Indians of Graton Rancheria, a federation of Coast Miwok and Southern Pomo peoples in Marin and Sonoma Counties, also sent a public comment endorsing our suggested revisions. In our supporting materials, we consistently referenced Indigenous scholarship alongside settler scholarship on Native American history.

Second, in the public comment process we grounded our fourth-grade California History and fifth-grade Early American History line-edit requests squarely in the scholarship. In *Making the Framework FAIR*, we urged that students "learn about gender/sexual systems that differed significantly from those of European explorers and colonizers. Some Native California cultures accepted third gender roles for females who preferred to assume men's social roles and males who assumed women's social roles. Such gender diversity often did not fit well with the gender roles of Spanish missionaries." The report also requested the Framework state, "Teachers may also explore the ways in which Spanish missionaries worked to fundamentally alter Native Californian cultures by trying to eliminate gender and sexual identities and practices among the Indians that Spanish felt were unacceptable."[43]

Next, our line edits sent as public comment to the History-Social Science Subject Matter Committee replaced that vague last statement from *Making the Framework FAIR* with more precise history: "Teachers can discuss how tribes such as the Klamath, Tolowa, Yuki, Gabrielino, and Chumash recognized males who preferred to dress and live as women and, in some cases, women who preferred to dress and live as men." We also recommended the Framework add: "Some California tribes granted such Two-Spirit people important spiritual and social roles, sometimes including marriage. To exemplify how the Spanish did not accept such Native Californian traditions, teachers and students could explore the well-documented eighteenth-century case of a Chumash male-to-female person who, after Santa Clara Mission friars ordered the person to give up women's clothing and work, ran away from the Mission and resumed a Two-Spirit identity in the tribe." While the language we suggested is fraught with problematic terms (such as "preferred to dress and live" and "male-to-female," both of which do not reflect current trans/Two-Spirit history best practices), the overall point was to make the unassailable case that Two-Spirit history is Indigenous Californian history. Resistance to what Indigenous scholar Deborah Miranda calls "gendercide" is important history for all of California's students.[44]

In the final Framework, this section of California History simply read, "Students should consider cultural differences, such as gender roles and religious beliefs, in order to better understand the dynamics of Native and Spanish interaction." The fifth-grade Early American History chapter was even more opaque. One paragraph mentions how "gender roles and family life varied between different tribes," while another references clashes between Indigenous and colonizer cultures.[45] These constituted enough basic scaffolding for highly motivated teachers to focus lessons on Native American gender and sexual diversity. However, by design, the Framework's vagueness made it highly unlikely that educators or textbook publishers would understand that these sections were addressing Two-Spirit history.

By the time the proposed Framework had been through the History-Social Science Subject Matter Committee and the IQC, advocates realized that the Framework's revisers were unlikely to include more specific and in-depth content at the lower grade levels, given their repeated rejections of our suggestions. We made a tactical decision to put our energies toward getting the term "Two-Spirit" into Grade 8 (Nineteenth-Century U.S. History). We made one last push in our final public testimony, before the State Board of Education. In addition to Two-Spirit young people testifying why it was important to them to have specific mention in the Framework, education specialists explained how the earlier grades' concepts of Indigenous gender and family diversity and clashing cultures should be latticed with more specific concepts in middle school. OFC's Rick Oculto testified on how these historical concepts and lessons also took on particular developmental importance in middle school, when all students were more self-consciously considering their own and others' sexual orientation, gender identity, and cultural/ethnic difference. Carolyn underscored how important it was to specifically use "Two-Spirit," which had for several decades been Indigenous communities' and scholars' preferred and agreed-upon term. Finally, Don's testimony focused on Two-Spirit historical scholarship, including the distribution of a one-page related bibliography to all board members. He indicated that this was the one place in the Framework they had a chance to accurately include this important history.[46]

In the end, we were successful. The Framework's eighth-grade section on the West mentions how "the American Indian wars, the creation of the reservation system, the development of federal Indian boarding schools, and the re-allotment of Native lands profoundly altered Native American social systems related to governance, family diversity, and gender diversity." It then makes explicit that this process included "breaking up Native lands into privately held units (largely based on the Anglo-American model of the male-led nuclear family), displacing elements of female and two-spirit authority traditionally respected in many tribal societies. Boarding schools in the late nineteenth and early twentieth centuries took Native children away from their parents for years at a time, imposing Christianity, U.S. gender binaries and social roles, and English-only education."[47]

The finalized History-Social Science Framework had LGBT-related content in elementary, middle, and high school. Approximately 60 percent of *Making the Framework FAIR*'s suggested content found its way, in some form, into the Framework. While the totality of that content is too substantial to detail here, the Framework includes:

- In grade two, students learn to connect their families to wider communities and histories. New content introduced the family diversity concept, which included LGBT-parented families along with many other types; and LGBT heroes, among other role models.
- In grade four (California History), students learn about California Indigenous gender diversity and its clash with colonialism; Gold Rush gender diversity; LGBT civil rights; and LGBT figures among Californian heroes.
- In grade five (Early American History), students learn about variations in gender roles across the colonies and Indigenous gender and family diversity.
- In grade eight (Nineteenth-Century U.S. History), students learn about shifting gender and sexual roles in industrialization and urbanization, clashes between Two-Spirit roles and settler colonialism, changing gender and sexual diversity in the American West and Northeast, and sexual violence and alternative family formation in enslavement and emancipation.

- In grade nine, LGBT issues, individuals, and movements are treated intersectionally with racialized communities and social movements in Ethnic Studies, Women's History, and other electives.
- In grade ten (World History), the persecution of homosexuals in the Holocaust is included. (The FAIR Education Act did not cover non-U.S. history, so LGBT advocates did not pursue content area revision.)
- In grade eleven (Modern U.S. History), substantial content is included in the Progressive Era, 1920s, Harlem Renaissance, World War II and the Cold War, postwar civil rights movements, the 1980s, and contemporary history.
- In grade twelve (American Government), students learn about major LGBT court cases and legislation related to equal protection, nondiscrimination and civil rights.

The Framework thus accomplishes a host of things. First, it demonstrates clearly how LGBT history content is appropriate for early, middle, and high school grades, aligned with developmentally meaningful concepts. Early grades emphasize families, gender diverse lives, and heroic figures. Middle grades begin to incorporate some concepts related to sexual diversity and sexuality as a field of power and meaning-making across time and cultures. Upper grades develop how gender- and sexually diverse peoples evolve into an "LGBT" community and a rights-seeking political movement across the twentieth and twenty-first centuries.

Second, it incorporates these concepts through individuals, events, and movements. This shows how LGBT history belongs in the U.S. history survey as it is taught across grade levels. Nothing requires teachers to set extra time aside for, say, LGBT History Month. Rather, it becomes an

132   Contested Curriculum

enrichment to core historical periods. This approach improves political, social, and cultural history as they are taught.

Third, the Framework's LGBT content contributes to the history education's civic project. It encourages students to evaluate similarities and differences from the past. It also demonstrates how sexual and gender diversity have existed across different cultures, and how this has shaped politics and society. Finally, it acknowledges that diverse LGBT people have mattered in the past, and, by extension, matter in the present.

Fourth, it establishes for all students, but especially for gender expansive and/or LGBTQ+ ones, ways to understand themselves through the interpretive lens of the past. As this book's introduction makes clear, this curricular intervention benefits all students in terms of school climate. It is especially impactful for students who might see aspects of themselves through this history. The Framework empowers many students to consider how it relates to their own processes of becoming, relating to one another, and understanding the world.

Government officials, the media, and researchers immediately recognized the 2016 Framework's far-reaching implications, especially its LGBT inclusion. Steven Camacia dubs the state "a model of transformative curriculum that supports critical democratic and LGBTQ-inclusive education." He adds that the Framework process "marks an increase in legitimacy of [the CDE's] democratic governance" through its "official curriculum." In an interview with Camacia, Tom Adams reflected, "To me, it's one of the best things I've done." In his evaluation of the new Framework, Camacia concludes that it builds toward "a curriculum that is integrated, encourages critical thinking, and focuses upon intersectionality. These goals are aligned with a new generation of standards that emphasize multiple perspectives and inquiry."[48]

In a full-circle moment, Bill Honig, the former California superintendent of public instruction who had overseen the 1987 History-Social Science Framework, served from 2014 to 2016 as chair of the CDE's History-Social Science Subject Matter Committee. In the late 1980s and early 1990s, Honig had (as chapter 2 details) repeatedly rebuffed LGBT education advocates. This time around, Honig oversaw substantial inclusion at many grade levels. By successfully reframing the problem definition, advocates had, in everything from *Making the Framework FAIR* to our Framework revision efforts, turned Honig, and the state's Board of Education and CDE leadership, into supporters.

The *Los Angeles Times* made the LGBT content the headline of their coverage about the new Framework, quoting State Superintendent of Public Instruction Tom Torlakson saying that it "will give our students access to the latest historical research and help them learn about the diversity of our state and the contributions of people and groups who may not have received the appropriate recognition in the past." An Associated Press story with international pickup similarly centered the LGBT-inclusive content. Numerous local media outlets utilized the Framework's passage to question their district officials regarding their reaction and plans for implementing the LGBT-related content, most of which were positive. Coverage was generally affirming or neutral, although most stories had a seemingly obligatory anti-LGBT interviewee.[49]

Over time, reporters investigated how the Framework led (or didn't lead) to classroom changes. This inevitably led to considerations of how textbooks would be revised. In a

September 2017 *Education Week* story, Bay Area educational consultant Olivia Higgins observed, "Some districts are working on creating lessons, and some individual teachers are, but when you have a textbook, it will be taught across the board in a way it can't be until we have those resources." In 2020, the *New York Times'* Jill Cowan compared Texas and California history textbooks side by side, and applauded California's 2016 "adoption of this massive doorstop, encyclopedic framework for the social sciences." Calling it a "truly a remarkable document," she specifically noted "this really groundbreaking through-line of LGBTQ history," adding that "it is kind of at the cutting edge of what we might be teaching." She credited the Framework with leading to unparalleled LGBT coverage in the state's U.S. history textbooks.[50]

Educational policy scholars and analysts saw the Framework as a best-practice model for socially relevant history education. In 2018, prominent curriculum and pedagogy professor Peter Seixas lauded its centering of history education as twenty-first-century citizenship training for liberal democracies under strain. In the context of rising fascist forces in the United States and around the globe, he noted the pressing importance of history education that cultivates "appreciation for a (qualified) narrative—open, of course to reasoned critique—of progressive opportunity and open democracy." He cited California's new Framework as a model. Steven Camacia and Juanjuan Zhu noted that the Framework invited a "transformational model for sexuality and gender history" by inviting accessible "inclusive language and discourse . . . to understand communities and social relations." They noted how dramatically this contrasted with other states' standards and related materials. Even the conservative Fordham Institute applauded the LGBT content as "well contextualized and integrated in the framework." It rated California as "exemplary" among states in its civics and U.S. history standards.[51]

In the years following the finalization of the 2016 History-Social Science Framework, the FAIR Education Act Implementation Coalition's strategies yielded downstream effects. Textbooks and other educational materials had to be aligned. Teachers and districts had to be trained. New lesson plans, primary source sets, and other teaching and learning documents had to be produced. In chapter 4, two practitioners describe that constantly unfolding process and suggest what challenges remain.

CAROLYN LAUB (she/her) is an activist and social entrepreneur based in San Francisco, California. She founded GSA Network in 1998 and organized with thousands of LGBTQ young people to create change, including winning passage of the FAIR Education Act. She currently consults with nonprofits to advance social justice.

FIG. 4.1. Maria Olivia Davalos Stanton, *Sally Ride's Adventures on Planet Lesbos*, 2021.

4

Resource FAIR

Materials and Trainings Empower Educators

WITH RICK OCULTO

The History-Social Science Framework approved in 2016 by the California Board of Education set a new precedent, with LGBT-related content in elementary, middle and high school. Yet the Framework, like the Fair, Accurate, Inclusive, and Respectful (FAIR) Education Act before it, would mean very little unless aligned with educational materials and professional development. Most educators neither grow up learning LGBTQ history nor receive related training. Textbooks, supporting materials, and trainings play an especially instrumental role in bringing this long-omitted content area into curriculums.

In this chapter, two of the principal LGBTQ history education specialists involved in California's textbook alignment, teacher training, and the development and distribution of other educational materials describe how those elements have unfolded since passage of the FAIR Education Act. Don Romesburg continued his work with the FAIR

Education Act Implementation Coalition (hereafter the FAIR Coalition) and as a trainer in LGBTQ history education long after the Framework's passage. Similarly, Rick Oculto, formerly of Our Family Coalition (OFC) and now an education consultant, was instrumental to textbook adoptions aligned with the Framework. He has helped educators and the state make LGBTQ history education more accessible and achievable. We argue that law- and policy-aligned materials and trainings are essential building blocks to factual, inclusive, and relevant history education. Even in California, this has yet to ensure that all districts, schools, and students have access to the curriculum they deserve.

Textbook Battles and the Limits of Revision

U.S. history textbooks are freighted with the transmission to students of how we have become a people and nation. Because of this, James LaSpina observes, they "occupy a space in education that is similar to traditional religion's sacred books. . . . Whose story gets told has always been a delicate question of critical importance."[1] Actual textbooks fall far short of the sacred. Publishing companies produce mass-market products. These have to meet state educational policy requirements, teachers' purposes, and culturally, linguistically, and neurologically diverse student needs. In the twenty-first century, digital platforms and teaching supplements mean that a textbook is never *just* a textbook. Over time, textbooks and their bundled materials amalgamate older and more contemporary historical and pedagogical framing, interpretation, and detail. Textbooks can feel less like grand narrative or deep historical inquiry than the result of sausage making.

Teachers, students, and education scholars across the ideological spectrum have long lamented that history textbooks don't live up to their promise, whether as a nationalistic progress narrative, a dynamic invitation into historical thinking, and/or an honest exploration of our nation's struggles for justice. Given the ambivalence, if not hostility, toward history textbooks, why is LGBTQ inclusion worth demanding? Most obviously, it's because many teachers and students still use them. In 2020, *New York Times* education reporter Dana Goldstein, after seeing a Michigan high school history teacher's textbook completely marked up and full of Post-its, declared that "the textbook is still important." At the same time, a recent fifty-state appraisal by the American Historical Association of K–12 history educators and instructional materials indicated that over 30 percent of teachers surveyed never use a textbook. Those who do are more likely to use it as a reference rather than a primary student tool.[2] Not all K–12 social studies teachers have deep subject-area knowledge, so textbooks end up being as necessary as they are insufficient. Moreover, LGBTQ presence in textbooks prompts students to bring it into the classroom and explore it in their projects, even if teachers choose not to cover it. As long as textbooks are assigned or used by teachers to guide their lessons, they should be honest reflections of the past's diversity and the scholarship being done on it.

Prior to California's 2017 textbook adoption alignment, LGBTQ inclusion was scarce but not completely absent. In 2014, social studies curriculum scholar Sandra Schmidt surveyed high school U.S. history textbooks published by Holt, Prentice Hall, McDougal Littell, and McGraw Hill. She found that none had pre–World War II LGBTQ content. Some mentioned Stonewall and/or AIDS. McGraw Hill's 2003 edition of *American History* was notable for its two-page "Gay Liberation" section that went from Stonewall through

Resource FAIR   141

the marriage equality movement. What this achieved in visibility it cordoned off as, at best, a brief stand-alone lesson.[3]

Much of what might be conventionally considered LGBTQ history—namely, the development of self-articulated queer and trans subcultures and communities and the evolution of the modern LGBTQ+ movement for justice and liberation—occurs in the twentieth- and twenty-first centuries. Since this is taught in the eleventh grade, it all falls outside of the state's textbook adoption process. Fortunately, as chapter 3 details, the 2016 History-Social Science Framework has LGBT-related content and concepts in grades two (Family Diversity and Heroes), four (California History), five (Early American History), and eight (American Revolution through Nineteenth-Century U.S. History). These became the basis through which the state's review process considered proposed textbooks' FAIR Education Act compliance.

In July 2016, the State Board of Education adopted evaluation criteria for Framework-aligned materials. The California Department of Education (CDE)'s Instructional Quality Commission (IQC) considered applicants to be state-appointed reviewers of submitted textbooks. Several educators applied who had been active in the Framework's LGBT inclusion, including David Donahue, coeditor of the *Making the Framework FAIR* report discussed in chapter 3, and Rob Darrow, a former teacher and administrator who directed research for the Safe Schools Project of Santa Cruz County. In 2017, the State Board of Education appointed dozens of reviewers, including Donahue and Darrow, to panels. Each panel of six to ten members reviewed materials from a particular publisher and grade area (K–5 or 6–8).[4]

The FAIR Coalition did not meaningfully enter the CDE's textbook adoption process until it was almost too late.

In early July 2017, Darrow urged the FAIR Coalition to consider submitting public comment. Initially, we resisted. The Genders and Sexualities Alliance (GSA) Network (formerly the Gay-Straight Alliance Network), central to the FAIR Education Act's passage, had undergone leadership change and deprioritized curriculum reform as it refocused on grassroots youth empowerment and movement building. Renata Moreira, who was then OFC's executive director, said the organization lacked dedicated funding to engage. Equality California (EQCA) was similarly unsure of how much they could do given other pressing demands.

Nonetheless, FAIR Coalition members quickly scanned the twelve proposed textbooks submitted by eight publishers. None fully incorporated the Framework's LGBT content. Application was highly uneven.[5] We realized we would have to take an approach similar to that we had for the History-Social Science Framework process, with painstaking attention to each line, image, and activity in the textbooks. Fortunately, OFC and EQCA stepped up.

In a rush of activity, a handful of people—Carolyn Laub, Don Romesburg, and OFC and EQCA staff and interns— closely read thousands of pages of student and teacher editions of all the textbooks, comparing them side by side with all of the LGBT-related Framework content. We identified where publishers had (or hadn't) included it, assessed quality and accuracy, and made recommendations. This was an intense project. We had two weeks to complete reviews, code each inclusion or edit based on how it aligned with the CDE's Instructional Materials Criteria and History-Social Science Framework, and provide rationales.[6]

During July 25–28, at the Sacramento DoubleTree Hotel, reviewers, state education staff, publisher representatives, and the public deliberated on the proposed textbooks. Each

Resource FAIR   143

day, panels followed a set schedule through which appointed reviewers discussed, grade by grade, how well the textbooks assigned to them met an array of criteria. Where panels agreed, either by consensus or, in cases of extreme deadlock, majority, they moved on. Otherwise, they continued to deliberate. They also generated questions for publisher's representatives, who responded to them midweek.

The dozens of criteria covered everything from accessibility to causation, and from chronology to spatial thinking. The most essential criteria were in the "History-Social Science Content/Alignment with Standards" category. If a panel found that a textbook did not meet the twenty-one criteria there "*in full*" (emphasis in original), the CDE instructed the panel to reject it, unless publishers could resolve the issues through "minor edits."[7] What constituted a "minor edit" versus a "major revision" was somewhat subjective. In general, a "minor edit" changed some phrasing, added or cut a sentence or two, or swapped out an image. A "major revision" required, for example, multiple new paragraphs or reconceptualization of a chapter.

Alignment with the Framework was key. While no textbook could be expected to include every Framework detail, they were supposed to include as many as possible. The FAIR Coalition highlighted each place where publishers did not present hard-won LGBT-related Framework victories. We insisted on their inclusion to the fullest extent that "minor edits" allowed. We also called for the rejection of textbooks that could not make necessary changes without major revisions.

The FAIR Coalition's critiques were less concerned with labeling this or that historical person as "gay" or "transgender" than with making sure textbooks captured the Framework's accurate and nuanced lenses of gender diversity and

144   Contested Curriculum

sexuality as fields of social power and meaning-making. Of the 106 total comments we made across the proposed textbooks, only thirteen (12 percent) had to do with biographies and/or adding labels to individual historical figures. Far more common were suggestions for discussion of gender roles, gender diversity, and diverse families in, for example, colonial America, Indigenous societies and their interaction with settler colonialism, western expansion, and enslavement and emancipation.

Much of this was lost in the deliberative processes. Biography tended to generate the most debate, none more so than for people we might today label as lesbian, gay, bisexual, transgender, nonbinary, and/or queer. Part of this was baked into the process. Called upon to address publishers' previously omitted discussion of people's same-sex relations or diverse gender expressions through "minor edits," panels sometimes landed on the quick fix of adding LGBTQ labels. While an anachronistic shorthand, this satisfied the FAIR Education Act and Framework's mandate.

In addition, what one reviewer describes as the "most controversial criterion" was embedded within the History-Social Science Content/Alignment with Standards category. This required "instructional materials [to] use biography to portray . . . the roles and contributions of lesbian, gay, bisexual, and transgender Americans" among "other ethnic and cultural groups to the total development of California and the United States." During deliberations, CDE staff confirmed to panelists that textbooks needed to address all of these groups, but sometimes suggested that "publisher materials did not need to explicitly identify an individual's gender identity [or sexuality] in order to meet the criterion." With Jane Addams or Langston Hughes, for example, it was unclear whether mere mention was sufficient or if

Resource FAIR   145

publishers should make edits to expressly identify them in relation to same-sex desires and relationships.[8]

The FAIR Coalition tried to spend our precious minutes within the brief twice-daily public comment periods explaining more substantial suggestions. Panels tended to fixate on labeling individuals. This produced what Rick and I call the "biography trap," which has several components. First, a focus on biographies fuels a long-standing anxiety that LGBT inclusion means the "outing" of prominent historical figures. Will LGBT activists "demand," for example, that Abe Lincoln be labeled as "gay" because of his romantic friendship with Joshua Fry Speed? This inevitably leads to a question about what constitutes the evidence for such labeling, which generally requires more interpretation than definitive "facts." This issue is not only confined to the early twentieth century and before. Sally Ride is featured prominently as the "first American woman astronaut" in second-grade "People Who Made a Difference" and fourth-grade California History. She lived openly with her longtime partner but her sexuality was only made public in her obituary. Review panels debated whether textbooks should mention Ride as the first known "gay" (or "lesbian" or "LGBT") astronaut, as the FAIR Coalition argued.[9] If not, why not?

Second, the labeling of past historical figures with today's identity terms smacks of poor historical practice. Inarguably, some people in most times and places have engaged in same-sex activities and affections and/or expressed expansive genders beyond Eurocentric binary categorizations. Terms such as "lesbian," "gay," "bisexual," "transgender," and all the other letters of today's sexual and gender diversity alphabet did not become self-identifying labels until sometime across the twentieth century (or, more generously for some terms, the late nineteenth century). Even then, it only occurred in culturally specific times and places. Rather than slap today's labels on past people, historians of the queer past generally assert that subjects' sexual and gender diversity should be described, contextualized, and explored. Publishers (with the exception of First Choice) lacked such care and nuance.[10] Had they done so, the FAIR Coalition would have applauded the adoption of their books. Yet publishers' claim that they sought to avoid anachronism often served as a cover for not discussing sexual and gender diversity in biographies at all. Even if they had wanted to, "minor edits" rarely allowed for publishers to substantially contextualize what their draft narratives had previously avoided. Labels became the next best option in a problem of publishers' own making.

The third element of the biography trap has to do with relevance. Some people question why historical figures' same-sex relationships and/or gender expansiveness are important for students to learn about. Does it only become worthy when it is central to the historical purpose of the person being mentioned, as with lesbian political foremothers Del Martin and Phyllis Lyon? While many scholars would assert that the romantic same-sex companionships of, say, Walt Whitman and Jane Addams deeply inform their life's work, K–12 textbooks have generally downplayed or ignored them. The FAIR Coalition believed that centering debates around biographical interpretation in educational materials could—and should—open up historical thinking practices.

One figure featured prominently in the History-Social Science Framework's fourth-grade California History and eighth-grade Nineteenth-Century U.S. History is illustrative in this regard: Charley Parkhurst. Parkhurst, assigned female at birth in New Hampshire in 1812, began dressing, working, and living as a man in the 1830s. Parkhurst moved out west to gold country in the 1850s, finding acclaim as a

FIG. 4.2. Charley Parkhurst, Los Gatos Footbridge Mural Project, Town of Los Gatos, California, 2017.

skilled stagecoach driver for Wells Fargo and others. Parkhurst later voted, operated a saloon, and worked as a lumberjack. In 1879, a doctor revealed Parkhurst's gender history after he died of cancer. This became a sensationalized national news story.

The section on Parkhurst in the 2016 History-Social Science Framework's grade-four chapter reads:

> Students may also read or listen to primary sources that illustrate gender and relationship diversity and engage students' interest in the era, such as . . . newspaper articles about the life of the stagecoach driver Charley Parkhurst, who was born as a female but lived as a male and drove

stagecoach routes in northern and central California for almost 30 years. Stagecoaches were the only way many people could travel long distances, and they served as a vital communication link between isolated communities. Parkhurst was one of the most famous California drivers . . .

In grade eight, it adds:

Many women of diverse racial and ethnic backgrounds felt trapped or limited by their gender in a place and time so dominated by men. Some . . . women handled the limitations of society by passing as or transforming themselves into men, thus benefiting from the greater opportunities men had in the West. California's Charley Parkhurst, for example, who was born a female but who lived as a male, drove stagecoach routes in northern and central California for almost 30 years . . . [11]

The fourth-grade version emphasizes engagement with primary sources, the concept of gender diversity, and biography as a way into in California's early transportation history. The eighth-grade version problematically frames Parkhurst as a woman "passing as or transforming . . . into" a man, rather than as someone who was assigned female at birth but lived as a man most of his life. Even so, it introduces students to social, economic, and potentially political limitations of culturally imposed gender roles in the nineteenth-century West, and how one individual navigated those constraints. This enables students to consider Parkhurst's possible reasons for doing so without landing on a definitive conclusion unsupported by known evidence.

Both of Parkhurst's Framework inclusions also highlight the existence of past gender expansiveness, which invites students' consideration in relation to contemporary LGBTQ+ lives. Late elementary and early teen years are meaningful developmental periods in all students' exploration of gender identity, roles, and stereotyping, both for themselves and in regard to others. The placement of Parkhurst in fourth- and eighth-grade curriculums is an efficient means of simultaneously practicing historical thinking, engaging history as a "story well told" through biography, considering gender in history, and contemplating past and present gender diversity. For all these reasons, Parkhurst's textbook inclusion was a priority for the FAIR Coalition.

Of the eleven proposed fourth- and eighth-grade textbooks we evaluated for the July meeting, nine mentioned Parkhurst. *California Studies* (fourth-grade) had a compelling biography, but we suggested they omit "One thing about Charley was a secret. Charley was actually a girl!" McGraw Hill's fourth-grade textbook wrote that "Parkhurst dressed as one [a man] to get the job." We explained that the authors could not decide the motive for Parkhurst based on extant evidence. We suggested that sentence be replaced with "What might be reasons that Parkhurst lived for many years as a man?" We also urged publishers to use they/them pronouns in deference to the inconclusive historical evidence as to why Parkhurst lived for so long as a man, or he/him pronouns since Parkhurst, at great personal risk, lived his adult life with masculine pronouns. The Teachers' Curriculum Institute (TCI)'s teacher's edition stood out for care with pronouns and language, use of a *San Francisco Call* primary source, and encouraging multiple perspectives.[12]

Almost all textbooks placed Parkhurst in a standard part of Californian and nineteenth-century surveys: a "Women in the West" (or, even more restrictively, "Pioneer Women") section. The FAIR Coalition urged publishers to retitle such

150   Contested Curriculum

sections as "Gender in the West" or "Gender and Women in the West" so that they could include racially and culturally diverse women's and men's gender roles, Indigenous two-spirit practices, shifting sex ratios, and how individuals dealt with all these across context and time. Parkhurst's placement in "Women in the West" lends an unwarranted authorial certainty regarding the primacy of birth-assigned sex as the "real" gender. It also erases the effort, risk, and skill through which Parkhurst functionally lived beyond birth assignment.[13] Designating Parkhurst as a woman conforms with the Framework wording, so the FAIR Coalition recognized our challenge on this front. Queer and trans scholars have taken great care not to side with doctors and sensationalized newspaper sources in "deciding" historical subjects' gender. The FAIR Coalition sought textbooks that presented gender-variant historical subjects with accuracy, which, in this case, necessitates ambiguity.[14]

In published versions of California's approved textbooks, the framing and language about Parkhurst has become more precise, albeit not to the extent that we requested. McGraw Hill's fourth-grade activity book (the *Inquiry Journal*) now centers Parkhurst in its section on the transportation revolution. While it still reads, "People found out that 'Charley' Parkhurst was really a woman named Charlotte Parkhurst," implying that assigned sex and birth name are the truth of one's existence, it ends with our suggested "What might be the reasons that Parkhurst lived for many years as a man?" It also provides a primary source in which Major Albert North Judd, one of Parkhurst's contemporaries, uses he/him pronouns to describe Parkhurst posthumously (even after the stagecoach driver's gender history was revealed). It prompts students to consider how Judd felt about Parkhurst and the words he used to describe him. Unfortunately, McGraw Hill undermines these best practices by using she/her pronouns in its own descriptions.[15]

The McGraw Hill eighth-grade U.S. history textbook presents Parkhurst at the start of its "California and Utah" chapter in a biography sidebar. Pronouns are not used. While it reads "*Charlotte* had transformed into a man," it highlights that "such transformations" could be due to "economic opportunities only open to men, or may have enabled different experiences or social freedoms." The *Teacher's Edition* prompts students to read the biography aloud and for the teacher to ask where and why there was a "surprising moment." The publisher undercuts itself by suggesting the surprise was the revelation of "*her* gender identification" (emphasis added).[16]

Our intention here is not to single out McGraw Hill for criticism. Its textbooks are relatively strong in terms of LGBT-related Framework content. Rather, we demonstrate that the state's textbook adoption process led to improvements in quality and accuracy, despite the constraint of "minor edits." Still, when it comes to correcting long-standing LGBTQ omissions and incorporating queer and trans historical scholarship's best practices, California's textbooks remain a work in progress.

When the instructional materials adoption deliberations began, the FAIR Coalition recommended that panels reject Houghton Mifflin Harcourt (HMH) publications as especially egregious. Its proposed textbooks generally left out most Framework LGBT-related content and concepts. During publisher responses during deliberations, its representatives seemed indifferent to input. Additionally, some of the little it did include violated the Framework's social content standards, which prohibited "adverse reflections" that stereotyped, demeaned, or patronized people in regard to gender role, sexual orientation, and gender identity.

In the grade-five "Revolutionary Women" section, for example, Houghton Mifflin Harcourt could have showcased Deborah Sampson as a female birth-assigned person who served as a male-presenting Revolutionary War soldier. Instead, its textbook asserted, "A woman could wear loose clothing and pretend she was a boy." In what can only be assumed to be a misguided attempt at humor, this was accompanied by a comic of HMH's own design entitled "Gals Disguised as Guys." In it, a presumably male soldier in Continental uniform gawks at another person who faces away from the viewer. This person also wears the tricorn hat and soldier's jacket but has what can only be described as capri pants and pink kitten heels. The viewer is clearly meant to identify with the gawker and find the idea of female birth-assigned people passing as men laughable. As the FAIR Coalition's report states, this "minimizes" such people's impact and "the struggles they had to endure to participate." We urged them to replace the comic with a historical image of Sampson.[17]

To the FAIR Coalition's disappointment, the review panels approved HMH's textbooks. Many reviewers either were overly deferential to publishers or minimized enforcement of the FAIR Education Act or LGBT-related Framework elements. Some felt other strengths outweighed weaknesses in these areas. HMH squeaked through by a narrow, contentious majority.[18]

In the FAIR Coalition's final assessment of the 365 minor edits and social content citations panels made across all proposed textbooks, just thirteen of them (3.5 percent) were in some way LGBT-related. Five were minor corrections to wording regarding Parkhurst, and seven were additions of "lesbian," "gay," or "bisexual" as biographical identity markers. Nine of the thirteen—and all of the identity

Resource FAIR   153

labels—were from the panel (McGraw Hill, K–5) on which Rob Darrow was a reviewer, which suggests how important LGBTQ+ representation on these panels was. The people that panel asked to be labeled were Ellen DeGeneres, Nikki Giovanni, Langston Hughes, Cleve Jones, Billie Jean King, and Sally Ride. McGraw Hill, in a subsequent letter to the IQC, took the position that addition of "lesbian," "gay," and/or "bisexual" would constitute a substantial "addition" rather than a minor "edit," and thus would be in violation of the state's own regulations. The FAIR Coalition strenuously rejected this interpretation, as did, eventually, the CDE.[19]

We hoped that in addition to the panels' spare edits, publishers would propose other "minor edits" and social content adjustments before the deliberations of the full IQC on September 28. In the interim, the FAIR Coalition organized over twenty people, including parents, students, teachers, content-area experts, children's book authors, and LGBTQ education advocates, to speak at a special August IQC meeting devoted exclusively to public comment. We also reached out to publishers, who were generally receptive. Representatives from Discovery's eighth-grade social science "techbook," Pearson's K–8 series, and First Choice's eighth-grade textbook were most responsive. Representatives from HMH met multiple times with members of the FAIR Coalition, but it was clear their textbooks would require major rewrites.[20] By the time the IQC met in late September, the FAIR Coalition again urged rejection of HMH.

The IQC is generally deferential to deliberation panels' recommendations, so the FAIR Coalition came prepared to press hard. In August and September, coalition added representatives from GSA Network, the American Civil Liberties Union, the Transgender Law Center, the National

FIG. 4.3. FAIR Education Act Implementation Coalition members after testifying before the Instructional Quality Commission at the California Department of Education in Sacramento, August 17, 2017. Top row: Maclain Pagenhart (Our Family Coalition intern), Don Romesburg (Committee on LGBT History), Kris Strangl (Berkeley Unified School District parent), unidentified, Julie Roberts-Phung (San Francisco Unified School District parent), Gaelynn Sparks (Oakland resident), Amanda McAllister-Wallner (California LGBTQ Health and Human Services Network), Rick Oculto (Our Family Coalition). Bottom row: Jo Michael (Equality California), Krystal Torres-Covarubias (Los Angeles LGBT Center), Renata Moreira (Our Family Coalition), Tarah Fleming (Our Family Coalition). Photo by Pauly Pagenhart, courtesy of Our Family Coalition.

Center for Lesbian Rights, and the Safe Schools Project of Santa Cruz County. These provided regional breadth and political clout. The FAIR Coalition's thirty-five-page report to the IQC detailed textbook line edits aligned with Framework-based rationales. In written and public testimony, LGBTQ advocates urged the IQC to "stand for the Framework's integrity and its relationship to the FAIR Education Act" where the review panels had not, and to "allow publishers to make the necessary minor LGBT edits and corrections to bring them into compliance." By the end of the meeting, the IQC had overridden the review panels' suggestions in several ways. First, it recommended that the State Board of Education reject HMH. Second, it approved the ten other submitted textbooks on the condition they incorporate a handful of the FAIR Coalition's edits.[21]

Media coverage of the IQC's decision often focused on the LGBT inclusion. By extension it tended to suggest that one of the main reasons for HMH's rejection was its lack of LGBT content.[22] Certainly, our push to exclude the publisher was based on that rationale, and we saw its rejection as a victory. What happened in terms of the data bears out a more complex truth.

The IQC required publishers in total to make 487 "edits and corrections." Only forty-seven (11 percent) were LGBT-related. Of the ninety-three total "social content citations" upon which the IQC conditioned approval, only eight (8.6 percent) were LGBT-related. Of 637 "publisher-submitted errata" recognized by the IQC, only twenty-three (3.6 percent) were LGBT-related. The vast majority of issues with textbooks in general and HMH specifically had nothing to do with LGBT omissions or misrepresentation. HMH, for example, was also cited for having too many factual inaccuracies as well as lack of balance regarding the world's religions.[23]

California's 2017 textbook adoption process was raucous. Over a thousand pages of public comments were submitted prior to the July deliberations. Online comments were submitted by 122 parties prior to early September. Indian Americans picketed outside the CDE. Approximately two hundred people gave public testimony before the IQC. When the State Board of Education met in early November to finalize adoption, the small handful of prepared, diverse, and on-message LGBTQ advocates mostly praised the process and the publishers.[24]

At the eleventh hour, HMH proposed dozens of edits, including LGBT ones, in an appeal to get the State Board of Education to overturn the IQC's ruling. At the meeting, Ted Levine, a HMH representative, said, "The public commentary that has been voiced over the last several months forces a company like mine to look at itself in the mirror. . . . I stand before you to say that you have been heard, and that adjustments have been made to the program, within the parameters and procedures that the state affords us." It was too large a pivot too late. In its written appeal, it also argued that "HMH feels that the terms *lesbian*, *gay*, *bisexual*, *transgender*, and *queer* are contemporary terms that may not map well on past lives and experiences." The publisher sought, instead, to provide biographical material in teachers' editions that contextualized the relationships and expressions of figures such as Whitman.[25]

In the media, HMH was less contrite. Deploying the biography trap, it positioned itself as an ethical player, the victim of activists and bureaucrats doing bad history with anachronistic labels. Journalist Theresa Harrington took up this framing in her *EdSource* stories. Harrington wrote that the publisher was rejected "in part because [it] . . . failed to detail the sexual orientation of historical figures such as literary luminaries Emily Dickinson, Ralph Waldo Emerson and Walt Whitman, and U.S. President James Buchanan." What goes unsaid is that the state would not have issued social content citations had the publisher's textbook provided nuanced language in the first place. Harrington also fails to mention that HMH was the only publisher not to submit publisher-submitted errata in the early fall, when issues may have been more readily rectified. The reporter quotes at length two of a small handful of the opposition letters the CDE received, overrepresenting their voice in the process. "I don't want sexual orientation in history and I don't want it to be highlighted as an attribute," wrote Sacramento business owner John Coburn, adding, "It has nothing to do with your accomplishment and I just think it's breaking down the family." The biography trap became a trope for other coverage as well.[26]

California's new textbooks were a mixed victory. Generally speaking, the state's approved K–8 history-social science textbooks now include at least the acknowledgment of same-sex-headed families and one or more LGBT role models (grade two); Charley Parkhurst and at least one twentieth-century LGBT California hero (often Harvey Milk, Billie Jean King, and/or Sally Ride) (grade four); an acknowledgment of gender diversity and changing sex ratio differences in the American colonies and colonization (grade five); Parkhurst again (often in a "Women and Gender in the West" section), shifting gender roles related to nineteenth-century urbanization and industrialization, and the recognition of two-spirit peoples in the effects of settler colonialism (grade eight). Some textbooks have more substantial content, whether biographical (such as Walt Whitman, Jane Addams, or Jose Sarria) or contextual (such as alternative families in enslavement or the rise in early queer urban subcultures).

Even when textbook mention is sparse, however, some educators have seized new opportunities to incorporate LGBT content into their lesson plans. Stephanie Kugler, who teaches eighth-grade history in West Sacramento, built a lesson on troops who could today be understood as transgender out of a brief mention in the TCI teacher's guide of Civil War soldiers assigned female at birth who fought and continued to live as men after the war. She coupled this with Black Union and Confederate soldier primary sources to explore how people overcame adversity.[27]

Approved K–8 educational materials could have been better. Language around identity, relationships, and gender could have been more precise. More contextualization could have generated better historical thinking practices. The content could have always appeared in student as well as teacher editions. When drafting their next versions of California's proposed textbooks, publishers should work in advance with LGBTQ scholars rather than relying on public comments and "minor edits" to fix what they omit.

A lack of state oversight makes the picture less clear for grade-eleven U.S. history. That said, after reviewing the textbooks of TCI and McGraw Hill, it appears that publishers followed the patterns within their K–8 texts. TCI's *History Alive! Pursuing American Ideals* only sparingly includes LGBT-related Framework content in its student edition. A student's first encounter is a brief World War II mention of Nazi genocide of "Jews, homosexuals, disabled people, captured Soviet soldiers, and Roma." LGBT history doesn't appear again until a chapter on the "widening struggle" for civil rights beyond Black freedom. Five paragraphs explain that a "gay rights movement" began in the late 1950s, held 1960s pickets outside Philadelphia's Independence Hall, and "became highly visible during the Stonewall Riots." From there it mentions the founding of Parents and Friends of Lesbians and Gays (PFLAG) and Harvey Milk. LGBT people appear three more times: in a section on evangelical Christians "distressed by rising divorce rates, drug use, gay rights, and feminism"; three paragraphs on HIV/AIDS and President Reagan's relative inaction; and three paragraphs on marriage equality in a contemporary section. The student edition lacks any mention of the government's systematic persecution during World War II and the Cold War era; any lesbian, bisexual, or transgender people; representation of nonwhite queer or trans people; and most LGBT-related Framework content. No image of an identified LGBT person shows up until Jim Obergefell in the final chapter.[28]

By contrast, the student edition of McGraw Hill's *IMPACT California Social Studies: United States History and Geography: Continuity and Change* features sixteen inclusions. Early twentieth-century mentions include Jane Addams's "romantic partner," Boston marriages, and LGBTQ subcultural possibilities in growing cities and the Harlem Renaissance. Midcentury elements include state persecution in World War II and the postwar era, Christine Jorgensen, the Beat movement, and civil rights discussions of Bayard Rustin. A small section on the "movement for LGBTQ rights" takes students from the 1920s Society for Human Rights and 1950s Daughters of Bilitis to the 2016 Stonewall National Historical Landmark nomination. The 1970s–1990s covers Gay Liberation, Milk, Reagan's AIDS indifference, ACT UP, and the rise of "advocacy groups" such as the Human Rights Campaign. In contemporary history, it discusses hate crimes and marriage equality. McGraw Hill's textbook also features an array of related images and primary sources. Its "Inquiry Journal" and teacher's edition invite further analysis and project-based learning.[29]

Following the State Board of Education's K–8 adoption, OFC contracted Darrow to develop a set of textbook evaluation tools aligned with LGBT-related Framework content. These documents, for K–5, 8, and 11 came out in January 2018 as some districts began local adoption processes. Each tool provides guiding questions on how well instructional materials meet the LGBT-related Framework content, tables

160   Contested Curriculum

for evaluators to quantify how the materials address each content area, and ways to indicate where a textbook's LGBT content might go beyond the Framework. Over the next several years, OFC consulted with ten county education offices directly.[30] This project was a part of a wider set of implementation initiatives in the decade after the FAIR Education Act.

Getting Implementation and Materials Right for Educators

While the FAIR Education Act, Framework, and state textbook adoptions provided a solid foundation, they would only be meaningful if school districts complied and educators steered them into classrooms. In the early years after the law passed, few teachers sought to incorporate more LGBTQ content. The lack of resources, support, and training largely left them to their own devices. Deficits of content knowledge and implementation strategies compounded with challenges of respectfully addressing the topic historically at the same time as contemporary language about gender and sexual diversity evolved. Finally, there was the issue of community perception. How and when to integrate LGBTQ history concepts and content as essential (rather than tokenizing or overly politicizing) was at the forefront of many educators' minds.

A number of individuals and organizations began creating resources in order to facilitate better understanding of the law and provide classroom content. Over time, resources included lesson plans, primary source sets, best practices in presenting LGBTQ-inclusive concepts in age-appropriate ways, primers on the law's requirements, and workshops. By May 2012, OFC, in conjunction with the FAIR Coalition, set up a website to educate teachers about the law. Soon after,

OFC collaborated with the ONE Archives Foundation in Los Angeles to transform the site into a central teaching resource hub. Eventually renamed Teaching LGBTQ History, it currently houses or links to many Framework-aligned lesson plans and primary source guides. It offers a brief history of California's LGBTQ-inclusive history education process, suggestions for advocacy, options for professional development, and evaluation rubrics for district textbook adoptions.[31]

Some educators created preliminary templates and guides based on their classroom experiences. Chapters 1 and 2 mention lessons and materials developed in the 1980s and 1990s. Education scholar Stacie Brensilver Berman describes how a handful of other projects across the country led up to the FAIR Education Act. In 2000, the University of Minnesota's Human Rights Resource Center worked with education scholar David Donahue to create activity-based lessons on changing laws and activism leading up to the marriage equality movement. In 2003, the *New York Times* Learning Network began posting LGBTQ history lessons on family, marriage, AIDS, culture wars, and the military. In 2009, GLSEN created a timeline and related lesson about important moments from the colonial era to the present, and two years later it launched its Unheard Voices program focused on historically contextualized biographies. In 2010, the Anti-Defamation League, which had partnered with GLSEN and StoryCorps on Unheard Voices, published an LGBTQ lesson for its Curriculum Connections program.[32]

In California, Will Grant had been an educator for twenty years when he created an LGBTQ studies high school course in 2009–2010 at the private Athenian School in Danville, in part as a response to the state's 2008 passage of Proposition 8 banning same-sex marriage. It ran for five years, until he left teaching to focus on consulting. At that point, having seen state law catch up to him, Grant started a training program named Fair Classrooms. In addition to providing classroom materials, Grant ran workshops to coach administrators on FAIR Education Act implementation and provided teachers with strategies to address language, framing, cultural competency, and community concerns.[33]

The ONE Archives Foundation also began laying groundwork in LGBTQ-inclusive history education training and materials prior to the FAIR Education Act's passage. It has continued to expand its reach ever since. Its earliest program, Youth Ambassadors for Queer History, has, since 2010, invited high school students to engage in archival projects that include presentations by community organizers and elected officials, workshops, and field trips. The final product is a program and exhibition at the ONE Gallery. From 2014 to 2019, ONE also developed a popular history panel series, each of which feature between fifteen and twenty-two panels. Schools, organizations, and companies can either purchase a full set or select particular panels.[34]

In addition, ONE committed to professional development. While it had conducted occasional workshops earlier, from 2017 to 2019, it partnered with the Los Angeles LGBT Center and Center X (the UCLA History-Geography Project), to run the OUT Curriculum Cohort. These weeklong summer symposiums for fifteen Southern Californian educators connected them with scholars and archives, encouraging teachers to develop and share lesson plans. Starting in 2014, ONE curriculum developers "combed through US history textbooks to find entry points" for LGBTQ integration and, by 2015, had generated initial lesson plans. Through its 2017 and 2018 summer workshops, ONE developed more Framework-aligned lessons, all of which are free downloads.

During the COVID-19 pandemic, ONE pivoted to online training, providing focused grade-level and topical webinars through 2022 in partnership with the global nonprofit Facing History and Ourselves. In 2024, now rebranded as One Institute, the organization resumed its in-person youth and educator programs. All of its low-cost or free professional development has been well received.[35]

At least one school district has gone another route, developing a stand-alone LGBTQ history elective course. In San Francisco, Lyndsey Schlax, history teacher at Ruth Asawa High School of the Arts, created in 2015 what came to be known as the first public high school class focused exclusively on LGBTQ+ history. As chapter 2 notes, the San Francisco Unified School District (SFUSD) began providing optional lesbian, gay, and bisexual lesson plans to educators by the mid-1990s. In 2006, SFUSD's Board of Education passed a resolution to affirm LGBTQ-inclusive family diversity curriculum for elementary school social studies. From 2008 to 2010, one of the authors of the 1990s curriculum, Barbara Blinick, taught a high school history and literature-focused LGBTQ studies pilot with fellow educators Pete Hammer and Jenn Bowman. Based on prior work the district had done developing Ethnic Studies, the pilot was taught on weekends through SFUSD's interdisciplinary institute for district high school students. In 2010, the Board affirmed its support of the pilot as part of the larger endorsement of LGBTQ Support Services.[36]

Schlax built upon this foundation and the FAIR Education Act to develop her semester-long elective taught during regular school hours. She described it as "broken into three units, beginning with basic terminology, followed by identities and the history of LGBT leaders including the late Supervisor Harvey Milk and the AIDS pandemic of the 1980s." She explained that the third unit looked at "the current portrayal of those who identify as LGBT." This innovative class included music, art, videos, and a trip to the GLBT Historical Society Museum down the hill from the school in the historic Castro neighborhood.[37]

The course received substantial media attention and was considered a success by the school, students, and district. Schlax reported that educators from across the Bay Area, Southern California, New York, Georgia, and Texas expressed interest in mounting something similar. In 2016–2017, the course expanded to Mission and Thurgood Marshall High Schools. The subsequent year (2017–2018), while Marshall discontinued the class due to low enrollment, Mission offered it again with its same teacher, Jenn Bowman. Schlax's course was then cross-listed with neighboring Academy High School.[38]

In 2018, when Schlax left Ruth Asawa and Bowman left Mission, the course was discontinued. By the time one of *Contested Curriculum*'s author's daughters took eleventh-grade U.S. history at Ruth Asawa in 2021–2022, there was no evidence that any of the elective's content—or much of the LGBT content in the History-Social Science Framework, for that matter—had migrated into the school's core U.S. history classes. At Mission and at Washington High School, where Bowman went after Mission, some of the content was folded into a Women's and Gender Studies elective. It is difficult to know whether U.S. history and social studies courses across SFUSD have generally had FAIR and Framework-related LGBTQ implementation, since the district does not assess this.[39] As such, the efficacy of the elective approach (rather than training and implementation across social studies) remains unclear.

From 2016 to 2019, Rob Darrow created a program to build Framework-aligned workshops for elementary, middle, and high school teachers in Santa Cruz and Salinas. Educators crafted and piloted LGBTQ-inclusive lesson plans, and Darrow provided ongoing feedback and peer support. Since then, he has continued to develop materials and guidance. As a result, Santa Cruz now has a fully accessible set of resources for teachers, including curriculum guides, teacher project pages, rubrics, and links. This also includes monthly fifteen-minute lesson plans for use in either classrooms or student groups (such as GSA clubs).[40]

During the framework adoption process, OFC learned more about the limited instructional resources available to educators. With the Framework as a guiding document, OFC in 2017 shifted the work of its education internships to help fill those gaps. Interns created Framework-aligned lesson plans and other resources, often also drawing on the *Making the Framework FAIR* report as a guiding document. While this approach went beyond the Framework as written, OFC reasoned that the CDE and its then–deputy superintendent Tom Adams had repeatedly stated that educators should understand the Framework as a "floor, not the ceiling" for how LGBT-inclusive content should be implemented. OFC also supported educators in conversations about overcoming resistance to lesson plan adoption.

The lesson plans were largely developed by college student interns drawn to OFC because of its inclusive history and social studies programming and advocacy. Prior to publication, OFC staff vetted the materials. These lesson plans utilize the inquiry model that the CDE seeks and focus on underrepresented aspects of LGBTQ history. One of the earliest, *Two-Spirit and Non-Traditional Families* (2018), seeks to introduce fourth-grade students to different family models. This lesson also introduces the two-spirit concept and cultural practice and invites student discussion of diverse family narratives. A fourth-grade lesson, *Chinese Laborers and the California Gold Rush: The Racialization of Masculinity* (2022), explores how Chinese workers were framed as a threat to both dominant gender norms and white men's economic prosperity. OFC also produced high school lesson plans such as *Christine Jorgensen: An Analysis of the Role That Privilege and Media Play in Access to Gender Confirmation Procedures* (2021). This compares barriers to physical and social transitioning in the 1950s and today. The lesson plan seeks to historically contextualize trans lives through an intersectional exploration of race, affluence, gender, age, and religion. Unfortunately, in 2023, OFC eliminated its education staffing and put education internships on hiatus, leaving the future of such programming uncertain.[41]

By 2017, many educators continued to be unaware of the FAIR Education Act, LGBT Framework content, or what to include in their curriculum. The CDE provided no implementation plan (nor did almost any local districts). An increasing amount of lesson plans, workshops, and other resources were available, but beyond the Teaching LGBTQ History website, there was no coordinated statewide presence. OFC's Director of Education Tarah Fleming and Education Manager Rick Oculto brought together the Santa Cruz Safe Schools Project's Rob Darrow and the Los Angeles LGBT Center's Krystal Torres-Covarrubias to plan LGBTQ+ History Stakeholder Forums for San Francisco and Los Angeles. These convened teachers, administrators, nonprofit representatives, and historians to discuss implementation needs, consolidate data, and provide a roadmap to better implementation. The first daylong event was held on October 12, 2018, in the Google Community Space in San Francisco. Over sixty attendees from across the state participated in an Open Space Technology process where, through consensus, they generated relevant topics. Erik Adamian from ONE Archives Foundation joined planning for the subsequent Los Angeles gathering at the offices of the American Civil Liberties Union the following February.[42]

The forums served two important functions: First, they helped identify areas where advocates and educators could create the most impact. Second, they solidified an informal network through which to better coordinate resources. This was a necessary evolution from the ad hoc FAIR Coalition, which had succeeded at shepherding the law's incorporation into the Framework and aligned textbooks but had not continued that momentum. The forums also created some collective movement and solidified the conveners as experts to which state and local education agencies could turn.

Unfortunately, the forums did not generate effective strategies to fundraise toward their goals. Ever since the FAIR Education Act had passed, those working on implementation had struggled to persuade funders, whether individual donors, foundations, or governmental agencies, that LGBTQ-inclusive history education should be a priority. We wonder how such funding would have accelerated change. In any case, today, as educators and districts around the state and the nation face a sustained attack on LGBTQ content in K–12 schools, we hope that funders can now see clearly how essential an investment this is.

In June 2018, the Sacramento County Office of Education reached out to OFC's Education Team to participate as a content expert for the Content, Literacy, Inquiry, and Citizenship (CLIC) Project. Funded through 2021 by the CDE, CLIC was a statewide professional development program that assisted educators in content adoption and inquiry-based teaching. Topics included the Bracero Program, Civic Education, LGBT History, Environmental Literacy, Filipino

168　Contested Curriculum

American Contributions to the Farm Labor Movement, Armenian Genocide, American Indian Genocide, Cambodian Genocide, Rwandan Genocide, and Challenging Injustice. On the CLIC website, introductory videos on each topic are accompanied by further resources. CLIC representatives from different California regions ensured that the new content was implemented there, meeting with the different content experts on a semiregular basis from 2018 to 2020. This resulted in OFC's Oculto, ONE's Erik Adamian, and Darrow providing LGBT CLIC trainings for Los Angeles, Monterey, Santa Clara, San Mateo, Santa Cruz, Sonoma, and Glenn County Offices of Education.[43] COVID derailed other planned trainings. As of 2024, they had not picked up again.

In California, most subject-area framework training comes from CDE contracts with related organizations and agencies. For the History-Social Science Framework, this primarily meant (in addition to county education offices and CLIC) the California History-Social Science Project (CHSSP). Headquartered at UC Davis, the CHSSP has regional offices at UC Berkeley, UC Irvine, UCLA, and UC Santa Cruz. The CHSSP collaborates with historians, education specialists, and K–12 educators to elevate history instruction and empower teachers through professional development, educational materials, and teaching aids. Once the FAIR Education Act passed, the CHSSP began very modestly incorporating more LGBT content into some of its model lesson plans.[44]

Following the Framework's finalization, the statewide CHSSP, which had also staffed the Framework's authorship, made substantial investments in LGBTQ-inclusive history education across elementary, middle school, and high school. CHSSP program coordinator Beth Slutsky noted that it was the mix of policy (the FAIR Education Act) and the

Resource FAIR   169

"community push" (what became the FAIR Coalition) that made the CHSSP step up. She said the ongoing biggest challenge in this area was educators' "content knowledge." Moreover, she explained, it "takes a while" for teachers to understand that LGBTQ-inclusive historical narratives exist for many periods and that this subject area has a scholarly "depth of knowledge."[45]

From 2017 to 2018 and then again from 2019 to 2020, the CHSSP led a series of History-Social Science Framework rollout events across the state. Nearly all of these included a FAIR content workshop. CHSSP assistant director Tuyen Tran credited Don Romesburg, who ran most of these workshops, with creating a "nonthreatening" forum where teachers and administrators trying to do this work "felt safe." The FAIR rollout sessions were well attended, consistently attracting between twenty and forty participants. The first round of workshops (2017–2018) introduced the breadth of LGBTQ-related Framework content, addressed basic concerns, and quelled anxieties. Based on participant feedback, the second round (2019–2020) featured more specific content, including, for elementary and middle school, two-spirit history in the context of Californian and Early American settler colonialism, and, for high school, the Harlem Renaissance and the Lavender Scare.[46]

In addition to rollouts, the various CHSSP affiliates around the state conducted dozens of their own LGBTQ-related educator workshops from 2017 through 2024, relying on a mix of K–12 teachers, university scholars, and LGBTQ education specialists. They have also included FAIR-related content in many of their more general workshops. The CHSSP provides related content, resources, and advice for districts that request them. Cumulatively, these formal and informal effects have had significant impact over time as teachers influence other teachers, even if, initially, the educators who participated were, as Slutsky put it, "in some respects preaching to the choir."[47]

The CHSSP has generated free and accessible lesson plans and primary source teaching sets aligned with the Framework's LGBTQ content across elementary, middle, and high school grades. Berkeley's History-Social Science Project features *Charley Parkhurst and the California Gold Rush* (grades four and eight), *Charity and Sylvia* (an early American same-sex couple) (grade five); a world history unit on Ancient Greece (grade six); and *Baron von Steuben and the Continental Army* (grade eight). In 2019, its grade-eleven lesson plan, *The Lavender Scare and McCarthyism*, won the Committee on LGBT History's inaugural Don Romesburg Prize for outstanding LGBTQ K–12 history curriculum. Center X (UCLA History-Geography Project) has two Cold War lesson plans in addition to the dozen relating to the late nineteenth through early twenty-first century that teachers developed through its summer seminar collaboration with the One Institute. The UC Davis History Project has developed several LGBTQ-inclusive primary source inquiry sets through the Teaching California Program, its partnership with the California Historical Society. These include, for grade-nine Ethnic Studies, *Political Activism in LGBTQ Communities* (2021); and, for grade-eleven, *The 1920s* (2019); *Civil Rights* (2018); *Civil Rights Movements* (2019); *Vietnam and Movements for Equality* (2020); and *Contemporary American Issues* (2020).[48]

Finally, in 2022, CHSSP, in conjunction with San José State University professor Wendy Rouse, produced the remarkable *LGBTQ+ History through Primary Sources*. This sprawling collection covers the following topics: the American Revolution, Gold Rush West, Women's Suffrage,

Slavery and Reconstruction, Industrialization and Urbanization, Early Twentieth Century Immigration, the Roaring Twenties, the Hays Code, World War II, the Lavender Scare, and Gay Liberation. These aligned and annotated primary sources provide ease of teacher incorporation into existing curriculums. They are in line with what the Stanford History Education Group's "Reading Like a Historian" program, which promotes strong practices of inquiry framing for issue-based learning, historical and sociocultural reasoning, and ability to scaffold with other lessons. Rouse was the ideal scholar-teacher to assemble, annotate, and align the over seventy-five primary sources in the project. Not only is she a prolific queer historian, she coordinates San José State's History and Social Science Teacher Preparation program. She trains emerging K–12 teachers to incorporate LGBTQ history into their pedagogies, curriculums, and classrooms, and publishes related articles.[49]

More recently, another Californian university, Sonoma State, has also begun to focus on LGBTQ-inclusive history and social studies preparation in its preservice program. In fall 2022, its School of Education's state-funded Teacher Residency Program for its TK–6 teachers in training brought on Professor Romesburg to develop a unit for mentors and mentees. This included LGBTQ+ cultural competency for elementary grades, bringing LGBTQ history into PK–6 classes (through which mentees developed and implemented a plan), and incorporating LGBTQ lessons year-round. A truncated version of this unit is now embedded each semester into the university's Multiple Subject Credential coursework.[50]

As Brensilver Berman notes, incorporating LGBTQ history into teacher education programs more broadly "would allow the information conveyed at the university level to trickle down to K–12 schools." This would, in turn, prepare "students for the courses to which they will have access" in college. It would also "alleviate one stated reason for the topic's omission in [K–12] classes," namely, a lack of educator knowledge and experience with that history and how to teach it. Indeed, the research bears out that educators with higher levels of self-efficacy in LGBTQ topics through preservice training will be more likely to develop inclusive curriculum and instruction, as well as support LGBTQ students and families.[51]

Where Are We Now?

In the 14 years since passage of the FAIR Education Act, California has taken incredible strides. Where textbooks previously had token mentions, if anything, they now have substantial elements in elementary, middle, and high school. Hundreds of PK–12 public school teachers and administrators have now had some LGBTQ history education professional development. Before there were very few related educational materials, while now they are abundant, diverse, and readily accessible. California could be seen as a model for the rest of the nation.

Even so, each step took a tremendous amount of sustained effort. For all the educators who have received training, there are thousands of others who have not. Some would be eager, or at least willing, to, while others would steadfastly refuse training or implementation. Even with all of the mandates, protections, and pathways to inclusive teaching, some will avoid it due to fear of parent, community, or administrative backlash. Others will refuse because of their own biases or because their view of what constitutes "proper" history refuses to allow LGBTQ+ lives into the frame. While a couple of state universities include LGBTQ history and social studies training in their credentialing programs, most do not. Creating all of the amazing lesson plans, primary source sets, and published guidance on how to incorporate LGBTQ content into K–12 history and social studies has been very labor-intensive. To date, we have no real way of assessing how much these are being utilized in California's classrooms or beyond.

Relatedly, those who have done this work have done so with a profound lack of funding. Where small pockets of state money appear, such as those linked to the Framework rollout, they are time-limited. This constrains long-range or universal implementation. Foundations and donors who usually emphasize education and/or LGBTQ+ issues rarely saw history education as a priority across the 2010s. This left OFC, the One Institute, and other nonprofit organizations very limited in their capacities. School districts, especially after being rocked by the COVID-19 lockdowns and disruptions, have understandably spent more time on learning-loss triage in STEM, reading, and writing, as well as on social-emotional learning, than on history and social studies. Focusing on how to align their materials and curriculums with the Framework's LGBT concepts and content risks being pushed even further down the list. This is unfortunate, given that LGBT-inclusive history education can improve student engagement, mental health, campus climate, and civic learning, beyond being just solid history.

Many of us who have been in the trenches doing this work for years have wondered, when, if ever, the wider public, politicians, and funders will see its importance. The book's conclusion sounds a note of despair in a time of unprecedented backlash. Just maybe, the current culture war will compel a broader movement to prioritize LGBTQ history education's implementation.

RICK OCULTO (HE/HIM) is a twenty-year nonprofit veteran specializing in justice, equity, diversity, and inclusion located in San Francisco, California. He has worked to implement LGBTQ+ inclusive practices to create welcoming and inclusive climates for youth and families of diverse backgrounds. Oculto has recently spearheaded efforts in California to implement LGBTQ+ inclusive history in schools.

FIG. C.1. Striff Striffolino, *Part of Me*, 2020.

Conclusion

As California Goes…?

In January 2020, when I began working on this book in earnest, the horizon was bright for LGBTQ-inclusive K–12 history education. Four more states—New Jersey, Colorado, Illinois, and Oregon—had recently passed inclusive curriculum legislation. In 2018, Massachusetts had added some LGBTQ content to its History-Social Science Framework. Two other states, Utah and Arizona (in 2017 and 2019, respectively), had done away with old "No Promo Homo" laws. In 2019, the National Council for the Social Studies had issued a position statement affirming LGBTQ history education as important and empowering.[1]

In 2021, however, storm clouds gathered. While two more states, Connecticut and Nevada, brought the total of those with inclusive curriculum legislation to seven, a wave of others passed anti-LGBTQ curriculum laws. Arizona, Arkansas, Florida, Montana, and Tennessee approved new legislation requiring teachers to give parents advance notice of any LGBTQ mention. While "No Promo Homo" laws from the 1980s and 1990s had been directed toward sex education, these were written more broadly.

In 2022 and 2023, no new states enacted inclusive education laws. In 2024, Washington did, rounding out inclusion by the four westernmost states in the continental United States. In those three years, seven states passed even more censorious "Don't Say Gay" legislation. The well-known Florida law initially restricted its mandate to K–3, then expanded to PK–8 and, through Board of Education rules, PK–12. Other states include Alabama, Arkansas, Indiana, Iowa, Kentucky, and North Carolina. These join Louisiana, Mississippi, Oklahoma, and Texas, which have old "No Promo Homo" laws still on the books. As of October 2024, eleven states have "Don't Say LGBTQ" laws and seven have parental restriction laws. More states have anti-LGBTQ curriculum censorship laws now than in a quarter century. If one more passes, the United States will have more than it ever has. In 2023, approximately 24 percent of PK–12 public school students lived in inclusive-law states, while 35 percent lived in prohibitive states.[2] In overall numbers of states and students, inclusive education laws are falling behind. In the many states where the government gives no directives regarding LGBTQ-inclusive history education, it is hard to imagine this culture war is not having a chilling effect.

The Movement Advancement Project (MAP) demonstrates how anti-LGBTQ curriculum censorship laws are part of two larger agendas. The first is an expansive scheme to censor historically accurate K–12 discussions of race, LGBTQ+ people, oppression, and social justice. As MAP writes, this "coordinated effort on behalf of well-financed, far-right lobbyists" seeks to undermine recent racial and LGBTQ+ progress. Across many states, identical "parental rights" and "protecting American history" language appears in bills, public relations, and social media. Seventeen states have passed related laws since 2020, and three others are subject to a similar executive order.[3] These often overlap with the states that have anti-LGBTQ curriculum laws.

The second agenda is, as MAP puts it, a "firestorm" that seeks to "erase LGBTQ people from schools and public life." Curricular laws are just the tip of the spear. Since 2020, legislatures in forty states have considered hundreds of curriculum censorship bills. Even when these do not become law, they promote mobilization at the local level. This has resulted in anti-LGBTQ library book bans, bans on drag performance in the presence of minors, removal of public school educational materials, restriction of curriculums, and harassing or criminalizing LGBTQ-inclusive educators, administrators, librarians, and school boards. Related are "hostile school climate bills," such as banning educator diversity trainings, requiring parental notification when students privately discuss sexual orientation or gender identity with staff, rolling back student gender identity nondiscrimination protections, and establishing anti–trans youth school policies regarding pronouns, bathrooms, and/or sports.[4]

These attacks have even made their way to California. In the most spectacular example, the Temecula Valley Unified School Board in Riverside County voted in May 2023 to reject K–5 social studies textbooks and related curriculum that had previously been approved through public evaluation, adoption, and piloting. This was ostensibly because fourth-grade supplemental material included mention of Harvey Milk. In November 2022, the three far-right evangelical Christian board members—Joseph Komrosky, Danny Gonzalez, and Jennifer Wiersma—had come to power with the support of Inland Empire Family PAC, which opposes what it calls "forced LGBTQ+ acceptance." The new majority rejected the Teachers' Curriculum Institute (TCI)'s *Social Studies Alive!*, leaving more than eleven thousand elementary students without materials for the upcoming fall. At the meeting, board president Komrosky, a philosophy professor, called Milk a "pedophile." This drew attention away from places in TCI's student edition where lesbian and gay content appears that he would have found much harder to scandalize. A section on major court decisions explains marriage equality, while a section on protest mentions Del Martin, Phyllis Lyon, and the Daughters of Bilitis.[5] The board majority sought to censor all of this as well. They doubled down by firing the superintendent, a district veteran for a quarter century.

Californian conservatives have harnessed the energies of COVID-19 anti-maskers and anti-vaxxers alongside parents outraged by pandemic online schooling and other social disruptions. The state's Republican Party, stymied a decade of Democratic governorship and legislative supermajority, prioritized local school boards for the 2022 and 2024 cycles. While electoral success so far has been spotty, victors make the most of it. Whether or not particular candidates win, the campaigns, with support and training from groups such as American Council, the Coalition for Parental Rights, California Policy Center, and Turning Point USA, feed into a national discourse regarding "gender ideology," "grooming," and "social contagion" that rallies and expands their base under the banner of "parental rights."[6] Although their primary target—and the place where they are getting the most traction—is trans youth, the Temecula battle reveals that stopping LGBTQ-inclusive and racial justice–related history education is a close second.

In this firestorm, it is easy to feel overwhelmed. Fixated on its awfulness, we can lose sight of the remarkable work that has been done building LGBTQ-inclusive history education for over four decades now, in materials, policies, advocacy, and practices. That history points us toward the future. Long after this culture war has burned out and the far right's politicians, lobbyists, and pundits have found some other politically expedient object for advancing their agenda, an LGBTQ-inclusive history education foundation will remain firm.[7]

Many Californian parents, community members, educators, and politicians are actively defending inclusive education. In Temecula, following protests against the renegade school board, Governor Gavin Newsom threatened to levy a $1.5-million fine and bill the district another $1.6 million to ship it textbooks. In July, the board backed down, approving TCI but deferring instruction on the chapter in which a few mentions of LGBT history appear to "allow for more public input." In August 2023, Newsom launched California's Family Agenda. In addition to encouraging parental engagement in district decisions and expansive access to skill-based learning in high school, he called for robust school-related health, nutrition, and safety programs. He centered this all in the "freedom to learn," protecting students' right to learn about "the world and themselves" without censorship. In addition, local parents, school, and community leaders founded the One Temecula Valley Political Action Committee. It led a successful June 2024 recall campaign against Komrosky, Gonzalez, and Wiersma, with allies including the National Association for the Advancement of Colored People (NAACP), League of United Latin American Citizens (LULAC), and Grandparents for Truth. The school board restored a majority that favored scholarly, fair, and diverse history education. Yet in November, Komrosky and others retook an anti-LGBTQ board majority. The fight continues.[8]

Conclusion   181

Beyond Newsom, other statewide leaders have stood in support of honest history curriculums and the rights of LGBTQ+ youth and families. In June 2023, Newsom, State Superintendent of Public Instruction Tony Thurmond, and Attorney General Rob Bonta issued a letter to superintendents and principals clarifying students' right to learn. It explains where California Education Code mandates LGBTQ-inclusive materials and instruction. Thurmond assembled a Task Force on Inclusive Education, and its June 21 hearing brought together textbook publishers and members of the legislature to hear from educational advocacy expert witnesses regarding racial diversity and LGBTQ history. At that hearing, publishers made a commitment to inclusive representation.[9]

Finally, a series of new laws emerged from California's LGBTQ Legislative Caucus. Assembly Bill (AB) 5 was introduced by Assemblymember Rick Zbur (D-Los Angeles), who led Equality California during the 2016 History-Social Science Framework process and 2017 textbook adoption struggle. Starting in 2025–2026, all grade 7–12 educators will annually receive a California Department of Education (CDE)–developed LGBTQ cultural competency training.[10]

Assemblymember Dr. Corey Jackson, a former member of the Riverside County Board of Education, introduced AB 1078. Jackson, a freshman Democrat, is also the first Black openly LGBTQ state lawmaker. His law, effective immediately, has three effects. First, it authorizes the state superintendent to provide textbooks at a school district's expense if its school board withholds them. Second, the law prohibits school districts from banning any "appropriately adopted textbook, instructional material, or curriculum on the basis that it contains inclusive and diverse perspectives." Third, it updates the Education Code language shaped by the FAIR Education Act to include "the roles and contributions of people of all genders, Native Americans, African Americans, Latino Americans, Asian Americans, Pacific Islanders, European Americans, LGBTQ+ Americans, persons with disabilities, and members of other ethnic, cultural, religious, and socioeconomic status groups." This amends "men and women" to recognize gender beyond the binary, adjusts an older language of "Mexican Americans" to recognize more diverse Latine peoples, and updates the "LGBT" language with more contemporary and expansive categories. By 2025, the CDE must provide districts guidance on related curriculum and materials.[11]

In the dozen years since California passed the FAIR Education Act, the state has deeply embedded it in its policy and practice. While censors seek to silence teachers, punish administrators, and limit student access, an expansive base of laws, policies, and resources supports those who follow the law. There is also the political will to counter bad faith actors who attempt to seize the reigns of local power, bully educators, disrupt community input practices, and deny history education mandates. While we still have a long way to go, we are a state transformed.

Other states with inclusive education mandates have also made strides. While beyond the scope of this book to detail their politics, policies, and processes, here's a snapshot of where they stand:

- New Jersey in January 2019 became the second state to pass an LGBTQ-inclusive education mandate. It covers the whole curriculum for middle and high school. A pilot program was to run in the spring of 2020 but the pandemic sidetracked it. Districts have erratically provided professional

Conclusion   183

development. Educators and curriculum specialists contracted with LGBTQ+ organizations Make It Better for Youth and Garden State Equality have developed forty-one free lesson plans, ten of which are history or social studies. In June 2023, the state's attorney general and Department of Education issued a statement urging adoption and a reporting hotline for noncompliant districts.[12]

- Colorado's openly gay governor Jared Polis signed House Bill (HB) 19-1192 in May 2019, focused on K–12 history and civic learning. In November 2021, a Colorado Social Studies Standards Review and Revision Committee proposed revisions, including mention of "LGBTQ people" in grades 1–5 and high school history and civics. Although two-thirds of public comments supported the revisions, the committee, citing "age appropriateness," removed most LGBTQ references throughout and all below fourth grade. They also replaced specific racial and ethnic references with the vague phrase "diverse perspectives." After an unprecedented mobilization of students, parents, and education, LGBTQ+, racial justice, and Indigenous advocates, in November 2022 the State Board of Education restored LGBTQ and racial/ethnic references to the final standards. The four Democratic Board members voted for inclusion, and the three Republicans voted against. The Colorado Department of Education has contracted with A Queer Endeavor, a University of Colorado, Boulder, School of Education program to support LGBTQ+ professional development for K–12 teachers, and the Colorado LGBTQ History Project, which is developing standards-aligned lesson plans and training.[13]

- Oregon's HB 2023, signed into law by openly bisexual governor Kate Brown in June 2019, requires LGBTQ inclusion in updated social studies standards and instructional material adoptions. The Oregon Department of Education integrated LGBTQ people into the "traditionally marginalized people" in its 2021 Ethnic Studies Overlay for all grade levels. Teachers have until 2026 for required implementation. Oregon also provides professional development and educational materials.[14]

- Illinois passed HB 246 in August 2019. It requires the study of LGBT "roles and contributions" in state and U.S. history, effective from 2020–2021. This law emerged due to the Legacy Project Education Initiative, established in 2013 to develop teaching tools and support preservice teacher education. Soon after, Equality Illinois, the Illinois Safe Schools Alliance, and the Legacy Project formed the Inclusive Curriculum Advisory Council of Illinois, which now has over seventy-five standards-aligned lesson plans across all grades in a searchable database. Illinois Social Science Standards are based on inquiry skills and disciplinary concepts rather than content. Its 2022 revision gives more attention to "marginalized communities," "historically oppressed peoples," and "multiple perspectives."[15]

- Nevada, in May 2021, passed AB 261, which ensures instruction about "persons of marginalized sexual orientation or gender identity" in "history and contributions to science, the arts and humanities." It also mandates updating standards and textbook adoptions, but this has yet to occur.[16]

- Connecticut, in June 2021, passed a budget provision that funded a K–8 Model Curriculum inclusive of LGBTQ+ studies. This is optional for all districts. The inclusive social studies elements are reflected in the state standards that were approved in October 2024.[17]

- Washington, in March 2024, passed SB 5462, which mandates "LGBTQ" inclusion among other "historically

Conclusion   185

marginalized and underrepresented groups" in K–12 curriculum and instructional materials across all subjects. The state is charged with creating a model policy and choosing related instructional materials by June 2025. By October, schools are supposed to have policies in place to incorporate the new curricular requirements.[18]

In our federal system, each new state has charted its own path. They can learn from one another but not simply transfer processes and materials. California's robust efforts cannot, for example, be put into practice wholesale in Colorado or Connecticut.

Still, commonalities exist. First, every state has linked LGBTQ inclusion to existing laws mandating inclusion of Indigenous peoples, people of color, women, people with disabilities, and other marginalized groups. All have been attentive to how related curriculum needs to be diverse and intersectional. Second, each state has understood that inclusive mandate laws must be followed up with standards and other supports. Third, states rely on LGBTQ history content experts to generate aligned materials and provide training. Education departments vary widely in terms of how much they fund or coordinate this work.

Those interested in accurate, relevant, and rigorous learning about our nation's diverse past will continue to build a better history education. They will be prevented in some parts of the country, but empowered in others and equipped in unprecedented ways. Across the country over the last decade, organizations, states, and cities have developed approaches beyond statewide legislation. Delaware, Massachusetts, Maryland, New York, Virginia, and Washington, DC, are creating inclusive standards and/or state materials without the legislative mandate. These suggest other pathways in a time of "Don't Say Gay" legislative assault.

History UnErased, founded in 2014, is the brainchild of former educator Debra Fowler. This Massachusetts-based national nonprofit seeks to put LGBTQ+ history into K–12 classrooms. It has two major programs. The "Intersections and Connections" U.S. history curriculum's integrated digital platform includes lesson plans, thematic modules, lenses of analysis, and primary sources. Training includes mentorship, cultural mindset awareness, methodology and pedagogy, and strategies for adoption, implementation, and assessment. History UnErased has reached over 1,500 schools across seventeen states. It consulted with the Massachusetts Department of Elementary and Secondary Education, which in 2018 approved a History and Social Science Framework with LGBTQ-related content in grades one, five, eight, and high school.[19]

In Maryland, dozens of state legislators submitted a July 2019 letter urging the state's Department of Education to include LGBT Americans in its History and Social Studies Standards. In the 2020 Standards, the Department of Education made good. There are three high school U.S. history references, in the 1920s, the mid-century civil rights movement, and contemporary history. In Delaware, similarly, the state's legislature in a 2022 resolution encouraged the Department of Education to identify "age-appropriate lessons" for grades 7–12 by 2024–2025. In June 2023, Washington, DC, approved LGBTQ-inclusive K–12 Social Studies Standards. These include in kindergarten (addressing diverse families), grade one (diversity in communities), grade three (political movements), grade five (civil rights movements), high school U.S. history (civil rights movements), and Washington, DC, history (diverse communities and justice).[20]

In 2021, Virginia's Democratic governor Ralph Northam assembled a Culturally Responsive and Inclusive Education Advisory Committee. It sought, among other things, to improve K–12 history and civics with an eye toward the 2023 state standards revision. At the time, committee members were considering how to incorporate sexual and gender diversity into history education across elementary, middle, and high school. On his first day in office in 2023, Republican governor Glenn Youngkin issued his first executive order to pledge an "end the use of inherently divisive concepts, including Critical Race Theory" in K–12 schools. A contentious process began with public outcry over a proposed standards revision that referred to Native Americans as the "first immigrants" and whitewashed the past. In April 2023, the Virginia Board of Education, with a Youngkin-appointed majority, approved its 2023 History and Social Science Standards of Learning. While it leaves a lot to be desired, it includes gay people twice, both in eleventh grade, where students are to learn about "social movements, including . . . the Gay Rights Movement" and "assessing the development of and changes in domestic policies due to Supreme Court decisions" including *Obergefell v. Hodges*. Token inclusion near the end of high school can hardly be counted as a major victory. Still, it offers some glimmer of hope when even a culture warrior–led state added something.[21]

Finally, New York City is proving how the nation's largest school district can continue this work with minimal state standards inclusion. In 2015–2016, when the New York State Department of Education (NYCDOE) updated its K–12 Social Studies Framework, it added just two LGBT mentions, both in the context of civil rights movements, in grades eight and eleven. The NYCDOE went much further in its 2021 *Hidden Voices: LGBTQ+ Stories in United States History.* This 238-page resource features twenty biographies and five historical eras spanning the precolonial to the present, aligned with the district's K–12 "Passport to Social Studies" curriculum. Each profile guides historical thinking, primary source analysis, and reflection for various grade levels. Developed by university historians and educational specialists under the leadership of Hunter College professor Daniel Hurewitz, the document is stunning in its scope, diversity, accuracy, and care. The NYCDOE engages in ongoing *Hidden Voices* professional development, including collaboration with education schools on preservice training. They have partnered with artists, scholars, archives, museums, and public television to generate everything from comic books to video segments, all funded through the NYCDOE. It is truly a model program.[22]

While some states opt for systematic erasure and others look toward substantial incorporation, still others will gradually add bits and pieces, most likely first in high school U.S. history. Cities such as Los Angeles, San Francisco, Chicago, and New York continue to produce and distribute relevant content. Through advocacy and scholarly organizations, many high-quality lesson plans, primary source sets, and other tools are widely available online to anyone who seeks them. These will find their way into classrooms and textbooks and, over time, more substantial development across grades.

As an LGBTQ history practitioner, K–12 inclusive education advocate, and, now, a scholar of the history of K–12 LGBTQ-inclusive U.S. history education, I have been reflecting on how we can harness lessons from the past to chart the future. Some final thoughts:

1. Use the Outstanding Resources That Exist

Over the past three decades, many books, lesson plans, primary source sets, and essays on teaching diverse and intersectional K–12 LBGTQ history have been produced. While some, particularly those created prior to widespread digital media, have gone out of print, many are just a few keystrokes away. In addition, the language in state laws, education codes, and district policies can be models for anyone interested in advocating for inclusive education in their communities. While each classroom, school, district, city, and state is different, no one has to reinvent the wheel at this stage. Stand on our shoulders!

2. Get Involved at Local Levels

Everyone should consider running for PTA and district school board positions. Vote. Raise your voice against those who would censor our past. Build and join diverse coalitions. If you're a parent or student, ask your teachers where they are including LGBTQ+ content. Guide them to online resources. Where possible, show them state standards, materials, and laws. Ask administrators how they invest in teachers in doing this work. If you're an administrator, reward teachers for related professional development. If you're a teacher in a state with inclusive laws and policies, demonstrate how it can be done. If you work where there is no mandate and no gag order, incorporate LGBTQ+ lives and themes into your classrooms, just as you would the

190   Contested Curriculum

histories of everyone else that make up our nation's rich past. If you work in a "Don't Say LGBTQ" state, consider education that can still occur through student groups such as Gay-Straight Alliances or through community centers, faith organizations, or public libraries. Showing through example serves as a powerful corrective to those who seek to silence inclusive history education. Research suggests that while educators tend to fear parental complaint far more than it occurs, LGBTQ+ teachers and teachers of color are more likely to actually face complaint for LGBTQ-inclusive education than their straight, white counterparts.[23] The latter thus have a particular duty to make history education a brave space.

3. Combine and Coordinate Bottom-Up Efforts with Statewide Work

Under-the-radar lessons made a lot of sense in a time before inclusive laws and standards, and before social media was an amplified rage machine. We're not in the 1980s anymore, though. Learn what your state mandates, encourages, and facilitates. Align your efforts accordingly. One teacher can make a difference, but it shouldn't all rely on that one teacher. In places where LGBTQ-inclusive history education is ambiguous or prohibited, teachers are left vulnerable to the pressures of a vocal minority. Promote inclusive education laws, and, where that is not viable, incremental state standards inclusion. Hold your state officials accountable. Collaborate with LGBTQ+ organizations, advocates for inclusive education in communities of color and religious minorities, teachers unions, parents, and students.

4. Position LGBTQ History Advocates as Allies to History Education Excellence

One of the most effective strategies in California was for LGBTQ+ historians and education advocates to present ourselves as collaborators to the CDE, publishers, and teachers in the process of developing excellent history education. The CDE, in particular, had been accustomed to seeing those calling for an expansion or reinterpretation of history education as disruptive and competing special interest groups vying to get "their version" into classrooms. By coordinating scholars, educators, and education advocates, we delivered well-researched, accessible, and grade-appropriate material linked to the CDE's own language of heritage, historical thinking, and civic development. Over time, that relationship built trust, and we became implementation partners. New Jersey, Colorado, and Illinois have followed similar paths. As you look toward law or standards reform and/or implementation, frame your efforts as promoting better education for *all* rather than primarily about LGBTQ+ youth or safe schools.

5. Build Bridges between Scholarly LGBTQ History and K–12 History Education

Whether you're a teacher, administrator, university-based education school, policymaker, state agency, or publisher, work with LGBTQ historians and education scholars. Consult with national organizations such as the LGBTQ+ History Association (LGBTQ+HA, formerly the Committee on LGBT History). In the past decade, those who study the queer and trans past have been more engaged with K–12 history education than previously. The LGBTQ+HA regularly hosts the Queer History Conference, an international

192 Contested Curriculum

gathering that features a K–12 education track. It also offers a prize for outstanding K–12 LGBTQ history curriculum. The American Historical Association (AHA), the Organization of American Historians (OAH), the LGBTQ+HA, and the OAH Committee on the Status of LGBTQ Historians and Histories have in recent years taken stands for LGBTQ-inclusive history education and against anti-LGBTQ censorship. The AHA and OAH annual conferences often have some K–12 LGBTQ programming. LGBTQ+ historians have been collaborating on K–12 educational materials, lessons, and primary source collections.[24] We are ready to help.

6. Urge University Education Programs to Incorporate LGBTQ-Inclusive History and Social Studies

Many schools of education mention LGBTQ+ cultural competencies in contemporary versions of "multicultural education" classes. That's great but not enough. Our future K–12 teachers need to learn LGBTQ-inclusive history state laws, policies, and standards. They should encounter related content and concepts in early grade multisubject and secondary single-subject history and social studies coursework. As those students move into teaching, their knowledge will mentor their mentors in areas for which many senior faculty have not received training. Preservice familiarization with grade-appropriate LGBTQ history education will lead to lasting classroom implementation.

7. Coordinate Local and Statewide Efforts Nationally (and Maybe Internationally)

At the end of chapter 2 I mention how back in the 1990s, activist Jessea Greenman created an incredible, if forgotten,

Conclusion   193

guidebook to making LGBTQ-inclusive education possible in all fifty states. At the time, she lamented the lack of political will to meet the challenge. As the Gay and Lesbian Alliance Against Defamation, with which she had worked previously, became a national organization, it stepped back from the attention its San Francisco chapter had given as a media watchdog to K–12 textbooks. Two decades later, in the years between California's passage of the FAIR Education Act and the History-Social Science Framework rollout, a handful of organizations struggled with little support from GLSEN, the Human Rights Campaign, and other national LGBTQ organizations with education initiatives, which were more focused on Safe Schools priorities. In recent years, GLSEN has stepped directly into inclusive history education implementation, most notably in Oregon. Still, there is no coalition, ad hoc or otherwise, for those doing this work across many districts and states. In the spirit of the original FAIR Education Act Implementation Coalition, maybe this begins just as a quarterly Zoom meeting and a shared Google doc. It could launch with a gathering at a national history, education, or advocacy conference. Over time continuity would necessitate infrastructure.

In a recent conversation with Colorado educator and LGBTQ-inclusive history education advocate David Duffield, he suggested I was thinking too small. He is conducting ongoing research on places around the globe where LGBTQ-inclusive history and social studies is being envisioned. He lamented what he called the "implementation gap." "People are learning from each other but not so much talking to each other," Duffield said, adding, "We need a larger format, an international conference for education. Once those lines of communication are built, it could become a self-organizing space."[25]

194   Contested Curriculum

8. Fund Bold, Long-Range Initiatives

Today, a well-coordinated, well-funded far-right agenda seeks to shrink public school history education by silencing many of the aspects making it a relevant civic education project for our diverse society. In California, Illinois, Massachusetts, New York, and elsewhere, educators, curriculum specialists, historians, and others have created excellent LGBTQ-inclusive history education law, policy, curriculum, training, and materials, despite shoestring budgets. Imagine what real investment could do. Teachers could be compensated better for the professional development in this area that is so sorely needed. Historians and education scholars could collaborate more fully with educators and policymakers to develop best practices to encourage engagement with the content and meet students with diverse learning needs where they are. Programs could be piloted, assessed, evolved, and more fully implemented. The scope could expand to global history education and, potentially, across the K–12 curriculum.[26] We could coordinate our efforts. All of this can be made far more accessible and widespread. It needs funding to do so.

LGBTQ-inclusive K–12 U.S. history education expands historical thinking, content knowledge, and civic learning for everyone. It improves school climate across the board, not just for LGBTQ+ youth. It also simply tells the truth by correcting a long-standing systemic failure to incorporate gender and sexual diversity as it has been expressed, policed, and transformed in our nation's politics, society, and culture for centuries. After decades of effort, we are now seeing how this can be done across primary and secondary education, in multiple states. It's up to all of us to steer it into the future.

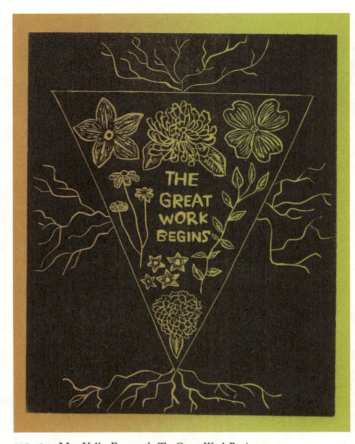

FIG. C.2. Mar Valle-Remond, *The Great Work Begins*, 2022.

Acknowledgments

Shortly after I began this book, COVID lockdowns and distance learning threw everything off course. I am grateful to Sonoma State University (SSU) for a semester-long sabbatical and summer research grants through which I was able to kickstart the project. The support of my fellow Women's and Gender Studies faculty, Lena McQuade and Charlene Tung, as well as the School of Education, has meant a great deal. Other universities should take a cue from SSU's consideration of my labor around LGBTQ-inclusive K–12 history education in tenure and promotion.

I am also indebted to the San Francisco Public Library's Special Collections staff, who let me in as one of the first masked researchers when they tentatively reopened in early 2021, and to Sonoma State's intrepid librarians, who tracked down and sent me so many sources when everything was still remote. Appreciation for Shawnte Santos and the Los Gatos Library for securing the Charley Parkhurst mural. Thanks, too, to N'Tanya Lee for digging up a copy of her *Transforming the Nation* teaching guide—I wish it was digitized and widely available!

My two chapter coauthors, Carolyn Laub and Rick Oculto, have been on California's K–12 LGBTQ-inclusive history education journey the whole way. Both have been vital partners in conceptualizing and conceiving their respective chapters and in all the experiences over the years leading up to them. Both are brilliant communicators, strategists, and implementers. They have been generous with their time and energy even when I moved at an academic's rather than an activist's pace. I cannot imagine anyone with whom I'd rather tell this story.

Deep gratitude to Erik Adamian, Jenn Bowman, Rob Darrow, David Duffield, Debra Fowler, Jennifer Gregg, Erik Martinez, Beth Slutsky, and Tuyen Tran for their time and expertise in interviews, emails, and last-minute fact-checking texts. Their sweat in the trenches with K–12 LGBTQ history education has allowed it to become a full, rich, real thing in classrooms and out in the world. Also thanks to the Committee on LGBT History (now renamed as the LGBTQ+ History Association) which trusted me to lead for the organization on *Making the Framework FAIR* and has supported K–12 work ever since, through its prizes, conferences, and ongoing advocacy. Special shout out to Stacie Brensilver Berman and Wendy Rouse, with whom I have shared many conversations about the past, present, and future of LGBTQ-inclusive history education. These all made this book possible.

Katie Gilmartin's incredible and ongoing Queer Ancestors Project was a perfect match for the artwork this book required. Since 2011—the year the FAIR Education Act passed—she has been working with young adult (18–26-year-old) queer and trans people in free, interdisciplinary LGBTQ+ history printmaking workshops. Those young artists have produced incredible work: check it out at queerancestorsproject.org. Their creativity appears on the cover and in each chapter. I am so grateful to Katie and to the artists for sharing the work with this book's readers.

198 Acknowledgments

Being on the Q+ Public Editorial Board kept me honest and grounded when, month after month in our meetings I would have to give book project status updates. Andy Spieldenner casually threw out the suggestion of "Contested Curriculum" for the title and it stuck. Stephanie Hsu, Ajuan Mance, and Maia Manvi gave the manuscript a close read at a crucial moment before final revisions. Thanks, also, to Kim Guinta at Rutgers University Press, who was endlessly patient and also a little pushy in the best ways when it mattered, and to the two anonymous reviewers who helped tighten and clarify the narrative. Thanks also to Carah Naseem who ably took over once Kim moved on.

There are so many legislators, policymakers, advocates, teachers, curriculum specialists, scholars, administrators, parents, and students who have built K–12 LGBTQ history education, especially here in California, but also around the country. If I try to thank you by name, these acknowledgments will never stop. You are often undervalued in this work, but I know how amazing you are and how important this is. This is your history, too.

Lastly, thanks to David, Asha, and Shailoe. You have supported me across my time as a professor and an LGBTQ+ history education advocate, especially just by being the family to whom I always want to come home.

Acknowledgments   199

Notes

Introduction

The title of this introduction riffs on Marshall Croddy's "Can Social Studies Teachers Save Democracy?," *Social Studies Review* 56 (2017): 19–21.

1. Gay, Lesbian, and Straight Teachers Network, "First Annual Lesbian, Gay, Bisexual History Month Essay Contest," media release, September 26, 1995, http://www.qrd.org/qrd/www/orgs/glstn/history.essay.winner.

2. A note on style: I use "LGBTQ+" to refer to contemporary students, advocacy, and people, in line with current terminology. I use "LGBTQ-" as a modifier, as in "LGBTQ-inclusive history," and when I am talking generally about the past. I also write generally about "LGBTQ history." When I am being specific about how particular authors used terminology and/or how they described their subjects (such as someone in the 1980s who uses the term "lesbian and gay"), I try to use their language to accurately reflect their conceptualization at that time.

3. James Van Kuilenburg, "What Happened When I Studied a Trans Civil War Soldier for History Class," *GLSEN Blog*, 2017, https://www.glsen.org/blog/what-happened-when-i-studied-trans-civil-war-soldier-history-class.

4. Thomas Jefferson, quoted in R. Freedman Butts, "History and Civic Education," in *History in the Schools: What Shall We Teach?*, ed. Bernard R. Gifford (New York: Macmillan, 1988), 61–63.

5. Butts, "History and Civic Education," 67–68; James Andrew LaSpina, *California in a Time of Excellence: School Reform at the Crossroads of the American Dream* (Albany: State University of New York Press, 2009), 50; California Department of Education (CDE), *History-Social Science Framework for California Public Schools, Kindergarten and Grades One through Twelve* (Sacramento: CDE, 1981), 3.

6. William Bennett, "The Homosexual Teacher," *American Educator* (Fall 1978): 23; Lynn Olson, "Opinions Clash at Conference to Define History Curriculum," *Education Week*, September 5, 1984, https://www.edweek.org/education/opinions-clash-at-conference -to-define-history-curriculum/1984/09; Diane Ravitch, *The Schools We Deserve: Reflections of the Educational Crisis of Our Time* (New York: Basic Books, 1985); *A Nation at Risk: The Imperative for Educational Reform* (Washington, DC: National Commission on Excellence in Education, 1983), 9.

7. Olson, "Opinions Clash"; Peter Stearns, "Social History in the American History Course: Whats, Whys and Hows," in Gifford, *History in the Schools*, 142–143.

8. Gary Nash, Charlotte Crabtree, and Ross Dunn, *History on Trial: Culture Wars and the Teaching of the Past* (New York: Vintage, 2000), 7–16.

9. Larry Cuban, *Teaching History Then and Now: A Story of Stability and Change in Schools* (Cambridge, MA: Harvard University Press, 2016), 1–2, 186; American Historical Association, *America's Lesson Plan: Teaching US History in Secondary Schools* (Washington, DC: American Historical Association, 2024), 131.

10. James Alan Lufkin, "A History of the California State Textbook Adoption Program" (EdD diss., University of California, Berkeley, 1968), 228–314.

11. Lufkin, "History of the California State Textbook," 157–160, 248; Jonathan Zimmerman, *Whose America? Culture Wars in the Public Schools* (Cambridge, MA: Harvard University Press, 2002), 117–118.

12. Harry N. Scheiber, "The California Textbook Fight," *The Atlantic* 220 (1967): 40; Clayton Howard, *The Closet and the Cul-de-Sac: The Politics of Sexual Privacy in Northern California* (Philadelphia: University of Pennsylvania Press, 2019).

13. Scheiber, "California Textbook Fight," 40.

14. Max Rafferty, "Should Gays Teach School?," *Phi Delta Kapan* 59, no. 2 (October 1977): 91–92.

15. Jonathan Alter and Lydia Denworth, "A (Vague) Sense of History," *Newsweek* 116, no. 10 (Fall–Winter 1990 special issue): 31–33; William F. Pinar, *What Is Curriculum Theory?*, 3rd ed. (New York: Routledge, 2019), 58; Zimmerman, *Whose America?*, 216–217; Nash, Crabtree, and Dunn, *History on Trial*; LaSpina, *California in a Time of Excellence*.

16. Gay issues related to these adoptions are briefly mentioned in Catherine Cornbleth and David Waugh, *The Great Speckled Bird: Multicultural Politics and Education Policymaking* (New York: St. Martin's, 1995), 22–23, 63–64, 86, and in Thomas R. Dunn, *Queerly Remembered: Rhetorics for Representing the GLBTQ Past* (Columbia: University of South Carolina Press, 2016), 97–109.

17. Diane Ravitch, *The Death and Life of the American School System: How Testing and Choice Are Undermining Education* (New York: Basic Books, 2010), 234.

18. Mark A. Chancey, "Rewriting History for the Christian American: Religion and the Texas Social Studies Controversy of 2009–2010," *Journal of Religion* 94, no. 3 (2014): 325–353; Pinar, *What Is Curriculum Theory?*, 65.

19. Terry Gross, "Uncovering Who Is Driving the Fight against Critical Race Theory in Schools," *Fresh Air*, NPR, June 24, 2021, https://www.npr.org/2021/06/24/1009839021/uncovering-who-is

-driving-the-fight-against-critical-race-theory-in-schools; Kmele Foster, David French, Jason Stanley, and Thomas Chatterton Williams, "We Disagree on a Lot of Things. Except the Danger of Anti-Critical Race Theory Laws," *New York Times*, July 5, 2021, https://www.nytimes.com/2021/07/05/opinion/we-disagree-on-a-lot-of-things-except-the-danger-of-anti-critical-race-theory-laws.html.

20. Organization of American Historians Committee on the Status of Lesbian, Gay, Bisexual, Transgender, and Queer Historians and Histories; and the Committee on LGBT History, "Major LGBTQ Historical Organizations Denounce New Wave of 'Don't Say Gay' Bills: Legislation in Multiple States Threatens K–12 Access to Inclusive and Accurate History," media release, May 11, 2021, https://www.oah.org/site/assets/files/8924/oah_teaching_lgbtq_history.pdf.

21. Janice Irvine, "One Generation Post-Stonewall: Political Contests over Lesbian and Gay School Reform," in *A Queer World: The Center for Lesbian and Gay Studies Reader*, ed. Martin Duberman (New York: New York University Press, 1997), 572–588.

22. Gentry-Fernandez, quoted in Robert Kim, *A Report on the Status of Gay, Lesbian, Bisexual, and Transgender People in Education* (Washington, DC: National Education Foundation, 2009), 47; Sharon Snapp et al., "Students' Perspective on LGBTQ-Inclusive Curriculum," *Equity and Excellence in Education* 48, no. 2 (2015): 255–256.

23. James T. Sears, "Sexuality: Taking Off the Masks," *Changing Schools* 11 (1983): 11–12.

24. In 2008, sociologist Stephen Russell summed up a decade of research on this topic: "Inclusion of GLBT issues in school curricula was the 'single strongest factor' in studies analyzing what produces better school climates for GLBT students. . . . When students learn about GLBT people and history . . . it makes students feel safer and dispels the notion that it is

inappropriate to study GLBT people or issues in an educational setting." Quoted in Kim, *Report*, 6.

25. Snapp et al., "Students' Perspective," 257–258; Sharon Snapp and Stephen T. Russell, "Inextricably Linked: The Shared Story of Ethnic Studies and LGBTQ-Inclusive Curriculum," in *Sexual Orientation, Gender Identity, and Schooling: The Nexus of Research, Practice, and Policy*, ed. Stephen T. Russell and Stacey S. Horn (New York: Oxford University Press, 2017), 154–156; GLSEN, *Inclusive Curricular Standards Representation of LGBTQ+ and Other Marginalized Communities Promotes Student Achievement and Wellbeing*, 2022, https://www.glsen.org/sites/default/files/2022-01/GLSEN_Inclusive_Curricular_Standards_Resource-2022.pdf.

26. Diane Ravitch, "Tot Sociology: Or What Happened to History in the Grade Schools," *The American Scholar* 56, no. 3 (1987): 343–344; Eric Rofes, "Opening Up the Classroom Closet: Responding to the Educational Needs of Gay and Lesbian Youth," *Harvard Educational Review* 59, no. 4 (1989): 452.

27. Margaret Smith Crocco, "Gender and Sexuality in History Education," in *The Wiley International Handbook of History Teaching and Learning*, ed. Scott Metzger and Lauren Harris (Medford, MA: Wiley, 2018), 335–337; Nelson Rodriguez, "(Queer) Youth as Political and Pedagogical," in *Queer Theory in Education*, ed. William Pinar (New York: Routledge, 1998), 148–149.

28. Barbara Smith, "Homophobia: Why Bring It Up?"; Leonore Gordon, "Why CBIC Is Dealing with Homophobia," *Interracial Books for Children Bulletin* 14, nos. 3–4 (1983): 3, 8.

29. Betsy Cahill and Rachel Theilheimer, "Stonewall in the Housekeeping Area: Gay and Lesbian Issues in the Early Childhood Classroom," in *Queering Elementary Education: Advancing the Dialogue about Sexualities and Schooling*, ed. William Letts and James T. Sears (Lanham, MD: Rowman and Littlefield, 1999), 39–48; David Fisher et al., "Advocacy to Support Gender Identity

Development in Schools in the Face of Organized Backlash," in Russell and Horn, *Sexual Orientation*, 219–220.

30. Stacie Brensilver Berman, *LGBTQ+ History in High School Classes in the USA since 1990* (London: Bloomsbury, 2022), 42; Stephen Camacia, "Synthesizing Multicultural, Global, and Civic Perspectives in the Elementary School Curriculum and Educational Research," *The Qualitative Report* 17, no. 52 (2012): 3; Christine Slater, "State Curriculum Standards and the Shaping of Student Consciousness," *Social Justice* 29, no. 4 (2002): 8–25; Louis Freedberg, "California Leads Drive to Reverse Focus on Standardized Tests," *EdSource*, November 30, 2015, https://edsource.org/2015/california-leads-drive-to-reverse-focus-on-standardized-tests/91114.

31. Stephen Camacia and Juanjuan Zhu, "LGBTQ Inclusion and Exclusion in State Social Studies Standards," *Curriculum and Teaching Dialogue* 21, nos. 1–2 (2019): 7–20; Brensilver Berman, *LGBTQ+ History*, 117–120, 233–234; Ingrid E. Castro and Mark Conor Sujak, "'Why Can't We Learn about This?' Sexual Minority Students Navigate the Official and Hidden Curricular Spaces of High School," *Education and Urban Society* 46, no. 4 (2012): 450–473; GLSEN, "LGBTQ-Inclusive and Supportive Teaching Practices:

The Experiences of LGBTQ and non-LGBTQ Educators," Research Brief, 2020, https://www.glsen.org/sites/default/files/2020-08/LGBTQ%20Supportive%20Teaching%20Brief%20.pdf; Cathy A. R. Brant and Cynthia A. Tyson, "LGBTQ Self-Efficacy in the Social Studies," *Journal of Social Studies Research* 40 (2016): 218–225.

32. Theresa L. Miller, Emilie L'Hôte, and Andrew Volmert, *Communicating about History: Challenges, Opportunities, and Emerging Recommendations*, FrameWorks Institute, 2020, https://www.frameworksinstitute.org/wp-content/uploads/2020/08/FRAJ8334-History-Strategic-Brief-200805-2-WEB.pdf.

33. David M. Donahue, "Learning from Harvey Milk: The Limits and Opportunities of One Hero to Teach about LGBTQ People and Issues," *Social Studies* 105 (2014): 37, 43; James Banks, *Multiethnic Education: Theory and Practice* (Boston: Allyn and Bacon, 1994).

34. Stephen P. Camacia, *Critical Democratic Education and LGBTQ-Inclusive Curriculum: Opportunities and Constraints* (New York: Routledge, 2016), 5–7, 16; bell hooks, *Teaching to Transgress: Education as the Practice of Freedom* (New York: Routledge, 1994), 21.

35. Gary B. Nash and Charlotte A. Crabtree, *National Standards for History* (Los Angeles: National Center for History in the Schools, 1996), 276.

36. Debra Fowler, interview with author, June 2, 2020.

37. James Baldwin, "The Nigger We Invent," *Integrated Education* 7, no. 2 (1969): 19–21.

Chapter 1   The Prehistory of LGBTQ History Education

1. James Alan Lufkin, "A History of the California State Textbook Adoption Program" (EdD diss., University of California, Berkeley, 1968), 8, 90–107.

2. Jonathan Zimmerman, *Whose America? Culture Wars in the Public Schools* (Cambridge, MA: Harvard University Press, 2002), 34–47; Gary Nash, Charlotte Crabtree, and Ross Dunn, *History on Trial: Culture Wars and the Teaching of the Past* (New York: Vintage, 2000 [1997]), 60–62.

3. Clayton Howard, *The Closet and the Cul-de-Sac: The Politics of Sexual Privacy in Northern California* (Philadelphia: University of Pennsylvania Press, 2019); Elaine Lewinneck, "Social Studies Controversies in 1960s Los Angeles: *Land of the Free*, Public Memory, and the Rise of the New Right," *Pacific Historical Review* 84, no. 1 (2015): 77–78; Matthew Dellek, *Birchers: How*

the John Birch Society Radicalized the American Right (New York: Basic Books, 2022), 214–216.

4. Nash, Crabtree, and Dunn, *History on Trial*, 62–63; Lufkin, "History of the California State," 252–254; Sara R. Smith, "Organizing for Social Justice: Rank-and-File Teachers' Activism and Social Unionism in California, 1948–1978" (PhD diss., University of California, Santa Cruz, 2014), 343; SB 48, Sess. of 2011 (CA 2011), http://www.leginfo.ca.gov/pub/11-12/bill/sen/sb_0001-0050/sb_48_bill_20110714_chaptered.html.

5. William Pinar, *What Is Curriculum Theory?*, 3rd ed. (New York: Routledge, 2019), 63; Zimmerman, *Whose America?*, 115; John Lescott-Leszcsynski, *The History of U.S. Ethnic Policy and Its Impact on European Ethnics* (New York: Routledge, 1984), ch. 4.

6. Janice Trecker, "Women in US History High School Textbooks," *Social Education* 35 (1971): 249–260; Smith, "Organizing for Social Justice," 301–343; William F. Pinar et al., *Understanding Curriculum: An Introduction to the Study of Historical and Contemporary Curriculum Discourses* (New York: Peter Lang, 1995), 366–370.

7. Deborah S. Rosenfelt, "'Definitive' Issues: Women's Studies, Multicultural Education, and Curriculum Transformation in Policy and Practice in the United States," *Women's Studies Quarterly* 22, nos. 3–4 (1994): 27–28; Suzanne Hurwitz, ed., *In Search of Our Past: Units in Women's History* (Newton, MA: Education Development Center, 1980).

8. Lewinneck, "Social Studies Controversies," 80–84; Tim Keirn, "History Curriculum, Standards, and Assessment Policies and Politics: U.S. Experiences," in *The Wiley International Handbook of History Teaching and Learning*, ed. Scott Metzger and Lauren Harris (New York: Wiley-Blackwell, 2018), 16–17.

9. Don Romesburg, "Introduction: Having a Moment Four Decades in the Making," in *The Routledge History of Queer America*, ed. Don Romesburg (New York: Routledge, 2018), 1–3;

Stacie Brensilver-Berman, *LGBTQ+ History in High School Classes in the USA since 1990* (New York: Bloomsbury, 2022), ch. 2; Gerard Koskovich, "The History of Queer History: One Hundred Years of the Search for Shared Heritage," in *LGBTQ America: A Theme Study of Lesbian, Gay, Bisexual, Transgender, and Queer History*, ed. Megan E. Springate (Washington, DC: National Park Service, 2016), ch. 4.

10. Jackie M. Blount, *Fit to Teach: Same-Sex Desire, Gender, and School Work in the Twentieth Century* (Albany: State University of New York Press, 2005), 76–92.

11. California Penal Code Section 291 mandated that police notify school boards when a teacher was detained or arrested. Education Code Section 12756 allowed suspension of credentials if teachers were convicted of "lewd acts" or other sex crimes. Karen M. Harbeck, *Coming Out of the Classroom Closet: Gay and Lesbian Students, Teachers, and Curricula* (New York: Harrington Park, 1992), 126–127; Blount, *Fit to Teach*, 92–97, 99–101, 106; Karen Graves, *And They Were Wonderful Teachers: Florida's Purge of Gay and Lesbian Teachers* (Urbana: University of Illinois Press, 2009); Craig Loftin, *Masked Voices: Gay Men and Lesbians in Cold War America* (Albany: State University of New York Press, 2012), 121–140; Howard, *Closet and the Cul-de-Sac*, 59–65.

12. Jeffrey Moran, *Teaching Sex: The Shaping of Adolescence in the Twentieth Century* (Cambridge, MA: Harvard University Press, 2000), 173–185; Sid Davis, *Boys Beware* (Inglewood, CA: Sid Davis Productions, 1961); available at the Internet Archive, https://archive.org/details/boys_beware. The film was co-produced by the Inglewood School District and Police Department.

13. George Kriegman, "Homosexuality and the Educator," *Journal of School Health* 39, no. 5 (1969): 309–310.

14. *Morrison v. State Board of Education*, 1 Cal.3d 214, 461 P.2d 375, 82 Cal.Rptr. 175 (1969); Chester M. Nolte, "Gay Teachers: March

from Closet to Classroom," *American School Board Journal* 160, no. 7 (1973): 28–32.

15. *Acanfora v. Board of Education of Montgomery*, 491 F.2d 498 (4th Cir. 1974); Blount, *Fit to Teach*, 112–114, 119–120; Nolte, "Gay Teachers," 29; PGN Staff, "30 Years Ago in PGN: Suburban Trans Teacher Reinstated," *Philadelphia Gay News*, April 30, 2009, https://epgn.com/2009/04/23/2430852-30-years-ago-in-pgn/; Salmacis Society, "Steve Dain Resigns," *The Gemini Yearbook* (1978), 40, in Francine Logandice Collection, GLBT Historical Society. In 2021, the Emeryville School District issued Dain a posthumous apology and named a street in front of the school in his honor. Rob Arias, "District Issues Official Apology to Trans-Rights Pioneer Steve Dain, Emeryville Street Renamed in His Honor," *The E'ville Eye*, March 24, 2021, https://evilleeye.com/news-commentary/education-news-commentary/district-issues-official-apology-to-trans-rights-pioneer-steve-dain-emeryville-street-renamed-in-his-honor/.

16. Smith, "Organizing for Social Justice," 436–439; Blount, *Fit to Teach*, 114–115; Harbeck, *Coming Out of the Classroom Closet*, 126; Jason Mayernick, *Not Alone: The First Gay Teacher Groups* (New Brunswick, NJ: Rutgers University Press, 2023).

17. Blount, *Fit to Teach*, 123–126; Tom Ammiano, *Kiss My Gay Ass* (San Francisco: Bay Guardian Books, 2020), 39–41; Queer Blue Light, "Board of Education Final Edit," June 17, 1975, Daniel A. Smith and Queer Blue Light Videotapes collection (#1999-52), GLBT Historical Society, https://archive.org/details/glbths_1999-52_093_sc; Mayernick, *Not Alone*.

18. Stephen Lane, *No Sanctuary: Teachers and the School Reform That Brought Gay Rights to the Masses* (Lebanon, NH: ForeEdge, 2019), 73, 82–83; Blount, *Fit to Teach*, 156–157; "Teacher in Flap Because of Gay Genocide Remark," *Honolulu Advertiser*, October 12, 1978, Gale Archives of Sexuality and Gender.

19. Lane, *No Sanctuary*, 85; Robert Birle and Jessea Greenman, "Project 21: A Brief History (First Draft)," GLAAD/SFBA, P.E.R.S.O.N. (Public Education Regarding Sexual Orientation Nationally) Project Records, San Francisco Public Library (SFPL), Box 11, "Project 21: A Brief History" (2 folders), 1991–[1992]; Blount, *Fit to Teach*, 121; Howard, *Closet and the Cul-de-Sac*, 273; Lester Kirkendall and Len Tritsch, "Educational Implications of the Dade County Imbroglio," *Phi Delta Kappan* 59, no. 2 (October 1977): 96.

20. Ammiano, *Kiss My Gay Ass*, 55.

21. Smith, "Organizing for Social Justice," 363–452.

22. Kirkendall and Tritsch, "Educational Implications," 95–96.

23. Aaron Lee Bachoffer II, "The Emergence and Evolution of Gay and Bisexual Male Subculture in Oklahoma City, Oklahoma, 1888–2005" (PhD diss., Oklahoma State University, 2006), 238–240, 245–252; *National Gay Task Force v. Board of Education of Oklahoma City*, 729 F.2d 1270 (1984), No. 82-1912.

24. *David O. Solmitz et. al. v. Maine School Administrative District No. 59*, 495 A.2d 812 (1985).

25. Nan Hunter, "Identity, Speech, and Equality," *Virginia Law Review* 79 (1993): 1710; Clifford Rosky, "Anti-Gay Curriculum Laws," *Columbia Law Review* 117, no. 6 (2017): 1461–1541. In 2003, California repealed its law: Act of September 24, 1988, ch. 1337, § 2, 1988 Cal. Stat. 4425, 4426, repealed by Act of October 1, 2003, ch. 650, § 10, 2003 Cal. Stat. 4984, 4989.

26. Smith, "Organizing for Social Justice," 439; Mayernick, *Not Alone*; Anthony Bowen, *Forty Years of LGBTQ Philanthropy, 1970–2010* (New York: Funders for LGBTQ Issues, 2012), 9–14.

27. Human Rights Foundation, *Demystifying Homosexuality: A Teaching Guide about Lesbians and Gay Men* (New York: Irvington, 1984); Sasha Alyson and Lynne Yamaguchi Fletcher, *Young, Gay and Proud!* (Boston: Alyson, 1980). Based on a pamphlet by the Melbourne Gay Teachers and Students Group

in Australia, the U.S. book went through four editions between 1980 and 1995.

28. Human Rights Foundation, *Demystifying Homosexuality*, 111–117, quoting Jonathan Katz, *Gay American History: Lesbians and Gay Men in the USA* (New York: Thomas Y. Crowell, 1976), 8.

29. Donna I. Dennis and Ruth E. Harlow, "Gay Youth and the Right to Education," *Yale Law and Policy Review* 4, no. 2 (1986): 466.

30. Rita Addessa, "Philadelphia Lesbian and Gay Task Force Education Equity Project Policy and Program Recommendations Report Excerpt," September 1989, Carnegie Mellon University Libraries Digital Collections, http://digitalcollections.library.cmu .edu/awweb/awarchive?type=file&item=553958; "Philadelphia School District, 102.4.1: Multiracial-Multicultural-Gender Education," January 24, 1994, P.E.R.S.O.N. Project Records, SFPL, Box 3, Curriculum Materials, 1984–1997; Jean Richter, "10.8.99 P.E.R.S.O.N. Project News," listserv email, October 8, 1999, http://www.qrd.org/qrd/education/1999/misc.news-10.08.99.

31. Pat Griffin and Matthew Ouellett, "From Silence to Safety and Beyond: Historical Trends in Addressing Lesbian, Gay, Bisexual, Transgender Issues in K–12 Schools," *Equity in Education* 36 (2003): 108–109; Lane, *No Sanctuary*, 5, 91–102.

32. Lane, *No Sanctuary*, 75–79, 132.

33. Lane, *No Sanctuary*, 80; Kevin Jennings, *Mama's Boy, Preacher's Son: A Memoir* (Boston: Beacon, 2006), 131–183.

34. Laurie Casa Grande, "Unfortunately, History Has Set the Record a Little Too Straight," poster (Minneapolis: Gay and Lesbian Community Action Council, 1988).

35. New York City Mayor's Office for the Lesbian and Gay Community, *Struggle for Equality: Lesbian and Gay Community*, New York City Board of Education Multicultural Education Curriculum (New York: Office of the Mayor, 1989), P.E.R.S.O.N. Project Records, SFPL, Box 6, New York—Textbook Policies, 1986–1997 Folder.

36. Ann Bradley to Jehan Agrama, "Re: Gay and Lesbian Panel at the LACOE Multicultural Curriculum Conference," October 17, 1990, P.E.R.S.O.N. Project Records, SFPL, Box 2, Los Angeles, 1990–1997 Folder; Martin Schoenhals, *Lesbian and Gay Affirmative Educational Initiatives in Selected U.S. Cities and Counties* (Philadelphia: Philadelphia Lesbian and Gay Task Force, June 1992), 30; Alan Hertzberg, "Pride and Prejudice," media release, May 15, 1991, Libraries: Women, June 1971–June 1992 (MS Folder No.: 08520), Lesbian Herstory Archives, Gale Archives of Sexuality and Gender.

37. N'Tanya Lee, Don Murphy, and Lisa North, "Sexuality, Multicultural Education and the New York City Public Schools," *Radical Teacher* 45 (Winter 1994): 12–16; New York City Mayor's Office for the Lesbian and Gay Community, *Struggle for Equality: The Lesbian and Gay Community* (New York: People About Changing Education, 1994), P.E.R.S.O.N. Project Records, SFPL, Box 3, Curriculum Materials, 1984–1997; Arthur Lipkin, *Understanding Homosexuality, Changing Schools* (Boulder, CO: Westview, 1999), 294–295.

Chapter 2   The State's the Place?

1. Wallace Turner, "Rafferty Is Defeated by a Negro as California Education Chief," *New York Times*, November 5, 1970, 1; Robert Lindsey, "California's Back-to-Basics Reformer," *New York Times*, August 3, 1986; "Honig Beats Supt. Riles in California," *Education Week*, November 10, 1982, https://www.edweek.org/education /honig-beats-supt-riles-in-california-8-other-incumbent-chiefs-re -elected/1982/11; James Andrew LaSpina, *California in a Time of Excellence: School Reform at the Crossroads of the American Dream* (Albany: State University of New York Press, 2009), 24–36.

2. LaSpina, *California in a Time of Excellence*, 41–44; *Summary of SB 813 and Related Legislation: Hughes-Hart Educational Reform*

Act of 1983 (Sacramento: California Department of Education, 1983), https://files.eric.ed.gov/fulltext/ED241155.pdf.

3. Diane Ravitch, "From History to Social Studies: Diemmas and Problems," in *History in the Schools: What Shall We Teach?*, ed. Bernard R. Gifford (New York: Macmillan, 1988), 52.

4. LaSpina, *California in a Time of Excellence*, 63–65; Francie Alexander and Charlotte Crabtree, "California's New History-Social Science Curriculum Promises Richness and Depth," *Educational Leadership* (September 1988): 10–13; Gary B. Nash, Charlotte Crabtree, and Ross Dunn, *History on Trial: Culture Wars and the Teaching of the Past* (New York: Vintage, 2000), 112–113.

5. Duane E. Campbell, "California Education to Latinos: Sorry, We Forgot That You Exist!," *La Presna San Diego*, May 16, 2008, 7; David Denby, "Public Defender," *New Yorker*, November 19, 2012.

6. LaSpina, *California in a Time of Excellence*, 63–66; Nash, Crabtree, and Dunn, *History on Trial*, 112–113; Bill Honig, "Teaching History Right: California Is Going to Try," *State Legislatures* 14, no. 8 (1988): 30; James Andrew LaSpina, *The Visual Turn and the Transformation of the Textbook* (Mahwah, NJ: Lawrence Erlbaum, 1998), 1–2, 20–21, 159.

7. Charles Linebarger, "Concern with Schools Moves to State Level: State Needs to Act on Textbooks, AIDS Education, Gay Activists Say," *Bay Area Reporter*, July 17, 1986, 14.

8. California Attorney General's Commission on Racial, Ethnic, Religious, and Minority Violence, *Final Report* (Sacramento: Office of the Attorney General, 1986), 58.

9. Charles Linebarger, "Honig Fears Backlash If Seen as Pro-Gay: Would Promote Tolerance in Schools but Not Allow Gays as Equals," *Bay Area Reporter*, July 24, 1986, 3.

10. Katherine Seligman, "History Would Be Franker under New Textbook Rules," *San Francisco Examiner*, August 10, 1987, 1;

Darrell Schramm, "The Right to Be Human," *Bay Area Reporter*, July 23, 1987, 8; California Department of Education, *Model Curriculum for Human Rights and Genocide: 1988 Edition with a New Forward and Preface* (Sacramento: California Department of Education, 2000 [1988]), 2.

11. Robert Birle, "In August of 1988 . . . ," personal communication with Bill Honig, April 16, 1991, and Project 21, "Notes of Meeting with Honig," April 6, 1992, P.E.R.S.O.N. (Public Education Regarding Sexual Orientation Nationally) Project Records, San Francisco Public Library (SFPL), Box 3, California State Superintendent [of Public Instruction], 1990–1995 Folder; Hollie Conley, "GLAAD Media Watch," *Bay Area Reporter*, February 20, 1992, 22.

12. Jessea Greenman, Project 21 recruitment flyer, 1990, P.E.R.S.O.N. Project Records, SFPL, Box 1, BANGLE, 1990–1997 Folder; Henri Donat, "Gays Lobby for Fair Textbooks," *San Francisco Sentinel*, July 19, 1990, P.E.R.S.O.N. Project Records, SFPL, Box 2, History, 1985–1995 Folder; Jessea Greenman, interview with author, November 18, 2023.

13. Jessea Greenman, "P21 History/Mission Statement for GLAAD/SFBA Board of Directors" report, May 7, 1994, P.E.R.S.O.N. Project Records, SFPL, Box 6, Organizing, 1990–1997 Folder.

14. Office of the Auditor General, *A Review of the Purchasing Practices and Conflict of Interest Policies in the Selection of School Textbooks* (Sacramento: Auditor General of California, 1990), 33–35.

15. Kevin Fagan, "Gay Educators Aim for Truth in Texts," *Oakland Tribune*, July 15, 1990, B1; David Tuller, "Gays' Campaign on Textbooks," *San Francisco Chronicle*, July 18, 1999; Greenman, interview.

16. William Trombley, "Proposed Textbooks Called Inaccurate, Stereotypical," *Los Angeles Times*, July 19, 1990, A-3; Donat, "Gays Lobby for Fair Textbooks"; M. R. Covino, "Gay Issues Raised at Textbook Hearings," *Bay Area Reporter*, July 26, 1990,

11, 15; Gilbert T. Sewall, "Report on California Textbook Selection," *Social Studies Review: A Bulletin of the American Textbook Council* (Fall 1990), P.E.R.S.O.N. Project Records, SFPL, Box 11, Project 21: A Brief History (2 folders), 1991–[1992]; Greenman, interview.

17. Greenman, interview.

18. Robert Birle, "Statements for Board of Education Public Hearing and Project 21 Rally," BANGLE, P.E.R.S.O.N. Project Records, SFPL, Box 1, California Textbook Policies, 1988–1995 Folder.

19. Jessea Greenman, "Public Comment before the California State Board of Education," September 13, 1990, P.E.R.S.O.N. Project Records, SFPL, Box 2, California State Board of Education I, 1986–1997 Folder; Robert Birle and Jessea Greenman, "Project 21: A Brief History (First Draft)," P.E.R.S.O.N. Project Records, SFPL, Box 11, Project 21: A Brief History (2 folders), 1991-[1992].

20. Birle and Greenman, "Project 21"; Nancy Boutilier, "School's Out? Homosexuality in SF Public Schools," *Sphere*, June 26, 1991, 10–11; David L. Kirp, "Battle of the Books," *IMAGE*, February 24, 1991, 19.

21. Tuller, "Gays' Campaign on Textbooks."

22. Thomas R. Dunn, "Queerly Remembered: Tactical and Strategic Rhetorics for Representing the GLBTQ Past" (PhD diss., University of Pittsburgh, 2011), 108–202.

23. Laurie Olsen, "Whose Culture Is This? Whose Curriculum Will It Be?," *California Perspectives* 2 (1991): 3–6, 11–13.

24. *Project 21 Newsletter*, P.E.R.S.O.N. Project Records, SFPL, Box 1, California Textbook Policies, 1988–1995 Folder; Olsen, "Whose Culture Is This?," 13; Robert Reinhold, "California Rewrites History," *This World, San Francisco Examiner*, October 27, 1991, 7–10; Jerry Taranto, "Textbook Controversy Continues," *San Francisco Sentinel*, August 22, 1991.

25. Gary Nash, *American Odyssey: The United States in the Twentieth Century* (Lake Forest, IL: Glencoe, 1991); Daniel Boorstin and Brooks Mather Kelley, *A History of the United States since 1861* (Needham, MA: Prentice Hall, 1990), 493; Boutilier, "School's Out?"; *Project 21 Newsletter* (December 1990).

26. Jessea Greenman, "School Superintendent Makes Homophobic Remarks," flyer, May 7, 1990, and Leland Yee, email to Jessea Greenman, "On October 12, 1990 . . . ," October 19, 1990, P.E.R.S.O.N. Project Records, SFPL, Box 11, San Francisco Unified School District, 1990–1992 folder.

27. Taranto, "Textbook Controversy Continues"; Martin Schoenhals, *Lesbian and Gay Affirmative Educational Initiatives in Selected U.S. Cities and Counties* (Philadelphia: Philadelphia Lesbian and Gay Task Force, June 1992).

28. Boutilier, "School's Out?"; Barbara Blinick, *Lesbian, Gay, and Bisexual Social Studies Lessons* (San Francisco: Support Services for Sexual Minority Youth, 1995). I thank Erik Martinez for his help tracking this down. See also Barbara Blinick, "Out in the Curriculum, Out in the Classroom: Teaching History and Organizing for Change," in *Tilting the Tower: Lesbians Teaching Queer Subjects*, ed. Linda Garber (New York: Routledge, 1994), 144–148.

29. Birle, "In August of 1988 . . ."; Conley, "GLAAD Media Watch."

30. GLAAD/SFBA, "Some Suggested Agenda Items for Project 21 Meeting with Superintendent Honig with Meeting Notes," April 6, 1992, P.E.R.S.O.N. Project Records, SFPL, Box 3, California State Superintendent [of Public Instruction], 1990–1995; "Project 21 Meets with Superintendent Bill Honig," *OurPaper* (San Jose, CA), April 22, 1992.

31. Associated Press, "Textbook Guidelines That Include Gays OKd," *Los Angeles Times*, December 12, 1992, https://www.latimes.com/archives/la-xpm-1992-12-12-mn-1796-story.html; Rachel Timmoner, "Gays, Fundies Square Off over Content of

Textbooks," *Bay Area Reporter*, June 4, 1992; David O'Connor, "A Textbook Case: New Gay-Positive Curriculum Adopted," *Bay Area Reporter*, December 17, 1992.

32. U.S. Department of Health and Human Services, *Report of the Secretary's Task Force on Youth Suicide* (Rockville, MD, 1989).

33. Arthur Lipkin, "The Case for a Gay and Lesbian Curriculum," in *The Gay Teen: Educational Practice and Theory for Lesbian, Gay, and Bisexual Adolescents*, ed. Gerald Unks (New York: Routledge, 1995), 38.

34. Kevin Jennings, *Mama's Boy, Preacher's Son: A Memoir* (Boston: Beacon, 2006), 199–200; Kevin Jennings, "Foreword," in *Safe Is Not Enough: Better Schools for LGBTQ Students*, ed. Michael Sadowski (Cambridge, MA: Harvard Education Press, 2016), viii–ix; Commonwealth of Massachusetts Commission on Gay, Lesbian, Bisexual, and Transgender Youth, *Annual Report* (Boston: Commonwealth of Massachusetts Commission on Gay, Lesbian, Bisexual, and Transgender Youth, 2009), 32; Arthur Lipkin, *Understanding Homosexuality, Changing Schools* (Boulder, CO: Westview, 1999), 277.

35. "Pleasure/Politics Conference Schedule, Harvard University," October 26–28, 1990, Colleges and Universities: Harvard University, October 1990–January 30, 1996 (MS Folder No.: 03620), Gale Archives of Sexuality and Gender; BANGLE and GLSTN, "United in Diversity: West Coast Conference on GLBT Issues in Education Conference Program," October 26, 1996, P.E.R.S.O.N. Project Records. SFPL, Box 1, BANGLE, 1990–1997 Folder.

36. Arthur Lipkin, *The Stonewall Riots and the History of Gay and Lesbians in the United States* (Cambridge, MA: Harvard Graduate School of Education, 1992); Lipkin, *Understanding Homosexuality*, 277, 337, 345–347; "Harvard University Project on K–12 Curriculum to Include Gender Issues," *Transgender Tapestry* 68 (Summer 1994), 68, 77.

37. Greenman, interview.

38. Nadine Brozan, "Another Curtain Lifts," *New York Times*, November 24, 1992, B4; David Richards, "Out in Print," *Washington Post*, October 27, 1995, https://www.washingtonpost .com/archive/lifestyle/1995/10/27/out-in-print/b50751f6-f712 -41de-b7f7-d2ac7caeedb0/. Other series biographies included Marlene Dietrich, John Maynard Keynes, T. E. Lawrence, Liberace, k.d. lang, Federico Garcia Lorca, Martina Navrati-lova, Georgia O'Keefe, Sappho, Gertrude Stein, Walt Whit-man, and Oscar Wilde.

39. The saga of Peterson and the East High GSA eventually ended in victory. But in 1996, the Salt Lake City Board of Education banned all noncurricular clubs to stop the GSA. In 1998, the students filed suit against the Board. In 2000, the district folded after it faced a second lawsuit for trying to deny a charter to the PRISM (People Respecting Important Social Movements) Club, an explicitly curricular student organization focused on LGBT history, social studies, and politics. Thus, LGBT-inclusive history education was key to establishing the right to form public school GSAs. See "Students and Salt Lake City School Board End Feud over Gay-Supportive Clubs," Lambda Legal, October 6, 2000, https://www.lambdalegal.org/news/ny _20001006_students-salt-lake-school-board-end-feud.

40. *Out of the Past*, directed by Jeffrey Dupre (A-PIX Entertain-ment, 1998).

41. GLSEN, "*Out of the Past* Teachers' Guide" (1999): https://www .glsen.org/sites/default/files/2020-04/Guide%20to%20Out%20 of%20the%20Past.pdf.

42. "Transgendered" was then the preferred terminology for what we now call "transgender" or "trans." N'Tanya Lee and Alex Robertson Textor, *Transforming the Nation: A Teaching Guide to Lesbian, Gay, Bisexual, and Transgendered US History Since the 1950s* (Brooklyn, NY: People About Changing Education, 2000);

N'Tanya Lee, Don Murphy, and Lisa North, "Sexuality, Multicultural Education and the New York City Public Schools," *Radical Teacher* 45 (1994): 12–16.

43. The Library of Congress hosts websites dedicated to Black History Month (https://www.blackhistorymonth.gov/), National Hispanic Heritage Month (https://www.hispanic heritagemonth.gov/), National Native American Heritage Month (https://www.nativeamericanheritagemonth.gov/), and Asian/Pacific Heritage Month (https://asianpacificheritage.gov /), all accessed September 10, 2024. See also "Women's History Month," National Women's History Museum, https://www .womenshistory.org/womens-history-month, accessed March 23, 2022.

44. Ben Carlson, "GLAAD Media Watch," *Bay Area Reporter*, February 7, 1992, 12; Kurt Johnson, "Gay Project 21 Takes Case," *Bay Area Reporter*, January 23, 1992; Greenman, interview. On May 7, 1995, Birle died from AIDS-related complications. The NEA-LGBTQ+ Caucus holds the Robert Birle Memorial Dinner at their annual conference.

45. Rodney Wilson, "Robert Birle said to contact you," email to Al Kielwasser, April 17, 1994, P.E.R.S.O.N. Project Records, SFPL Box 4, History; Jennings, *Mama's Boy, Preacher's Son*, 214–215; *Taboo Teaching: A Profile of Missouri Teacher Rodney Wilson*, dir. Dan Steadman (Circa 87 Films, 2020); Rodney Wilson, "Knowing LGBT History Is Knowing Yourself," *Advocate*, October 1, 2015.

46. Rodney Wilson, "Telling Our Stories, Winning Our Freedom," in *One Teacher in Ten: Gay and Lesbian Educators Tell Their Stories* (Boston: Alyson Publications, 1994), 200–207; *Taboo Teaching*.

47. Wilson, "Telling Our Stories"; Connie Farrow, "More Gay Teachers Are Coming Out of the Closet," *Los Angeles Times*, January 29, 1995, https://www.latimes.com/archives/la-xpm-1995 -01-29-mn-25614-story.html; *Taboo Teaching*.

48. National Coordinating Council for Lesbian and Gay History Month, "Work Plan for Local Organizing of Lesbian and Gay History Month," report, Chicago, 1994, P.E.R.S.O.N. Project Records, SFPL, Box 3, Curriculum Materials, 1984–1997; Rodney Wilson, "October Declared Lesbian & Gay History Month," media release, July 18, 1994, http://www.qrd.org/qrd /culture/1994/october.declared.lgb.history.month-08.09.94.

49. National Coordinating Council for Lesbian and Gay History Month, "Secondary Schools Packet for Lesbian and Gay History Month," August 1994, P.E.R.S.O.N. Project Records, SFPL, Box 5, NLGHM, 1994.

50. Ginny Beemyn, "I am writing to express my disappointment . . . ," email to Jessea Greenman, October 7, 1994; Jessea Greenman, "Notes on Wilson's Secondary Schools Packet for Lesbian and Gay History Month," August 31, 1994; and Jessea Greenman, "Comments on History Month Primer," email to Kim Felipe, August 18, 1996, all in P.E.R.S.O.N. Project Records, SFPL, Box 5, NLGHM, 1994 Folder; Jessea Greenman, "I am sending out the more current version," email to qrd listserv, August 9, 1994, http://www.qrd.org/qrd/culture/1994 /october.declared.lgb.history.month-08.09.94.

51. Pat Wingert and Steven Waldan, "Did Washington Hate Gays? Fighting to Take Homosexual History Out of the Closet," *Newsweek*, October 16, 1995, 81; Robley S. Jones, email communication to Kevin P. Filocamo, October 12, 1995, P.E.R.S.O.N. Project Records, SFPL, Box 6, NEA, 1991–1997 Folder; Jeanne Ponessa, "NEA Backing for Gay Month Sparks Firestorm," *Education Week*, October 25, 1995, https://www.edweek.org /education/nea-backing-for-gay-month-sparks-firestorm/1995/10.

52. "History Resolution Sparks Debate," *Caucus Connection* 8, no. 2, December 1994, 1; Ken Walker, "NEA Stance on Homosexuality Protested by Christian Groups," *Baptist Press*, September 29, 1995, Southern Baptist Historical Library and Archives, Nashville,

Tennessee, http://media.sbhla.org.s3.amazonaws.com/8055,29 -Sep-1995.pdf.

53. Jessea Greenman, "CWA's Half Page Ad Running in Newspapers across America," email to qrd listserv, October 13, 1995, http://www.qrd.org/qrd/religion/anti/CWA/ad.about.lg.history .month-10.13.95.

54. "History Month Proclamation Withdrawn in Oregon," *Baltimore Gay Press*, October 6, 1995, P.E.R.S.O.N. Project Records, SFPL, Box 6, Oregon—General Content, 1991–1997; Jan Garbosky, "Removal of LGBHM Display," email correspondence to schools@critpath.org listserv, October 17, 1995, P.E.R.S.O.N. Project Records, SFPL, Box 1, California General Context, 1990–1997 Folder.

55. Greenman, "CWA's Half Page Ad"; GLAAD National, "Exploitation, Not Education, Is Real Goal of CWA Ad against Lesbians & Gays," media release, October 17, 1995, http://www .qrd.org/qrd/religion/anti/CWA/glaad.response.to.ad-10.17.95.

56. Ponessa, "NEA Backing for Gay Month Sparks Firestorm"; Jesse Fox Mayshark, "Tennesseans' Role Noted in Defeat of Gay History Month," *Knoxville News-Sentinel*, July 17, 1996; John Linder, "NEA Adopts New Resolution Language," personal email correspondence to Jessea Greenman, July 10, 1996, P.E.R.S.O.N. Project Records, SFPL, Box 6, NEA, 1991–1997 Folder.

57. Charlotte Crabtree and Gary B. Nash, *The National Standards for History* (Los Angeles: National Center for History in the Schools, UCLA, 1996).

58. Lynne Cheney, "The End of History," *Wall Street Journal*, October 20, 1994, A22; Nash, Crabtree, and Dunn, *History on Trial*.

59. Liz Tracey, "'Charting the Future, Reclaiming the Past': October Is Lesbian and Gay History Month," media release, GLAAD, August 7, 1997, P.E.R.S.O.N. Project Records, SFPL, Box 4, History; Jan Garbosky, "L/G History Month Celebration," email

222   Notes to Pages 86–89

correspondence to schools@critpath.org listserv, September 19, 1997, P.E.R.S.O.N. Project Records, SFPL, Box 1, California General Context, 1990–1997 Folder. For Equality Forum, see "About LGBT History Month," LGBT History Month, https://lgbthistorymonth.com/background, accessed April 20, 2022.

60. Lipkin, *Understanding Homosexuality*, 307.

61. Diane Brooks, "Thank you for your letter of February 17, 1995," correspondence with Jessea Greenman, March 8, 1995, P.E.R.S.O.N. Project Records, SFPL, Box 2, History, 1985–1995 Folder.

62. California State Assembly, AB 22, Session 1994–1995; "Re: AB 22 (Archie-Hudson)," email correspondence from Jessea Greenman to Jennifer Richard, May 24, 1995, P.E.R.S.O.N. Project Records SFPL, Box 1, California General Context, 1990–1997 Folder.

63. Ellen McCormick, "California Legislative Update: The Good News and the Bad News," media release, LIFE: California's Lesbian, Gay, Bisexual, Transgender, and HIV/AIDS Lobby, June 4, 1997, P.E.R.S.O.N. Project Records, SFPL, Box 1, AB 1001 and AB 101, 1995–1997 Folder; Katie Folmar, "Trustees Aim to Fight Bill Protecting Gay Students," *Los Angeles Times*, March 17, 1997, 1; Elizabethe Payne and Trevor Raushi, "Charting California's Protection of LGBTQ Students through Legislation," Queering Education Research Institute, Fall 2013, 2, https://www.academia.edu/5469689/Payne_and_Raushi_2013 _Charting_California_s_Protection_of_LGBT_Students _Through_Legislation_1987_2013_PART_TWO.

64. California State Legislature, AB 537: Student Safety and Violence Prevention Act of 2000, Session 1999–2000, https://leginfo.legislature.ca.gov/faces/billTextClient.xhtml?bill_id =199920000AB537.

65. Jessea Greenman, David Marshall, and Robert Kaplan, *The P.E.R.S.O.N. Organizing Manual* (Oakland, CA:

P.E.R.S.O.N. Project, 1995), P.E.R.S.O.N. Project Records, SFPL, Box 10; Greenman, interview. The P.E.R.S.O.N. Project continued in some form through 2004.

66. Stacie Brensilver Berman, *LGBTQ+ History in High School Classes in the USA since 1990* (London: Bloomsbury, 2022), 117–119.

Chapter 3 Making California FAIR

1. Thomas Dunn, *Queerly Remembered: Rhetorics for Representing the GLBTQ Past* (Columbia: University of South Carolina Press, 2016), 99, 109–125.

2. Dunn, *Queerly Remembered*, 125; "California to Include Gays in School Texts," *UPI Newswire*, May 12, 2006, https://www.upi .com/Top_News/2006/05/12/California-to-include-gays-in -school-texts/UPI-91841147467478/; Susan Jones, "One 'Sexual Indoctrination' Bill Dead, Two to Go, Conservatives Say," *Christian News Service*, October 7, 2006, https://cnsnews.com /news/article/one-sexual-indoctrination-bill-dead-two-go -conservatives-say.

3. "California History: What's Sexual Preference Got to Do with It?" *Sacramento Bee*, May 8, 2006, B4; "Politically Correct History," *Los Angeles Times*, May 9, 2006.

4. Jonathan Zimmerman, "Straight History: The Danger of Trying to Put a 'Positive' Face on the Past," *San Francisco Chronicle*, May 7, 2006.

5. Jonathan Zimmerman, *Whose America? Culture Wars in the Public Schools* (Cambridge, MA: Harvard University Press, 2002), esp. 5.

6. Julian Grant, letter to the editor, *San Francisco Chronicle*, May 14, 2006.

7. California State Senate, SB 777, Session 2006–2007, http://www .leginfo.ca.gov/pub/07-08/bill/sen/sb_0751-0800/sb_777_bill _20071012_chaptered.html.

8. California State Senate, SB 572, Session 2008–2009, https://leginfo.legislature.ca.gov/faces/billTextClient.xhtml?bill_id=200920100SB572; SB 572 Bill Analysis, California Assembly Committee on Education, June 17, 2009, http://www.leginfo.ca.gov/pub/09-10/bill/sen/sb_0551-0600/sb_572_cfa_20090616_120206_asm_comm.html.

9. Nancy McTeague, "Sharing Past and Present in California: The State of History Education," *Social Studies Review* 48, no. 2 (2009): 79–80; Rosemary Blanchard, "The Framework Revision That Almost Was," *Social Studies Review* 50, no. 1 (2011), 9–10.

10. Stacie Brensilver Berman, *LGBTQ+ History in High School Classes in the United States since 1990* (London: Bloomsbury, 2022), 90.

11. "The Overton Window," Mackinac Center for Public Policy, https://www.mackinac.org/OvertonWindow, accessed August 9, 2023; Maggie Astor, "How the Politically Unthinkable Can Become Mainstream," *New York Times*, February 26, 2019.

12. These briefs are on the California Safe Schools Coalition website, http://www.casafeschools.org/getfacts.html.

13. Russell Toomey et al., "High School Gay-Straight Alliances (GSAs) and Youth Adult Well-Being: An Examination of GSA Presence, Participation, and Perceived Effectiveness," *Applied Developmental Science* 15, no. 4 (2011): 175–185.

14. Eric W. Robelen, "Calif. May Mandate Inclusion of Gay History in Curricula," *Education Week*, April 27, 2011, 10; Carolyn Laub and Hilary Burdge, "The Use of Research in Policy and Advocacy for Creating Safe Schools for LGBTQ Students," in *Sexual Orientation, Gender Identity, and Schooling: The Nexus of Research, Practice, and Policy*, ed. Stephen T. Russell and Stacey S. Horn (New York: Oxford University Press, 2017), 324.

15. Assembly Committee on Education, "Instruction: Prohibition of Discriminatory Content," Sacramento, CA, June 22, 2011,

https://leginfo.legislature.ca.gov/faces/billAnalysisClient.xhtml ?bill_id=201120120SB48.

16. Callisyn Zielenski, interview with Carolyn Laub, March 15, 2018, in Laub's possession.

17. Robelen, "Calif. May Mandate Inclusion of Gay History."

18. Lisa Leff, "Gay History in Textbooks: California Debates Adding New Curriculum," Associated Press, April 18, 2011; Charlotte Crabtree and Gary B. Nash, *The National Standards for History* (Los Angeles: National Center for History in the Schools, UCLA, 1996).

19. Office of the Governor, "Governor Brown Signs SB 48 to Recognize Contributions of LGBT Americans, Pacific Islanders and Persons with Disabilities," media release, July 14, 2011, https://www.ca.gov/archive/gov39/2011/07/14/news17124/index .html; GSA Network and Equality California, "Governor Signs Landmark LGBT Education Bill," media release, July 14, 2011, in Romesburg's archives.

20. Los Angeles Times Editorial Board, "Gays in Textbooks: Best Told by Historians, Not Politicians," *Los Angeles Times*, April 8, 2011; "Gaps in the Lesson Plan," *Los Angeles Times*, October 19, 2011; "A Textbook Case of Politicization," *Los Angeles Times*, October 25, 2011.

21. Mark Leno, "California's FAIR Education Act: Addressing the Bullying Epidemic by Ending the Exclusion of LGBT People and Historical Events in Textbooks and Classrooms," *QED* 1, no. 1 (2013): 108; Los Angeles Times Editorial Board, "Gays in Textbooks."

22. Lorri L. Jean and C. Scott Miller "Why Calif. Students Should Know That Harvey Milk Was Gay," *Los Angeles Times*, October 28, 2011.

23. Ryan Schwartz and Carolyn Laub, "From 'Dignity' to 'Success': Using Strategic Communication to Change Policies and Perspective," in Russell and Horn, *Sexual Orientation*, esp. 281–282.

24. Seth Hemmelgarn, "Decline to Sign Campaign Developing," *Bay Area Reporter*, August 3, 2011, https://www.ebar.com/story .php?241778.

25. Lisa Leff, "Calif. Gay History Referendum Faces Uphill Battle," *San Diego Union-Tribune* [Associated Press], September 3, 2011, https://www.sandiegouniontribune.com/sdut-calif-gay-history -referendum-faces-uphill-battle-2011sep03-story.html; Lisa Leff, "Effort to Undo California Gay History Law Fails," *East Bay Times* [Associated Press], July 12, 2012, https://www.eastbay times.com/2012/07/17/effort-to-undo-california-gay-history-law -fails/.

26. Theresa Watanabe, "How Do You Teach Gay Issues in the First Grade?," *Los Angeles Times*, October 16, 2011; Margaret Nash and Karen Graves, *Mad River, Marjorie Rowland, and the Quest for LGBTQ Teachers' Rights* (New Brunswick, NJ: Rutgers University Press, 2022), 78. In 2019, Frost received $850,000, the largest employment discrimination settlement Lambda Legal had ever secured. The district had to revise its nondiscrimination training. "Settlement Reached in Lawsuit Brought by Lesbian Teacher against Hesperia USD," Lambda Legal, April 18, 2019, https://www.lambdalegal.org/blog/ca_20190418_settlement -reached-frost-v-hesperia.

27. McClatchy-Tribune, "Calif. Districts Unclear on Gay-History Content," *Education Week*, January 12, 2012; California Department of Education [CDE], *2017 History–Social Science Adoption Report* (Sacramento: CDE, 2017), 8.

28. Watanabe, "How Do You Teach?"; Brensilver Berman, *LGBTQ+ History*, 17; Sandra J. Schmidt, "Civil Rights Continued: How History Positions Young People to Contemplate Sexuality (In) Justice," *Equity and Excellence in Education* 47, no. 3 (2014): 353–369.

29. Teaching LGBTQ History: https://lgbtqhistory.org/, accessed October 20, 2023.

30. Michael Sadowski, *Safe Is Not Enough: Better Schools for LGBTQ Students* (Cambridge, MA: Harvard University Press, 2016), 32–35.

31. FAIR Education Act Symposium Planning Meeting notes, March 5, 2012, in Romesburg's possession.

32. CDE, *Standards for Evaluating Instructional Materials for Social Content* (2013 ed.), https://www.cde.ca.gov/ci/cr/cf/lc.asp.

33. GSA Network secured $5,000 from an anonymous donor for the whole project. In an email to Laub, the donor, a gay man who had an education philanthropy background, wrote, "I frame all of my work around expanding and shifting consciousness and this aligns perfectly!" This paid modest honoraria to the editors and contributors and funded the report's design and distribution. Anonymous donor, email with Carolyn Laub, May 30, 2013, in Laub's possession.

34. Don Romesburg, Leila J. Rupp, and David Donahue, eds., *Making the Framework FAIR: California History-Social Science Framework Proposed LGBT Revisions Related to the FAIR Education Act* (San Francisco: Committee on LGBT History, 2014), 1–2.

35. Romesburg, Rupp, and Donahue, *Making the Framework FAIR*, 9.

36. Jal Mehta, "How Paradigms Create Politics: The Transformation of American Educational Policy, 1980–2001," *American Educational Research Journal* 50, no. 2 (2013): 291–293.

37. Paul Pierson, *Politics in Times: History, Institutions, and Social Analysis* (Princeton, NJ: Princeton University Press, 2004); James Andrew LaSpina, *California in a Time of Excellence: School Reform at the Crossroads of the American Dream* (Albany: State University of New York Press, 2009).

38. "Standardized Testing and Reporting (STAR)," CDE, https://www.cde.ca.gov/re/pr/star.asp, accessed June 20, 2023; Steven P. Camacia, *Critical Democratic Education and LGBTQ-Inclusive Curriculum* (New York: Routledge, 2016), 63.

39. Instructional Quality Commission, "History-Social Science Committee Recommended Edits" (2014), https://www.cde.ca.gov/be/cc/cd/hisocscieqcsep17182014.asp, accessed February 6, 2015, pp. 4, 7.

40. Camacia, *Critical Democratic Education*, 65–66.

41. Romesburg, Rupp, and Donahue, *Making the Framework FAIR*, 6–7.

42. Instructional Quality Commission, "Summary List of Public Comments Received" (2014), https://ww.cde.ca.gov/be/cc/cd/dechssmtg.asp, accessed February 6, 2015.

43. Romesburg, Rupp, and Donahue, *Making the Framework FAIR*, 13.

44. Judy Appel, Don Romesburg, Rick Zbur, and Carolyn Laub, public comment correspondence with History-Social Science Subject Matter Committee, October 7, 2015, in Romesburg's possession; Deborah Miranda, "Extermination of the *Joyas*: Gendercide in Spanish California," *GLQ* 16, nos. 1–2 (2010): 253–284.

45. CDE, *History-Social Science Framework for California Public Schools* (Sacramento: CDE, 2016), 76–77, 98.

46. Romesburg's meeting notes; J. B. Mayo and Maia Sheppard, "New Social Learning from Two-Spirit Native Americans," *Journal of Social Studies Research* 36, no. 3 (2012): 263–282; Maia Sheppard and J. B. Mayo, "The Social Construction of Gender and Sexuality: Learning from Two-Spirit Traditions," *Social Studies* 104 (2013): 259–270; J. B. Mayo, "GLBTQ Issues in the Social Studies," *Contemporary Social Studies: An Essential Reader*, ed. William B. Russell III (Charlotte, ND: Information Age, 2014), 258. See also Harper Keenan, "The Mission Project: Teaching History and Avoiding the Past in California Elementary Schools," *Harvard Educational Review* 91, no. 1 (2021): 109–152.

47. CDE, *History-Social Science Framework*, 274.

48. Camacia, *Critical Democratic Education*, ix, 63, 67–68, 75.

49. Joy Resmovits, "California's Students Will Soon Learn More LGBT History in Schools," *Los Angeles Times*, July 14, 2016; Lisa Leff, "LGBT History Lessons Heading for California Classrooms," Associated Press, July 14, 2016; Janis Mara, "Marin Gay Rights Advocates, School Officials Applaud New Guidelines," *Marin Independent Journal*, August 9, 2016; Jill Tucker, "California School Officials Adopt Landmark LGBT Coursework," *San Francisco Chronicle*, July 14, 2015; Stephanie Magagini, "California's New Public School History Standards Reflect State's Diversity," *Sacramento Bee*, August 1, 2016.

50. Stephen Sawchuk, "LGBT Curricula Spreads Slowly, Despite Mandate," *Education Week*, September 6, 2017, 14; Jill Cowan, "What California's History Textbooks Tell Us," *New York Times*, February 6, 2020.

51. Peter Seixas, "Foreword: History Educators in a New Era," in *The Wiley International Handbook of History Teaching and Learning*, ed. S. Metzger and L. Harris (New York: Wiley-Blackwell, 2018), xiii–xviii; Steven Camacia and Juanjuan Zhu, "LGBTQ Inclusion and Exclusion in State Social Studies Standards," *Curriculum and Teaching Dialogue* 21, nos. 1–2 (2019): 7–20; Jeremy A. Stern et al., *The State of State Standards for Civics and U.S. History in 2021* (Washington, DC: Fordham Institute, 2021), 69.

Chapter 4   Resource FAIR

1. James A. LaSpina, *The Visual Turn and the Transformation of the Textbook* (Mahwah, NJ: Lawrence Erlbaum, 1998), 1.

2. Jill Cowan, "Textbooks' Enduring Importance," *New York Times*, 14 January 2020; Nicholas Kryczka et al., "Culture Warriors—on Both Sides—Are Wrong about America's History Classrooms," *Time*, March 14, 2024, https://time.com/6917632/history-wars-teacher-survey/; American Historical Association,

American Lesson Plan: Teaching US History in Secondary Schools (Washington, DC: American Historical Association, 2024).

3. Sandra J. Schmidt, "Civil Rights Continued: How History Positions Young People to Contemplate Sexuality (In)Justice," *Equity and Excellence in Education* 47, no. 3 (2014): 353–369, esp. 366. In the early 1990s, Barbara Blinick reviewed more than fifteen textbooks and found no mention of lesbians and only a couple mentions in gay men in passing in the context of AIDS. Barbara Blinick, "Out in the Curriculum, Out in the Classroom: Teaching History and Organizing for Change," in *Tilting the Tower: Lesbians Teaching Queer Subjects*, ed. Linda Garber (New York: Routledge, 1994), 146.

4. California Department of Education (CDE), *2017 History-Social Science Adoption Report* (Sacramento: CDE, 2017), 5, 11. In California, since the 1927 creation of the Instructional Quality Commission (IQC)'s precursor, the CDE has only been charged with evaluating and adopting elementary and middle school (K–8) materials. Local school districts evaluate textbooks for grades 9–12. In 1976, the adoption process was codified to occur every eight years. CDE, *A History of the California State Department of Education, 1900–1967* (Sacramento: CDE, 1986), 23. A 2016 amendment allows for a second review during that cycle in extenuating circumstances: Calif. Ed. Code, Stats. 1976, Ch. 1010, amended by Stats. 2016, Ch. 550, Sec. 1. (AB 575).

5. The eight publishers were Discovery Education, First Choice, Houghton Mifflin Harcourt (HMH), McGraw Hill, National Geographic, Pearson, Studies Weekly, and Teachers' Curriculum Institute (TCI). Studies Weekly only had proposed K–6 textbooks, while Discovery, First Choice, and National Geographic only had grade 6–8 textbooks. The others had proposed educational materials across K–8. CDE, *2017 History-Social Science Adoption Report*, 17–30.

6. The assessments of the FAIR Education Act Implementation Coalition (hereafter FAIR Coalition) are in Romesburg's personal archives. People centrally involved included Carolyn Laub (independent consultant); Don Romesburg (Committee on LGBT History); Rick Oculto, Renata Moriera, Tarah Fleming, Matt Klein, Aiden Wigda, and Cate Barber (Our Family Coalition); and Tami Martin and Jo Michael (Equality California).

7. See "Criteria for Evaluating Instructional Materials: Kindergarten through Grade Eight," in California State Board of Education, *History–Social Science Framework for California Public Schools* (Sacramento: CDE, 2016), esp. 622. For a description and analysis of the process from one panelist, see Dave Neumann, "Textbooks in the Balance," *The History Teacher* 52, no. 4 (2019): 653–676.

8. Neumann, "Textbooks in the Balance," 662–663; California State Board of Education, "Criteria for Evaluating Instructional Materials," 626.

9. The IQC required McGraw Hill to name Ride as the first "lesbian" astronaut. The FAIR Coalition supported how the publisher met this request in a photo caption: "Sally died in 2012. She was awarded the Presidential Medal of Freedom in 2013. Her life partner, a woman named Tam O'Shaughnessy, accepted the medal." James Banks et al., *IMPACT California Social Studies: People Who Made a Difference* (Chicago: McGraw Hill, 2019), Reading Companion, 268. O'Shaughnessy recounts their coming-out decision in Madeline K. Sofia, "Loving Sally Ride," *Short Wave*, NPR, June 24, 2021, https://www.npr.org/2021/06/22/1009098412/loving-sally-ride. Their relationship is prominently featured on the website of Sally Ride Science; see "Dr Sally Ride," Sally Ride Science @ UC San Diego, https://sallyridescience.ucsd.edu/about/sallyride/about-sallyride/.

10. Mark Jarrett, *E Pluribus Unum: The American Pursuit of Liberty, Growth, and Equality, 1750–1900* (Lafayette, CA: First Choice, 2020), 232–233.

11. California State Board of Education, *History-Social Science Framework*, 79, 264.

12. HMH included Parkhurst in its fourth-grade textbook but not its eighth-grade one; National Geographic omitted Parkhurst. All examples come from FAIR Coalition textbook reports in Romesburg's possession.

13. See Jarrett, *E Pluribus Unum*, 359–360, where a strong biography of Parkhurst is located in "Notable Pioneer Women." The eighth-grade textbook is the only approved one with a featured "Gay, Lesbian, and Bisexual Americans" section (232–233).

14. For teaching gender-expansive subjects prior to the modern categories of "transsexual" and "transgender," see Genny Beemyn, "Transforming the Curriculum: The Inclusion of the Experiences of Trans People," in *Understanding and Teaching U.S. Lesbian, Gay, Bisexual, and Transgender History*, ed. Leila J. Rupp and Susan K. Freeman (Madison: University of Wisconsin Press, 2014), 111–122.

15. James Banks et al., *California: A Changing State* (Chicago: McGraw Hill, 2019), Inquiry Journal, 172–175, Teacher's Edition, T432–T435.

16. It could have preferably read, "Charley's assigned sex and lived gender identity." Joyce Appleby et al., *IMPACT California Social Studies United States History and Geography: Growth and Conflict* (Chicago: McGraw Hill, 2019), Student Edition, 416, Teacher's Edition, 416.

17. FAIR Coalition assessment of HMH, Romesburg's archives.

18. CDE, *2017 History-Social Science Adoption Report*, 12; Neumann, "Textbooks in the Balance," 668.

19. Rob Darrow, "Evidence of LGBT History by Textbook Review," internal report for the FAIR Coalition, August 10, 2017; Carolyn Laub, Don Romesburg, and Rob Darow, email correspondence, September 11 and 25, 2017, both in Romesburg's possession; IQC, *2017 History-Social Science Adoption:*

Instructional Quality Commission Advisory Report (Sacramento: CDE, 2017), 76–77.

20. FAIR Coalition members, email correspondence with Carolyn Laub, August 11, 2017; Marty Creel and Daniel Byerly (Discovery Education), email correspondence with Don Romesburg and Carolyn Laub, September 1–18, 2017; First Choice Educational Publishing, "Response to Comments and Suggestions of the FAIR Education Act Coalition for *E Pluribus Unum*," submitted to the IQC, n.d. [September 2017]; Rick Oculto, email correspondences with Roderick Spellman and Rhonda Haynes (HMH), September 12–18, 2017; all in Romesburg's possession.

21. FAIR Coalition Report to IQC Chair Lizette Diaz and Vice Chair Bill Honig, September 12, 2017, via email; FAIR Coalition, "Sample Talking Points," September 27, 2017; Don Romesburg, speech notes for History-Social Science Subject Matter Committee and IQC testimony, September 27 and 28, 2017; all in Romesburg's possession.

22. Jonathan Cooper, "LGBT Groups Protest Potential California Textbooks," Associated Press, September 27, 2017; Stephen Sawchuk, "California Panel Adopts History Texts with LGBT-Inclusive Themes," *Education Week*, October 5, 2017, 5; Theresa Harrington, "California State Board Asked to Reject Textbooks That Fall Short on LGBT Contributions," *EdSource*, November 6, 2017; Theresa Harrington, "After Hours of Testimony, California State Board Rejects Two History Textbooks, Approves 10 Others," *EdSource*, November 9, 2017. Debates regarding representation of Hinduism and South Asian/Indian history were also mentioned.

23. Data on edits, corrections, social content citations, and publisher errata comes from IQC, *Instructional Quality Commission Advisory Report*. HMH was the only publisher to submit no errata to the IQC.

24. CDE, *2017 History–Social Science Adoption Report*, 12–13; CDE, *2017 History–Social Science Adoption: List of Public Comment Received*, September 27, 2017, https://www.cde.ca.gov/be/cc/cd /documents/hsspubliccomment.pdf; President Dr. Michael Kirst and Vice President Ilene Straus (State Board of Education), correspondence with FAIR Coalition, October 23, 2017, in Romesburg's possession.

25. Harrington, "California State Board."

26. Harrington, "California State Board"; IQC, *Instructional Quality Commission Advisory Report*, 73; Laura Moorhead, "LGBTQ+ Visibility in the K–12 Curriculum," *Phi Delta Kappan* 100, no. 2, March 24, 2018, 22–26; John Murawski, "How LGBTQ Education Is Gaining in Tax-Funded Schools, from Pre-K on Up," *RealClear Investigations*, November 13, 2019, https://www .realclearinvestigations.com/articles/2019/11/14/how_lgbtq_ed_is _gaining_from_pre-k_through_grade_12_121157.html.

27. Dana Goldstein, "Two States. Eight Textbooks. Two American Stories," *New York Times*, January 12, 2020.

28. Diane Hart and Bert Bower, *History Alive! Pursuing American Ideals* (Rancho Cordova, CA: TCI, 2019), 411, 523, 534, 535, 626, 631, 688. We identified another nineteen places in the student edition where TCI could have included LGBT-related Framework content.

29. Joyce Appleby et al., *IMPACT California Social Studies: United States History and Geography: Continuity and Change* (Columbus, OH: McGraw Hill, 2019), Interactive Student Edition, 75, 101, 104, 142, 157, 167, 187, 188, 204, 210, 232, 234, 242, 266.

30. Rob Darrow, *History Textbook Alignment: Grades K–5*, *History Textbook Alignment: Grade 8*, and *History Textbook Alignment: Grade 11*, Our Family Coalition, January 2018, https:// lgbtqhistory.org/textbook-evaluation-tools/. County offices of education included Los Angeles, San Mateo, Santa Clara,

Sonoma, Glenn County, Petaluma, Santa Cruz, Monterey, and San Francisco, notes of meetings in Oculto's possession.

31. Teaching LGBTQ History: https://lgbtqhistory.org/, accessed July 10, 2023.

32. Stacie Brensilver Berman, *LGBTQ+ History in High School Classes in the United States since 1990* (London: Bloomsbury, 2022), 65–79.

33. Daniel Hurewitz, "Putting Ideas into Practice: High School Teachers Talk about Incorporating the LGBT Past," in Rupp and Freeman, *Understanding and Teaching U.S. Lesbian, Gay, Bisexual, and Transgender History*, 48–49, 68.

34. In 2014, ONE created the panel sets *History of the LGBTQ+ Civil Rights Movement*, *Heroes of the LGBTQ+ Civil Rights Movement*, *Legendary Lesbians*, *Lesbian History*, and *AIDS Timeline*. In 2017, it added *Transgender History*. In 2019, it added *Road to Stonewall* and *A Retrospective on AIDS, 1981–2019*. Erik Adamian, Educational Director, and Jennifer Gregg, Executive Director (ONE Archives Foundation), interview with Romesburg, February 21, 2020; Trevor Ladner, Education Programs Manager (ONE Archives Foundation), email correspondence with Romesburg, October 10, 2023; "Education," One Institute, https://www.oneinstitute.org/education/, accessed March 20, 2024.

35. Adamian and Gregg, interview; Brensilver Berman, *LGBTQ+ History*, 104–106, 230n.18; One Institute, "Education."

36. Erik Martinez, Manager in the Student and Family Services Division (San Francisco Unified School District), email correspondence with Romesburg, October 5, 2023; San Francisco Board of Education, "Implementational of the Family Diversity Curriculum," Resolution 69–26A1, October 10, 2006; San Francisco Board of Education, "In Support That the San Francisco Unified School District Strengthen the Anti-Discrimination Program in Schools in Order to Effect a Healthier Learning Environment for Lesbian, Gay, Bisexual,

Transgender and Questioning (LGBTQ) Students," Resolution 912-8A3, February 9, 2010.

37. Laura Dudnick, "Curriculum Completed for First-Ever LGBT Studies Course at SF Public High School," *San Francisco Examiner*, June 22, 2015.

38. Jill Tucker, "Gay History Class a First at Public SF High School," *San Francisco Chronicle*, July 27, 2015; Sherry Posnick-Goodwyn, "California's First Gay Rights High School Class," *California Educator*, April 2016, 16; Michael Barba, "Trailblazing Class Expands in San Francisco," *San Francisco Examiner*, June 12, 2016; Moorhead, "LGBTQ+ Visibility"; Martinez correspondence.

39. Jenn Bowman, correspondence with Romesburg, October 11, 2023; Martinez correspondence.

40. These can all be found at https://safeschoolsproject.org/ under "Curriculum," "LGBTQ History," and "Resources" (accessed October 10, 2023).

41. "LGBTQ Lesson Plans," Teaching LGBTQ History, https://lgbtqhistory.org/lesson-plans/, accessed October 10, 2023.

42. Rick Oculto, "Announcing the LGBTQ History Stakeholder Forum," Our Family Coalition, August 25, 2018, https://ourfamily.org/announcing-the-lgbtq-history-stakeholder-forum/.

43. "LGBT History," The Content, Literacy, Inquiry, and Citizenship Project, https://californiahss.org/LGBThistory.html, accessed August 22, 2023.

44. "About Us," California History-Social Science Project (CHSSP), https://chssp.ucdavis.edu/about, accessed June 10, 2023; Bill Honig, "An Educator's Life: The Backstory," Building Better Schools, 2016, http://www.buildingbetterschools.com/bill-honig/, accessed June 2, 2021; "Cold War America #3: Anti-Communism at Home," *History Blueprint*, Regents of the University of California, Davis, 2013, https://chssp.ucdavis.edu/sites/g/files/dgvnsk8426/files/inline-files/Containment%20at%20Home%20%28CWA3%29.pdf.

45. Beth Slutsky, Deputy Director, and Tuyen Tran, Assistant Director (CHSSP), interview with Romesburg, February 7, 2020.

46. Slutsky and Tran interview; workshop slide decks and handouts in Romesburg's possession; Brensilver Berman, *LGBTQ+ History*, 108–109, 168–169.

47. Slutsky and Tran interview.

48. "UCBHSSP and the FAIR Act," UC Berkeley History-Social Science Project, https://ucbhssp.berkeley.edu/teacher-resources/lgbtq, accessed October 12, 2023; Don Romesburg Prize, Committee on LGBT History, http://clgbthistory.org/prizes/don-romesburg-prize, accessed July 10, 2023; "Lesson Plans and Resources," UCLA History-Geography Project, https://centerx.gseis.ucla.edu/history-geography/curriculum-resources-2/, accessed October 12, 2023; "Teaching California," California History-Social Science Project, https://chssp.ucdavis.edu/resources/teachingcalifornia, accessed October 18, 2023.

49. Wendy Rouse, *LGBTQ+ History through Primary Sources*, CHSSP, 2022, https://chssp.ucdavis.edu/lgbtq-primary-sources; Brad Fogo, Abby Reisman, and Joel Breakstone, "Teacher Adaption of a Document-Based History Curricula: Results of the Reading Like a Historian Curriculum-Use Survey," *Journal of Curriculum Studies* 51, no. 1 (2019): 62–83. The Stanford History Education Group only has one LGBT-related lesson: "Stonewall Riots," 2015, https://sheg.stanford.edu/history-lessons/stonewall-riots, accessed July 10, 2021. See some of Rouse's published work on LGBTQ+ teaching at her website, https://wendylrouse.com/resources-for-educators/, accessed October 12, 2023.

50. Slide decks, correspondence, and content for the Sonoma model are in Romesburg's possession.

51. Brensilver Berman, *LGBTQ+ History*, 56–58; Cathay A. R. Brant and Cynthia A. Tyson, "LGBTQ Self-Efficacy in the Social Studies," *Journal of Social Studies Research* 40, no. 3 (2016): 218; Todd Jennings, and Ian Macgillivray, "A Content Analysis of Lesbian,

Gay, Bisexual, and Transgender Topics in Multicultural Education Textbooks," *Teaching Education* 22, no. 1 (2011): 40, 50, 58.

Conclusion

1. "Equality Maps: LGBTQ Curricular Laws," Movement Advancement Project (MAP), https://www.lgbtmap.org /equality_maps/curricular_laws, accessed October 4, 2023; Massachusetts Department of Elementary and Secondary Education (DESE), *2018 History and Social Science Framework, Grades Pre-Kindergarten to 12* (Malden: DESE, 2018); Debra Fowler and Steven LaBounty-McNair, "Contextualizing LGBT History within the Social Studies Curriculum," National Council for the Social Studies, 2019, https://www.socialstudies .org/position-statements/contextualizing-lgbt-history-within -social-studies-curriculum.

2. MAP, *LGBTQ Youth: LGBTQ Curricular Laws*, last updated September 25, 2023, https://www.lgbtmap.org/img/maps /citations-curricular-laws.pdf; National Center for Education Statistics, "Enrollment in Public Elementary and Secondary Schools, by Region, State, and Jurisdiction: Selected Years, Fall 1990 through Fall 2031," https://nces.ed.gov/programs/digest/d22 /tables/dt22_203.20.asp, accessed October 6, 2023.

3. MAP, *Policy Spotlight: Curriculum Censorship and Hostile Climate Bills*, March 2022, https://www.lgbtmap.org/file/2022-spotlight -school-bills-report.pdf; PEN America, "Educational Censor- ship," https://pen.org/issue/educational-censorship/, accessed October 5, 2023; Woody Holton, "Chilling Affects: The Far Right Takes Aim at Black History," *American Historical Review* 129, no. 1 (2024): 199–216.

4. MAP, *The War on LGBTQ People in America*, Under Fire Series Report No. 2, March 2023, https://www.mapresearch.org/file /MAP-Under-Fire-Erasing-LGBTQ-People_2023.pdf, p. 4.

5. Diana Lambert, John Fensterwald, and Mallika Sashardi, "Temecula Valley Unified Reverses Course and Adopts State-Approved Social Studies Curriculum," *EdSource*, July 22, 2023, https://edsource.org/2023/temecula-valley-unified-reverses-course-and-adopts-controversial-social-studies-curriculum/694593.

6. Mackenzie Mays, "Fights for Local School Boards Not Over; Despite Losses at Polls, Conservatives Say Now They Have a Playbook," *Los Angeles Times*, November 29, 2022; Laurel Rosenhall, Hannah Wiley, and Mackenzie Mays, "Lacking Political Power in California, Conservatives Turn Focus to Local School Boards," *Los Angeles Times*, August 15, 2023; Kevin Rector, Howard Blume, and Mackenzie Mays, "How Conservatives Are Bringing a Well-Coordinated Culture War to California's Schools," *Los Angeles Times*, October 15, 2023. For a wider view on the phantasm of gender ideology and its relationship to discourses of "grooming" and anxieties of contagion, see Judith Butler, *Who's Afraid of Gender?* (New York: Farrar, Straus and Giroux, 2024), 93–111.

7. Stacie Brensilver Berman and Daniel Hurewitz, "LGBTQ+ Americans: History Is on Our Side," *Advocate*, July 29, 2022, https://www.advocate.com/commentary/2022/7/29/lgbtq-americans-history-our-side.

8. Lambert, Fensterwald, and Sashardi, "Temecula Valley Unified Reverses Course"; Governor Gavin Newsom, "California's Family Agenda Promotes Educational Freedom," media release, August 14, 2023, https://www.gov.ca.gov/2023/08/14/californias-family-agenda-promotes-educational-freedom/; One Temecula Valley Political Action Committee: https://onetvpac.com/, accessed October 19, 2023; "Temecula Valley Unified School District Recall, California (2023–2024)," Ballotopedia, https://ballotpedia.org/Temecula_Valley_Unified_School_District_recall,_California_(2023-2024), accessed March 21, 2024; Mallika Seshardi, "Joseph Komrosky's Recall Leaves Temecula

Valley Unified's Future Uncertain," EdSource, June 20, 2024, https://edsource.org/2024/joseph-komroskys-recall-leaves-temecula-valley-unifieds-future-uncertain/714450.

9. Governor Gavin Newsom, Attorney General Rob Bonta, and State Superintendent of Public Instruction Tony Thurmond, "Educational Rights and Requests to Remove Instructional Materials," June 1, 2023, https://www.gov.ca.gov/wp-content/uploads/2023/06/Book-Bans-Letter-6.1.23-1.pdf. The author's testimony at the June 21 hearing is in his possession.

10. Safe and Supportive Schools Act, AB 5, California State Legislature (2023), https://leginfo.legislature.ca.gov/faces/billStatusClient.xhtml?bill_id=202320240AB5.

11. Instructional Materials and Curriculum: Diversity, AB 1078, California State Legislature (2023), https://leginfo.legislature.ca.gov/faces/billStatusClient.xhtml?bill_id=202320240AB1078; Andre Scheeler and Lindsey Holden, "California Lawmakers Pass Bill Barring School Boards from Banning Inclusive Books, Curricula," *Sacramento Bee*, September 8, 2023, https://www.sacbee.com/news/politics-government/capitol-alert/article279074994.html.

12. Tennyson Donyéa, "N.J.'s LGBTQ Curriculum Still Faces Hurdles Three Years after It Was Mandated," WHYY, April 7, 2022, https://whyy.org/articles/nj-lgbtq-curriculum-still-faces-hurdles-three-years-after-mandated/; "Pilot: Executive Summary," Garden State Equality and Make It Better for Youth, 2020, https://www.teach.lgbt/research/pilot-executive-summary/; "Lesson Plans," Garden State Equality and Make It Better for Youth, https://www.teach.lgbt/lesson-plans/, accessed October 19, 2023; Matthew J. Platkin and Angelica Allen-McMillan, "AG Platkin and Acting Commissioner Allen-McMillan Announce Joint Statement from Division of Civil Rights and Department of Education on School-Based Anti-Bias Initiatives and the Law Against Discrimination,"

media release, New Jersey Departments of Law and Public Safety and of Education, June 26, 2023, https://www.njoag.gov/ag-platkin-and-acting-commissioner-allen-mcmillan-announce-joint-statement-from-division-on-civil-rights-and-department-of-education-on-school-based-anti-bias-initiatives-and-the-law-against-discrimin/.

13. "About Us," A Queer Endeavor, University of Colorado Boulder, https://www.colorado.edu/center/a-queer-endeavor/, accessed December 15, 2022; Social Studies Standards Review and Revision Committee, "Draft Revision Recommendations," Colorado Department of Education, November 2021, https://www.cde.state.co.us/standardsandinstruction/socialstudiesrevisionrecommendationsnov-21; Jenny Brundin, "In a Divided Vote, Colorado Board of Education Approves New Inclusive Social Studies Standards after a Tumultuous Year-Long Debate," Colorado Public Radio, November 10, 2022, https://www.cpr.org/2022/11/10/colorado-state-board-of-education-approves-new-inclusive-social-studies-standards/; David Duffield, conversation with author, October 20, 2023.

14. Oregon Department of Education, *2021 Social Science Standards Integrated with Ethnic Studies*, 2021, https://www.oregon.gov/ode/educator-resources/standards/socialsciences/Documents/2021%20Social%20Science%20Standards%20Integrated%20with%20Ethnic%20Studies%20(3-2-2021).pdf; GLSEN, "Inclusive Curricular Standards," https://www.glsen.org/activity/inclusive-curricular-standards, accessed October 15, 2023. In March 2023, Oregon congresswoman Suzanne Bonamici introduced the Bill of Rights for Students and Parents in the U.S. House of Representatives. It would, among other things, include LGBTQI+ peoples in its urging of "the adoption of educational materials by elementary and secondary schools that are historically accurate, reflect the powerful diversity of the Nation, and prepare students to think critically and participate

actively in a multiracial and multi-ethnic democracy." While symbolic given Congress's current political balance, it could build federal inclusive education rights over time. Suzanne Bonamici, "Bill of Rights for Students and Parents," March 10, 2023, https://bonamici.house.gov/sites/evo-subsites/bonamici .house.gov/files/evo-media-document/final-bill-of-rights-for -students-and-parents.pdf.

15. "About," Legacy Project, https://legacyprojectchicago.org/about, accessed October 20, 2023; Inclusive Curriculum Advisory Council of Illinois: https://icl.legacyprojectchicago.org/, accessed October 20, 2023; Illinois State Board of Education, *Illinois Social Science Standards*, 2016, https://www.isbe.net /Documents/K-12-SS-Standards.pdf; "Revisions to the Illinois Social Science Standards for the 2022–23 School Year," Illinois Civics Hub, https://docs.google.com/document/d/1zF4XkXlV RiiUDloQ6Jp6EcM-yIOGYBmTif_cPm8heDE/edit#heading =h.3kw7z3ydcsu0.

16. AB 261, 81st sess., Nevada State Assembly, 2021, https://www.leg .state.nv.us/App/NELIS/REL/81st2021/Bill/7727/Text#.

17. File No. 649, Connecticut General Assembly, 2021, https://www .cga.ct.gov/2021/FC/PDF/2021HB-06619-R000649-FC.PDF; GLSEN, "Connecticut Funds K–8 Model Curriculum That Includes LGBTQ+ Studies," media release, July 2, 2021, https:// www.glsen.org/news/connecticut-funds-k-8-model-curriculum -includes-lgbtq-studies; Alison Cross, "There's a Lot of New Curriculum in CT Schools for 2023," Hartford Courant, August 28, 2023, https://www.courant.com/2023/08/28/whats -new-in-connecticut-schools-curriculum-for-2023-and-whats -ahead/; Connecticut Department of Education, *Connecticut Elementary and Secondary School Standards* (Hartford: Connecti- cut Department of Education, 2024), esp. 4, 24, 46, 56, 66, https://portal.ct.gov/-/media/sde/social-studies/socialstudies standards.pdf.

18. SB 5462, 2023–24 sess., Washington State Legislature, 2024, https://lawfilesext.leg.wa.gov/biennium/2023-24/Pdf/Bills/Session%20Laws/Senate/5462.SL.pdf?q=20241011095305; Alexandra Yoon-Hendricks, "What to Know About WA's Law Requiring LGBTQ+ History in Public Schools," *Seattle Times*, March 21, 2024, https://www.seattletimes.com/education-lab/what-to-know-about-was-law-requiring-lgbtq-history-in-public-schools/.

19. DESE, *2018 History and Social Science Framework*, 41, 77, 78, 110, 132, 136, 156, 159. History UnErased also consulted on model curriculums: "Inclusive Curriculum Materials," Safe Schools Program for LGBTQ Students, https://www.mass.gov/info-details/safe-schools-program-for-lgbtq-students#inclusive-curriculum-materials-, accessed October 20, 2023; Debra Fowler, interview with author, June 2, 2020.

20. Samantha Schmidt, "Maryland Schools Aim to Include LGBT and Disability Rights in History Curriculum," *Washington Post*, August 16, 2019, https://www.washingtonpost.com/dc-md-va/2019/08/16/maryland-schools-aim-include-lgbt-disability-rights-history-curriculum/; Maryland State Department of Education, *High School United States History Framework*, https://marylandpublicschools.org/about/Documents/DCAA/SocialStudies/HSUS.pdf, pp. 2, 11, 15, 21; Delaware General Assembly, House Concurrent Resolution 90, 2022, https://legis.delaware.gov/BillDetail?LegislationId=109613; Office of the State Superintendent of Education, *Washington, DC K–12 Social Studies Standards* (Washington, DC: Office of the State Superintendent of Education, 2023), https://osse.dc.gov/sites/default/files/dc/sites/osse/page_content/attachments/Adopted%20Standards.pdf.

21. Austin Houch, correspondence with author, January 2021, in author's possession; Rick Hess, "How One State Found Common Ground to Produce New History Standards,"

Education Week, July 20, 2023, https://www.edweek.org/teaching
-learning/opinion-how-one-state-found-common-ground-to
-produce-new-history-standards/2023/07; Board of Education
for the Commonwealth of Virginia, *History and Social Science
Standards of Learning for Virginia Public Schools* (Richmond:
Board of Education for the Commonwealth of Virginia, 2023).
Drafts and public comments can be found on the Virginia
Department of Education's website: https://www.doe.virginia
.gov/teaching-learning-assessment/k-12-standards-instruction
/history-and-social-science/standards-of-learning/review
-revision-of-the-history-social-science-standards-of-learning.
See also mention of the "LGBTQ Movement" as one of twenty
examples to meet the state's 2021 eleventh-grade history
standard "Explain how various individuals and groups strategized, organized, advocated and protested to expand or restrict
freedom and equality" in North Carolina Department of Public
Instruction, *North Carolina Unpacking Document for American
History*, July 15, 2021, https://www.dpi.nc.gov/american-history
-unpacking-document-fall-2021-implementation.

22. New York State Education Department, *New York State K–8
Social Studies Framework*, 2016 (rev. 2017), https://www.nysed
.gov/sites/default/files/programs/curriculum-instruction/ss
-framework-k-8a2.pdf; New York State Education Department,
New York State Grades 9–12 Framework, 2015 (rev. 2017), https://
www.nysed.gov/sites/default/files/programs/curriculum
-instruction/framework-9-12-with-2017-updates.pdf; New York
City Department of Education (NYCDOE), *Hidden Voices:
LGBTQ+ Stories in United States History*, 2021, https://www
.weteachnyc.org/media2016/filer_public/61/19/6119a2aa-af90
-4389-88af-757a0ed217c4/hv_lgbtq_v17f_web.pdf; WNET,
*Understanding the LGBTQ+ Identity: A Toolkit for Educators
Collection*, https://www.pbslearningmedia.org/collection/lgbtq
-identity/, accessed October 23, 2023; Danny Lore et al.,

Recognized: A Civics for All Comic (New York: NYCDOE, 2022). See also the NYCDOE's middle school resource on the Stonewall Riots: "Stonewall National Monument Middle School Collection," WeTeachNYC, 2018, https://www.weteachnyc.org/resources/collection/stonewall-national-monument-middle-school-collection/.

23. Elizabeth Meyers et al., "Elementary Teachers' Experiences with LGBTQ-Inclusive Education: Addressing Fears with Knowledge to Improve Confidence and Practices," *Theory into Practice* 58, no. 1 (2019): 6–17; Wendy Rouse and Don Romesburg, "Tips on Teaching K–12 LGBTQ+ History," *The American Historian* (Spring 2023), https://www.oah.org/tah/sports-and-leisure/tips-on-teaching-k-12-lgbtq-history/.

24. "Conferences," Committee on LGBT History, http://clgbthistory.org/conferences, accessed October 10, 2023; "Don Romesburg Prize," Committee on LGBT History, http://clgbthistory.org/prizes/don-romesburg-prize, accessed October 10, 2023; Organization of American Historians (OAH), "OAH Committee on the Status of LGBTQ Historians and Histories Co-Issues Statement on 'Don't Say Gay' Laws," media release, May 12, 2021, https://www.oah.org/2021/05/12/oah-committee-on-the-status-of-lgbtq-historians-and-histories-co-issues-statement-on-dont-say-gay-laws/; Committee on LGBT History, "Statement on New Wave of 'Don't Say Gay' Bills," media release, March 8, 2022, http://clgbthistory.org/statement-on-new-wave-of-dont-say-gay-bills; OAH, "OAH Endorses Statement Condemning Exclusion of LGBTQ+ History in Florida," media release, May 17, 2023, https://www.oah.org/2023/05/17/oah-endorses-statement-condemning-exclusion-of-lgbtq-history-in-florida/; Rouse and Romesburg, "Tips on Teaching."

25. Duffield, conversation.

26. Queer Global Heritage: https://globalqueerheritage.com/, accessed August 10, 2023.

Index

Acanfora v. Board of Education of Montgomery County (1974), 35–36

Adamian, Eric, 168, 169, 198

Adams, Tom, 112, 115, 117, 121, 133, 166

Addams, Jane, 145, 147, 158, 160

Adolescent Family Life Act (1981), 43–44

age-appropriateness and grade-appropriateness, 18–19, 73, 93, 105–106, 113, 117–118, 161–164, 192–193

AIDS and HIV, 3, 44, 72, 81, 220n44. *See also* history education, LGBT-inclusive: AIDS

American Civil Liberties Union, 126, 168

American Historical Association (AHA), 8, 33, 114, 126, 141, 193

Ammiano, Tom, 37, 69

anti-LGBTQ: animus, 33–35, 38, 48, 64, 69–70, 111–112, 134, 240n6; falsehoods and scare tactics, 5, 11, 39–44, 85–86, 97, 105–107, 178–181

Appel, Judy, 117

Asian American history, xi-xii, 61, 68, 81, 90, 125, 167, 183

Baldwin, James, xii, xxii, 24, 49, 78

Bay Area Network of Gay and Lesbian Educators (BANGLE), 59–61, 64, 66

Bay Area Teachers Caucus. *See* Gay Teachers and School Workers Coalition

Bennett, William, 5–7, 11, 57–58

Berner, Larry, 40

Bias-Free Curriculum Act (2006), 96–100, 104

"biography trap," 147–152, 157–158

Birle, Robert, xiii, 59–67, 71–72, 76–77, 81–82, 220n44

bisexual (as specific rather than in "LGBTQ+"), 75, 84, 126, 146, 153–154, 157, 160, 184

Black/African American history, 9–11, 22, 28–32, 46, 87, 98–99, 106. *See also* history education, LGBT-inclusive

Blinick, Barbara, 71, 164, 231n3

Bowman, Jenn, 164–165

Brensilver Berman, Stacie, 93, 162, 172, 198

Briggs, John. *See* Briggs Initiative

247

Briggs Initiative (Proposition 6), 11, 29, 39–44, 100
Brown, Governor Jerry, 102, 108
Bryant, Anita, 11, 38, 39, 42, 64, 86

California: Berkeley, 5, 31, 57, 68, 155, 169, 171; Board of Education, 10–12, 35, 56–73, 81, 90, 116–135, 142, 156–160; Curriculum Committee (or Curriculum Commission), 9, 27, 31, 63–66, 71–72, 90; Department of Education, 5, 9–12, 27–28, 59–72, 95–136, 142–161, 166–169, 182–183, 231n4–5; Federation of Teachers, 30–31, 36; History-Social Science Framework, 5–6, 12–13, 18–19, 23, 28, 55–73, 81, 90, 95–174; History-Social Science Standards, 116; Instructional Quality Commission, xiv, 122–130, 142, 154–157, 231n4, 232n9; Los Angeles, 90, 108–114, 124, 134, 162–169, 189, 235n30; Los Angeles Unified School District and schools, 47, 93, 106, 113; Orange County, 28–29, 34, 40–41; San Francisco, 39, 44–46, 99–101, 105, 124, 150, 189, 194; San Francisco Unified School District, Board of Education, and schools, 37, 38, 69–71, 93, 164–165; San José State University, 171–172; Santa Cruz, 64, 142, 155, 165–167, 169, 235–236n30; Sonoma, 40, 128, 169, 235–236n30; Sonoma State University, 172; Standards for Evaluating Instructional Materials for Social Content ("Social Content Standards"), 116–117, 152–153; State Legislature, 9, 27, 30, 34, 44, 90–93, 96–114, 182–183; Supreme Court, 35; Temecula Valley Unified School Board, 179; University of California, Berkeley (and California History-Social Science Project), 5–7, 57, 169–171; University of California, Davis (and California History-Social Science Project), 114, 169–172; University of California, Los Angeles (and Center X), 57, 88–89, 163–164, 169–171

California Safe Schools Coalition, 103, 106

California Student Safety and Violence Prevention Act (2000), 91, 96, 103

Camacia, Stephen, 23, 133, 135

Capitol Resource Institute, 111

Cather, Willa, 49, 63, 78

Cheney, Lynne, 58, 88–89

civic education: and civic engagement, 3, 6, 174; history education as, 20, 56–59, 119, 124, 133, 168, 192, 195

civil rights, 9–10, 29–30, 39–45, 102, 242–243n14; and human rights, 60. *See also* history education, LGBT-inclusive: social justice movements

Clio Conference (1984), 5–7, 57

College, Career, and Civic Life (C3) Framework for Social Studies State Standards, 20, 124

Colorado, 4, 177, 184, 186, 192, 194

Committee on Lesbian, Gay, Bisexual, and Transgender History (CLGBTH), 33, 114, 116–125, 171, 192, 232n6

Common Core, 20, 114, 124

common story/common cultural narrative, 6–7, 12, 57–58, 89, 99, 120

248 Index

Concerned Women for America, 85–89, 97

Connecticut, 177, 185

Content, Literary, Inquiry, Citizenship (CLIC) Project, 168–169

COVID-19, 164, 169, 174, 180, 197

Crabtree, Charlotte, 23, 57, 88

Cuban, Larry, 8

Dain, Steve, 36, 210n15

Darrow, Rob, 142–143, 154, 160, 165–166, 167

Daughters of Bilitis, 38, 160, 180

D'Emilio, John, 33, 118

democracy, xix, 3–8, 14, 18, 20–25, 57–58, 88, 135–136, 242–243n14

Democrats, 42, 90–91, 102, 120, 180, 182, 184, 188

Demystifying Homosexuality: A Teaching Guide about Lesbians and Gay Men (1984), 45–46, 49

disability and disability history advocacy, 30, 59, 87, 99, 114, 118, 125, 183

Donahue, David, 22–23, 117, 142, 162

"Don't Say Gay"/"Don't Say LGBTQ"/"No Promo Homo" bills and laws, xix, 44, 110, 177–179, 187, 191

Duberman, Martin, 33, 52, 78; "Lives of Notable Gay Men and Lesbians" series, 78

Duffield, David, 194

Dunn, Thomas, 66, 96–97

educational materials. *See* textbooks and other educational materials

Elementary and Secondary School Education Act (1965), 30–31

elementary school (PK/TK-5), 28, 36, 40, 71, 231n4; and LGBT-inclusive

history education, 18–23, 38, 99, 112, 121, 127–131, 146–172, 179–187, 233n12

Equality California, 110, 114, 126–127, 143, 155, 182, 232n6

Ethnic Heritage Studies Act (1972), 30–31

ethnic studies, 30–31, 66, 105, 132, 164, 171, 185

Facing History and Ourselves, 164

Fair, Accurate, Inclusive, and Respectful Education Act (FAIR Education Act) (2011), xiii–xiv, 3, 13–15, 27, 95–169, 173, 183, 194

FAIR Education Act Coalition or FAIR Education Act Implementation Coalition (FAIR Coalition), xiv, 110–130, 136, 139–161, 168, 170, 194, 232n6, 233n12

family diversity (as history and social studies concept), 19, 32, 71, 118, 130–131, 142, 164

fascism and anti-fascism, 21, 82, 135, 159

feminism, 12, 29–32, 71, 80–81, 118, 132, 159–160, 171–172

Ferreria, Al, 47

Florida, 11, 29, 34, 39, 177–178

Franklin, John Hope. See *Land of the Free*

Funding, 24, 174, 195; donors, foundations and organizations, 36, 44–45, 62, 85, 92, 143, 168, 228n33; federal, 30–32, 44, 88; local/state, 13, 46–47, 108–109, 112, 172, 185, 189

Gay, Lesbian, and Straight Teachers Network (GLSTN). *See* GLSEN

Gay, Lesbian, Bisexual, Transgender (GLBT) Historical Society, 49, 77, 112, 165

Gay and Lesbian Alliance Against Defamation (GLAAD), 61–62, 64, 78, 81–82, 84–89

Gay and Lesbian Community Action Council of Minneapolis, 49

Gay-Straight Alliance Network (later Gender and Sexualities Alliance Network, GSA Network), 102–106, 110, 113–115, 117–118, 124, 136, 143, 154, 228n33

Gay Straight Alliances (GSAs), 17, 47–48, 73, 78–79, 92, 104, 112, 166, 191, 219n39

Gay Teachers and School Workers Coalition, 37, 44, 69

gender in history education: gender diversity, viii, 22–23, 144–161, 179, 183–185, 188, 233n14; gender fluidity, 78; gender identity, xiv, 2, 4, 14, 99–100, 109–110, 116–117, 167; gender roles, 17–19, 31–32, 45, 121, 127–133. *See also* trans/transgender history; women's history

Gerber, Henry, 79, 160

Gerber/Hart Gay and Lesbian Library and Archives, 83

Gilmartin, Katie, xi

Gittings, Barbara, 33, 79

GLSEN, 1–2, 48, 73–75, 79, 82–83, 92, 103, 162, 194

Grant, Will, 162

Greenman, Jessea, xiii, 62–72, 83–84, 90–92, 115, 193

Harlem Renaissance, 22, 51, 71, 160, 170

Hart-Hughes Educational Improvement Act (1983), 56

Harvey Milk Day, 100–102, 111

hate crimes, 42, 99–100, 160

health education. *See* sex education

Helms Amendment (1987), 44

heritage vs. historical thinking/ inquiry models of history education, 7–20, 45–46, 119–122, 147–150, 159, 189, 192, 195

heroes. *See* history education, LGBT-inclusive: role models and heroes

heteronormativity, 17–19, 60, 98

Hidden Voices: LGBTQ+ Stories in United States History (2021), 189

high school (9–12), 36–39, 47–48, 59, 102; assertion LGBT content should only appear in high school, 60, 65, 107; LGBT-inclusive history education, 42–43, 70–71, 112–113, 185–186; LGBT content and the California History-Social Science Framework, 121, 125, 132; LGBT content and textbooks and materials, 68–69, 74–84, 141–142, 159, 172, 189, 244–245n21

history and social science education policy, 8–10, 27–32, 90; and LGBT history censorship, 13–14, 52, 177–180; and LGBT-inclusive history education, 24, 27, 46–47, 50–52, 55–74, 95–136, 139–161, 177–189

history education, LGBT-inclusive: global, 71, 75, 76, 82, 132, 171, 195; U.S.: AIDS, 68–69, 76, 113, 141, 159–162, 164, 231n3; Black/African American, 22, 51, 71, 79–81, 84, 131–132, 158–160, 170–172, 187–189; Californian, 19, 30, 101, 127–131, 147–154, 158, 166–172, 180; colonialism, 18–19, 76, 127–131, 145, 158, 170; contemporary (1990s-present), 121, 142, 159–160, 162, 180; early American history,

250 Index

63–64, 75–76, 84, 127–131, 153, 162, 170, 171; gay liberation, 50–51, 71, 76, 88, 113, 141–142, 150–160, 171–172; homophile movement, 50–51, 75–76, 147, 159–160, 171, 180; Latino/a/x/e, xii, xxii, 158; Lavender Scare, 22, 75, 84, 122, 132, 160, 170, 171, 172; nineteenth century, 45, 75–79, 84, 127–131, 142–152, 158, 167, 171–172; opt-in/supplemental, 12, 16, 48–50, 55, 68–71, 76–93, 161–173, 179, 185; Progressive Era and 1920s, 22, 45, 51, 84, 71, 132, 160, 170–172, 187; role models and heroes, xii, xxii, 2, 16, 18–19, 38, 45–46, 49–50, 63–65, 77, 78, 83, 97–98, 104–105, 118, 131, 142, 158; "roles and contributions," 19, 31, 85, 90, 96, 99–102, 117, 122, 183–185; social justice movements, xii–xiii, 50–52, 74–80, 84, 88, 131–132, 159–172, 187–189; World War II, 61, 71, 75, 132, 159–160, 172
History UnErased, 24, 187, 244n19
"History Wars" as culture wars, 7–14, 21, 55, 72–73, 88–89, 98–99, 174–175, 178–183
Holocaust, 71, 75, 82, 132
Holzer, Allison, 1–2, 16
Honig, Bill, 5, 11–12, 57–61, 67, 71–72, 134
Hughes, Langston, 107, 145, 154
Human Rights Campaign, 112, 160, 194
Human Rights Foundation, 44–46
Hurewitz, Daniel, 118, 189

identity and labels (as an LGBTQ+ historical project), xii–xiv, 2, 19, 74–76, 97–98, 121, 144–154, 157–159

Illinois, 4, 15, 83, 177, 185, 189, 192, 195; Chicago, 15, 83, 189
"inclusionists" and "pluralists," 7, 22, 66–68
Indigenous/Native American, xii, 6, 58, 67–68, 99, 145, 151, 184–186; Two-Spirit, vii, 19, 26, 127–131, 158, 166–167
In Search of Our Past (1980), 31–32
Interracial Books for Children Bulletin, 17–18
intersectionality as a historical approach, 7, 16–18, 22, 79–80, 118–119, 131–134, 167, 186

Jackson, Corey, 182
Jennings, Kevin, 48, 73–76, 79, 80, 82–83, 92; *Becoming Visible: A Reader in Gay and Lesbian History for High School and College Students* (1994), 74–76, 82, 83
Jorgensen, Christine, 160, 167

Katz, Jonathan Ned, 33, 45; *Gay American History* (1976), 33
King, Bille Jean, 158
Komrosky, Joseph, 179–181
Kuehl, Sheila, 90–91, 96–100, 107, 108

labor and unions, 24, 31, 35–43, 52, 56, 169, 191
Land of the Free (1966), 10–11, 29, 32
Lane, Stephen, 37–38, 48
LaSpina, James, 140
Latino/a/x/e history, 30–31, 58, 81, 86, 90, 105, 181, 183. *See also* history education, LGBT-inclusive: Latino/a/x/e
Laub, Carolyn, 95–136, 143, 228n33, 232n6

Index   251

Leno, Mark, 100–103, 106–109

Lesbian and Gay History Month. *See* LGBT History Month

LGBT History Month, 1, 12, 55, 80–89, 92, 101, 109, 132

LGBTQ+ educators, 5–6, 34–48, 61, 81–83, 93, 112, 162–163, 210n15, 227n26

LGBTQ+ historians, 33, 52, 78, 116–118, 122, 147, 167, 189, 192–193

LGBTQ+ History Association. *See* Committee on Lesbian, Gay, Bisexual, and Transgender History (CLGBTH)

LGBTQ+ History through Primary Sources (2022), 171–172

LGBTQ+ students and youth, 34–38, 47, 73–74, 82, 90–92, 126, 179, 201n2, 219n39; and history education, 1–3, 14–19, 44, 50, 78–79, 96–98, 102–106, 133, 163

libraries, 30, 39, 51–52, 74, 78, 83, 103, 179, 191

Lipkin, Arthur, 47, 73–74, 76, 80, 89; *The Stonewall Riots and the History of Gays and Lesbians in the United States* (1992), 76

Lorde, Audre, xii, xiii, 17, 51

Los Angeles Gay and Lesbian [now LGBT] Center, 109–110, 113–114, 155, 163, 167

Los Angeles Times, 97, 108–110, 112, 134

Lyon, Phyllis, 147, 180

Maine, 42–43

Making Schools Safe for Gay and Lesbian Youth (1993), 12

Making the Framework FAIR: California's History-Social Science Framework Proposed Revisions Related to the FAIR Education Act (2014), xiii, 117–124, 126, 128, 131, 134, 142, 166

marriage equality, 100, 110, 120–121, 142, 159–162, 180, 188

Martin, Del, 147, 180

Maryland, 2, 36, 186–187

Massachusetts, 38, 47, 55, 73–76, 80, 177, 186–187, 195; Governor's Commission on Gay and Lesbian Youth, 12, 73–74

middle school (6–8), 10–11, 29–32, 37–39, 182, 231n4; and LGBT-inclusive history education, 19, 50–52, 127–131, 147–159, 170–171, 182, 234

Milk, Harvey, 22–23, 47–48, 83, 97, 100–102, 111, 121, 158–164, 179–180

Missouri, 81–83

Model Curriculum Guide for Human Rights and Genocide (1985), 60, 62, 90

Moreira, Renata, 143, 155

Morrison v. State Board of Education (1969), 35–37

multiculturalism, 7, 11–12, 20–23, 47, 52, 57–58, 66–73, 88–89, 120, 193

Nash, Gary, 23, 68, 88, 107–108

National Association for the Advancement of Colored People (NAACP), 28, 66, 181

National Coming Out Day, xii, 49–50, 82, 101

National Council for the Social Studies, 124, 177

National Education Association (NEA), 36–37, 82–83, 85–88

National History Standards (1994), 12, 23, 107

Nation at Risk, A (1983), 6, 11, 56

Nestle, Joan, 33, 52
Nevada, 4, 177, 185
New Jersey, 4, 36, 177, 183–184, 192
New Right, 10, 29, 40–44
Newsom, Governor Gavin, 181–182
New York: Gay Teachers Association, 36–37; New York City, 47, 50–52, 58, 73–74, 79, 162, 189; State Department of Education, 188–189
nonbinary and agender, xiii, xv, 145
"no promo homo" laws. *See* "Don't Say Gay"/"Don't Say LGBTQ"
North Carolina, 178, 245n21

Oculto, Rick, 124, 130, 139–175
Oklahoma, 42
ONE Archives Foundation (One Institute), 113, 162–164, 168, 171, 174, 236n34
Oregon, 4, 39, 41, 87, 177, 184–185, 194, 242n14
Organization of American Historians (OAH), 21, 193
Our Family Coalition (OFC), 95, 113–118, 124–126, 130, 140–144, 155, 160–174, 232n6
Out of the Past (1998), 78–79
Overton window, 102–103, 127

Parents and Friends of Lesbians and Gays (PFLAG), 60, 64, 159
Parkhurst, Charlie, xiv, 147–153, 158, 171, 233n12–13
path dependency, 120
patriotism and nationalism (as reasons for history education), 4, 8–11, 57, 88
Pennsylvania, 36, 159; Philadelphia Lesbian and Gay Task Force, 46–47
P.E.R.S.O.N. Project, 91–92

primary sources (as used in LGBT-inclusive history education), 18, 75, 148–151, 159–162, 171–172, 187–190, 193
problem definition, 119–120, 122, 134
professional development in LGBTQ-inclusive education, 21–24, 51, 75–76, 80–82, 92–93, 124, 139, 161–175
Project 10, xiii, 47, 69, 70
Project 21, xiii, 61–73, 77, 81, 91
Proposition 8, 100–101, 110–111, 162
Public Universal Friend, xiii, 94

Queer Ancestors Project, xi–xv, 198

race and racism in history education, 9–10, 13–18, 24–32, 51, 58–61, 65–80, 84–85, 90, 118–119. *See also* history education, LGBT-inclusive; intersectionality as a historical approach; *various specific BIPOC histories*
Rafferty, Maxwell, 11
Ravitch, Diane, 6–7, 12, 16, 57–58, 67
Reagan, Ronald, 5–6, 10, 29, 30, 43, 56–57, 81, 159, 160
religious right/Christian Right, 10–13, 41–43, 69, 79–80, 85–89, 97, 110–111, 179–180
Report of the Secretary's Task Force on Youth Suicide (1989), 73
Republicans, 5–6, 10, 11, 29–30, 43, 56–57, 81, 159, 160
Ride, Sally, xiv, 138, 146, 154, 158, 232n9
Rofes, Eric, 38
Rouse, Wendy, 171–172
Rupp, Leila, 117
Rustin, Bayard, xii, 54, 79, 111, 160

Sacramento Bee, 86–87, 97

Safe Schools movement, 48, 55, 73–74, 90–92, 113, 142, 167, 194; and LGBT-inclusive history education, 3, 15–16, 96–107, 119, 185, 192

Sampson, Deborah, 153

"Save Our Children." *See* Bryant, Anita

Schlax, Lyndsey, 164–165

school boards, local, 37–43, 106, 164, 190, 209n11; and LGBT-inclusive history education, xiii, 46–47, 50–52, 68–71, 164, 179–182, 219n39

Schwarzenegger, Governor Arnold, 99–101

Sears, James T., 15

sex education, 12, 14, 29, 34–39, 41–45, 72–73, 109, 177

Sheldon, Reverend Lou. *See* Traditional Values Coalition

Smith, Barbara, 17–18

Smith-Rosenberg, Carroll, 33

social justice model (for history education). *See* transformative model for history education

speakers bureaus, LGBTQ+, 37–39, 42, 44

Stanford History Education Group, 122, 238n49

Stearns, Peter, 6

Stonewall Riots, 50–51, 71, 76, 113, 121, 141, 159–160

Stop SB 48, 110–111

Struggle for Equality: Lesbian and Gay Community (1989), 50–52

Student Civil Rights Act (2007), 100

student success, as rationale for LGBTQ-inclusive history education, 3, 15–16, 102–107, 119

teacher preparation and residency programs, 21, 172–173, 185, 189, 193

Tennessee, 13, 177

Texas, 12, 135, 165, 178

textbooks and other educational materials, 9–12, 24–32, 56–58, 134–136, 231n3; and LGBT-inclusive history, 2–3, 21, 24, 49–52, 60–80, 108–109, 134–183, 189, 233n12; First Choice Publishers, 147, 154, 231n5; Houghton-Mifflin (and Houghton-Mifflin Harcourt), 64, 68–69, 152–158, 231n5, 233n12; McGraw Hill, 141–142, 147, 150–154, 159–160, 231n5, 232n9; Teacher's Curriculum Institute (TCI), 50, 158–160, 179–181, 231n5, 235n28

Thurmond, Tony, 182

Traditional Values Coalition, 41, 47, 64, 72, 107

transformative model for history education, 17, 20, 22–25, 93, 118–119, 133, 135, 178

Transforming the Nation: A Teaching Guide to Lesbian, Gay, Bisexual, and Transgendered U.S. Histories since the 1950s (2000), 79–80

Transgender Law Center, 126, 154

trans/transgender history (as specific rather than in "LGBTQ" or "queer and trans"), 75, 80, 85, 118, 122, 125, 160, 167; as role models and heroes, xii–xv, 2–3; and terminology, 219n42, 233n14. *See also* Parkhurst, Charlie

Van Kuilenburg, James, 2, 14

Virginia, 4, 85, 186, 188

254   Index

Washington, 4, 178, 185–186
Washington DC, xii, 82, 84, 186–188
Weld, William, 12, 74
Whitman, Walt, 49, 107, 157–158
Wilson, Hank, 37, 61–64
Wilson, Rodney, 81–84
"windows and mirrors" as inclusive education metaphor, 17
Women's Education Equity Act (1974), 31

women's history, 29–32, 80–81, 87, 118, 132, 147, 159, 171. *See also* gender in history education; history education, LGBT-inclusive; trans/transgender history
women's studies and gender studies, 66, 165

Zbur, Rick, 182. *See also* Equality California
Zimmerman, Johnathan, 98–99, 107–108

About the Author

DON ROMESBURG (HE/HIM) is a professor of women's and gender studies at Sonoma State University in California. He is editor of the *Routledge History of Queer America* and was the lead scholar working to bring LGBTQ content into California's 2016 K–12 History-Social Science Framework and subsequent textbooks. He trains educators on implementation.

Available titles in the Q+ Public series:

E. G. Crichton, *Matchmaking in the Archive: 19 Conversations with the Dead and 3 Encounters with Ghosts*

Shantel Gabrieal Buggs and Trevor Hoppe, eds., *Unsafe Words: Queering Consent in the #MeToo Era*

Andrew Spieldenner and Jeffrey Escoffier, eds., *A Pill for Promiscuity: Gay Sex in an Age of Pharmaceuticals*

Alexander McClelland and Eric Kostiuk Williams (illus.), *Criminalized Lives: HIV and Legal Violence*

Stephanie Hsu and Ka-Man Tse, eds., *My Race Is My Gender: Portraits of Nonbinary People of Color*

João Florêncio and Liz Rosenfeld, *Crossings: Creative Ecologies of Cruising*

Don Romesburg, *Contested Curriculum: LGBTQ History Goes to School*